JOURNEY THROUGH THE
Old Testament

D0506651

Harcourt
Religion Publishers

Harcourt Religion Publishers

Our Mission

The primary mission of Harcourt Religion Publishers is to
provide the Catholic and Christian educational markets with the
highest quality catechetical print and media resources.
The content of these resources reflects the best insights of current
theology, methodology, and pedagogical research. The resources are
practical and easy to use, designed to meet expressed market needs,
and written to reflect the teachings of the Catholic Church.

Nihil Obstat
Rev. Richard L. Schaefer

Imprimatur
✢ Most Rev. Jerome Hanus OSB
Archbishop of Dubuque
September 21, 2000
Feast of Saint Matthew

"The Ad Hoc Committee to Oversee the Use of the
catechism, National Conference of Catholic Bishops,
has found this catechetical text, copyright 2002, to be
in conformity with the *Catechism of the Catholic Church.*"

The Imprimatur is an official declaration that a book or pamphlet is free of doctrinal or moral
error. No implication is contained therein that anyone who granted the Imprimatur agrees
with the contents, opinions, or statements expressed.

The Scripture quotations contained herein are from the New Revised Standard Version Bible:
Catholic Edition copyright (c) 1993 and 1989, by the Division of Christian Education of the
National Council of the Churches of Christ in the U.S.A. Used by permission. All rights
reserved.

Photo credits are on page ix.

Printed in the United States of America

ISBN 0-15-900691-0

10   9   8

Contents

Hear my prayer, O Lord . . .
answer me in your righteousness.
Teach me the way I should go,
for to you I lift up my soul.
Let your good spirit lead me on a level path . . .
for I am your servant.

Psalm 143:1, 8, 10b, 12b

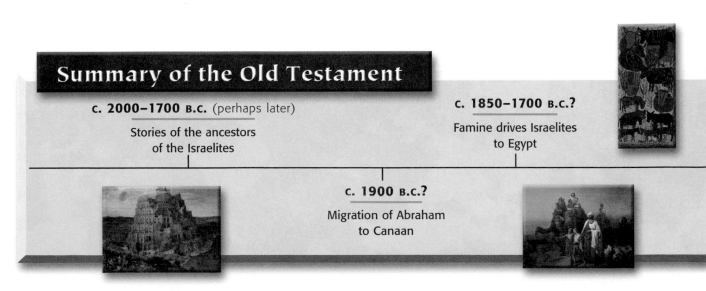

Summary of the Old Testament

c. 2000–1700 B.C. (perhaps later)
Stories of the ancestors
of the Israelites

c. 1850–1700 B.C.?
Famine drives Israelites
to Egypt

c. 1900 B.C.?
Migration of Abraham
to Canaan

Chapter 5

Claiming the Promised Land 84

Chapter 6

Building a Kingdom .104

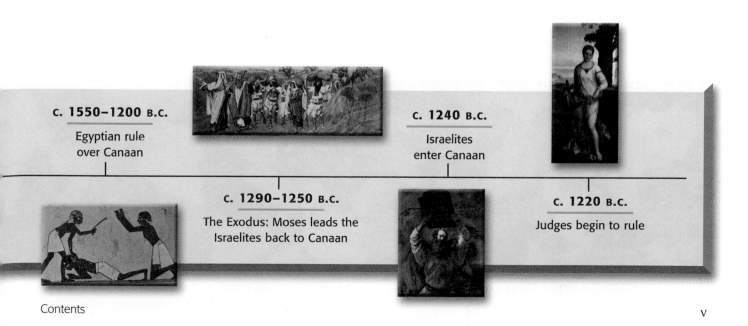

c. 1550–1200 B.C.
Egyptian rule
over Canaan

c. 1290–1250 B.C.
The Exodus: Moses leads the
Israelites back to Canaan

c. 1240 B.C.
Israelites
enter Canaan

c. 1220 B.C.
Judges begin to rule

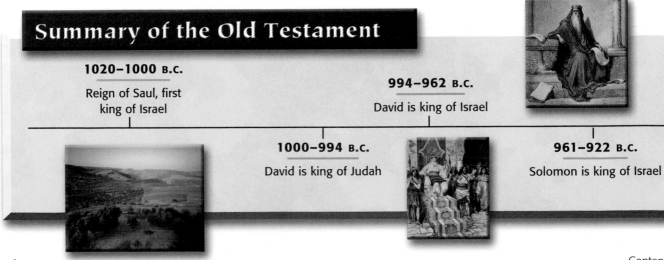

Summary of the Old Testament

1020–1000 B.C.
Reign of Saul, first king of Israel

994–962 B.C.
David is king of Israel

1000–994 B.C.
David is king of Judah

961–922 B.C.
Solomon is king of Israel

c. 960 B.C.
Solomon builds a temple
in Jerusalem

869–849
The prophecy of Elijah

922–587 B.C.
Divided monarchy

c. 730–722 B.C.
Assyrian invasion of
northern Israel

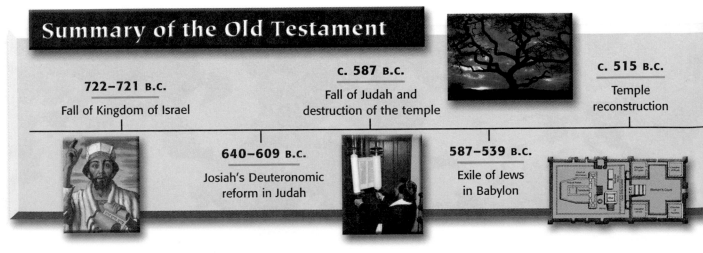

Summary of the Old Testament

722–721 B.C.
Fall of Kingdom of Israel

C. 587 B.C.
Fall of Judah and destruction of the temple

C. 515 B.C.
Temple reconstruction

640–609 B.C.
Josiah's Deuteronomic reform in Judah

587–539 B.C.
Exile of Jews in Babylon

The colored boxes at the end of paragraphs indicate point of use for the following:

■ FAitH SHARiNG

■ ActiviTy

■ OPENiNG THE Word

■ JOURNAL

Photo Credits

Academy of the Sacred Heart—176; **AP/Wide World Photos**—18; **Art Resource**—Erich Lessing: 33, 51, 64, 66, 70, 72, 76, 131(1), 132, 186, 190; Giraudon: 100, 215; Scala: 38, 117, 119; The Jewish Museum: 36, 75, 201; The Pierpont Morgan Library: 94; Werner Forman: 205; **Bardstown Art Gallery**—212; **British Museum**—168; **Buklarewicz**—25; **Corbis**—216, 224; Bettman: 73; David Lees: 140; Joseph Sohm/ChromoSohm, Inc.: 99; Reuters: 80; **FPG International**—Barbara Leslie: 223; Gerard Fritz: 144; Mike Smith: 156; **1994 Fr. John Giuliani**—116; **Image Works**—Nancy Richmond: 200; **Marquette University Archives**—102; **James M. Mejuto**—24; **North Wind Picture Archives**—79; **Oriental Institute of the University of Chicago**—91, 169; **Photo Edit**—Bill Aron: 60(bottom), 218, 219, 220, 222; Bill Brachmann: 196(left); Myrleen Cate: 64; Myrleen Ferguson Cate: 162; Myrleen Ferguson: 19, 214; Jose Galvez: 59; William Hart: 177; Erich Lessing: 125, 142; Michael Newman: 45; A. Ramey: 134, 166; Mark Richards: 157, 163; David Young-Wolf: 213; **Photo Researchers, Inc.**—George Gerster: 81; **Gene Plaisted/The Crosiers**—35; **School Sisters of Saint Francis, Milwaukee, WI**—47, 165(left); **James L. Shaffer**—106, 135, 179, 182, 197, 209; **St. Thérèse of the Child Jesus**—57; **SuperStock**—2, 7, 21, 32, 39(left), 48, 61, 67, 77, 83, 84, 86, 92, 103, 104, 118, 124, 138, 145, 149, 154, 155, 165(right), 173, 183, 191, 196(right); Barnes Foundation: 41; Chartres Cathedral, France: 122; Dahlem Staatliche Gemaldegalerie, Berlin: 17; Hermitage Museum, New York: 192; Jewish Museum, New York: 10, 54, 68, 75, 89, 112, 131(2), 136; Kunsthalle, Mannheim, Germany: 164; Kunsthistorisches Vienna, Austria: 8; Musee du Petit-Palais, Avignon, France: 55; Museum Des Beaux Arts, Tours, France: 50; Museum of Chandigarh, Chandigarh, India: 184; National Gallery, Budapest, Hungary: 12; Silvio Fiore: 141; Stock Montage: 206; Warehouse and Dodd, London: 174; **Don O. Thorpe**—62; **Tony Stone Images**—Alan Abramowitz: 152; Bill Aron: 107; David Ash: 4; Bruce Ayres: 126; Bushnell/Soifer: 188; Paul Chesley: 121; Cosmo Condina: 198; Sylvain Grandam: 128; Ernst Haas: 146; Zigy Kaluzny: 58; Hulton Getty Picture Library: 194; Richard Passmore: 14; Tom Raymond: 108; Ian Shaw: 127, 159; Tom Till: 180; Charlie Waite: 160; Jeremy Walker: 22, 39(right); Denis Waugh: 110; Art Wolfe: 42; **Trustees of the British Museum**—168; **U.S. Army Photo**—88; **Jim Whitmer**—11, 44, 195; **Bill Wittman**—60(top), 139

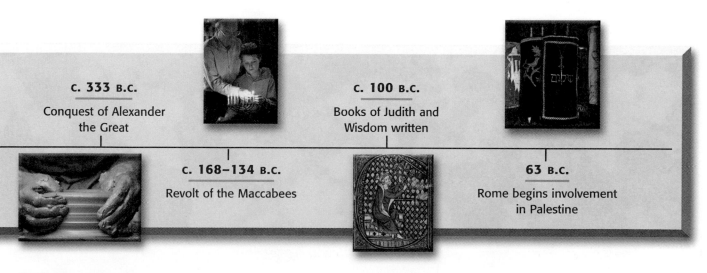

c. 333 B.C. Conquest of Alexander the Great

c. 100 B.C. Books of Judith and Wisdom written

c. 168–134 B.C. Revolt of the Maccabees

63 B.C. Rome begins involvement in Palestine

Make me to know your ways, O Lord;
  teach me your paths.
Lead me in your truth, and teach me,
  for you are the God of my salvation;
  for you I wait all day long.

Psalm 25:4–5

Events in Old Testament History

c. 1900 B.C.?
Migration of Abraham
to Canaan

c. 1290 B.C.
Exodus of Israelites from
Egypt

c. 960 B.C.
Building of first temple

c. 2000–1700 B.C. (PERHAPS LATER)
Stories of the ancestors
of the Israelites

c. 1000–962 B.C.
Reign of King David

922 B.C.
Division of kingdom into
Israel and Judah

CHAPTER 1

Understanding the Old Testament

CHAPTER GOALS

Increase knowledge of the meaning of the Old Testament and deepen understanding of its value by studying the following:

- Old Testament literary characteristics
- geographical and historical background of the Old Testament
- the authority of the Scriptures
- the enduring significance of the Old Testament

CHAPTER OUTLINE

Literary Interpretation: Structure, Sources, Forms

Historical Interpretation: Overview

Theological Interpretation: Natural Moral Law

Witness: Mother Teresa

Personal Challenge: Our History

Summary

722–721 B.C.
Fall of Kingdom of Israel

587 B.C.
Fall of Kingdom of Judah; destruction of first temple

515 B.C.
Completion of second temple

C. 333 B.C.
Conquest of Alexander the Great

587–539 B.C.
Exile of Jews in Babylon

539–333 B.C.
Persian rule

C. 168–134 B.C.
Revolt of the Maccabees

Cleaning the basement on a rainy afternoon late in summer vacation, you come across some cartons containing a lot of papers and photographs. You ask your mother about them, and she tells you the cartons contain different kinds of materials that she has been collecting over the years with the hope of being eventually able to arrange them into a sort of family history that she could share with her children. "I want you to know what kind of people your grandparents and great-grandparents were—in what they believed, how they lived, what they achieved, and what their hopes and dreams and joys and sorrows were. But, of course," she admits, "I never seem to find the time or energy to organize the material. Maybe you could help me."

You agree to help. You begin by identifying the different kinds of material in the cartons. You find letters, diaries, photographs, school report cards, business ledgers, birth and death certificates, marriage licenses, newspaper clippings, children's drawings, records of military service, and other types of documents. Next, using dates and other evidence, you decide to which generation of your family the items belong, and you arrange the materials into chronological order as best as you can. Then you spend days reading the documents and studying the photographs, sometimes discussing them with your mother and father. Finally, you make a selection of the materials that you and your parents agree are the most important in telling the story of your family.

Keep this story in mind as you study the Old Testament. The Old Testament tells the story of the family of God.

Literary Interpretation

FAITH SHARING

Create a list this week of important times in the history of your family. Be sure to include celebratory events such as birth dates and vacations. Also include events that marked difficult times, such as moving to a new home or school, or the death of a loved one. Write a short summary describing how all of these events represent the story of your family.

JOURNAL

Review the chart below. Write a few sentences noting the Old Testament stories with which you are most familiar. How are these stories important to you? (Journal responses will not be shared or read by anyone.)

Like you, those who assembled the Old Testament wanted to tell the story of their family—the family of God, which descended from Abraham. And like you, the Old Testament assemblers selected from a variety of materials certain documents that they felt best told that story. The process of assembling the Old Testament, however, did not occupy a week or two. It went on for hundreds of years. ■

A COLLECTION OF BOOKS

Jesus and Christians recognize God as the first author of Scripture. The Old Testament is not a single book but a collection of books written by different human authors at different times, and it includes different types of literature. Some individual books, such as the 150 sacred songs included in the Book of Psalms, are themselves collections assembled over hundreds of years. Despite these differences of authorship, date of composition, and literary form, the basic subject of all the books of the Old Testament is the same—God's role in shaping human events. Christians understand this to mean that the Old Testament also prepares for and declares in prophecy the coming of Christ, who is the redeemer of all humankind.

Jews, Catholics, and Protestants differ in the number of books they include in their respective versions of the Old Testament. Catholics include forty-six books; Jews and Protestants include thirty-nine. The chart below lists the books included in the Catholic version of the Old Testament. Works not included in the Jewish and Protestant versions of the Old Testament appear in *italics*. ■

Structure of the Old Testament

Books of the Law	Historical Books	Wisdom Books	Prophetic Books
Genesis	Joshua	Job	Isaiah
Exodus	Judges	Psalms	Jeremiah
Leviticus	Ruth	Proverbs	Lamentations
Numbers	1 Samuel	Ecclesiastes	*Baruch*
Deuteronomy	2 Samuel	(Qoheleth)	Ezekiel
	1 Kings	Song of Solomon	Daniel
	2 Kings	(Song of Songs)	Hosea
	1 Chronicles	*Wisdom of Solomon*	Joel
	2 Chronicles	*Sirach* (Ecclesiasticus)	Amos
	Ezra		Obadiah
	Nehemiah		Jonah
	Tobit		Micah
	Judith		Nahum
	Esther		Habakkuk
	1 Maccabees		Zephaniah
	2 Maccabees		Haggai
			Zechariah
			Malachi

STRUCTURE OF THE OLD TESTAMENT

Torah Hebrew, "law"; Jewish name for the first five books of the Old Testament

Pentateuch the first five books of the Old Testament, the Torah

The books of the Old Testament fall into several large groups. The first five books form a group referred to as "the Law." Jews refer to the books of the Law as the **Torah** (from Hebrew, "law"); these books are also referred to as the **Pentateuch** (from Greek, "five books"). They provide accounts of the creation of the world, stories of the ancestors of the Jews, early Israelite history, and codes of Jewish law. The historical books give an account of Jewish history from the conquest of Canaan to the kingdom of the Maccabees, which was the last independent Jewish state in ancient times. The wisdom books include poetry about religion and love, collections of wise sayings, and the Book of Job—a moral drama that examines the mystery of why the innocent suffer. The prophetic books include the visions and sermons of a group of Jewish religious reformers known as the prophets.

SOURCES OF THE OLD TESTAMENT

The writers of the Old Testament histories relied on both oral and written sources. Oral tradition existed before the invention of writing (and continued afterward to some degree). In an oral tradition, historical chronicles, genealogies, laws, and other kinds of cultural lore are memorized and passed down from one generation to the next. There is striking evidence that complex records can be preserved by oral tradition over great lengths of time. The oral historians of West Africa, for example, the griots, preserved an oral epic of the deeds of the hero-king Sundiata, who founded the Mali Empire in A.D. 1200. When African American author Alex Haley was researching his book *Roots*, he encountered a griot who knew 200-year-old details of the history of Haley's family.

However, inconsistencies inevitably develop in oral traditions that are preserved over long periods; further discrepancies develop during the period in which a culture moves from oral tradition to writing. The written sources for the Old Testament histories were letters, memoirs, genealogies, palace and temple records, reports of settlements and military campaigns, and other documents. ■

JOURNAL

In your journal, record some examples of oral tradition—such as stories, rhymes, and sayings that have been passed down from generation to generation in your family. What meaning does this oral tradition have for you? Why is it important or not important to you?

BIBLICAL PARALLELS IN OTHER LITERATURES

While the Bible is unique and inspired by God, its first author, the human writers of the Old Testament were indirectly influenced at times by the other cultures of the ancient Near East, particularly those of Mesopotamia and Egypt. This is reflected in a number of parallels between the Old Testament and ancient Mesopotamian and Egyptian literature. In the early 1870s a scholar working in the British Museum made a startling discovery in examining some clay tablets from ancient Mesopotamia. The tablets revealed an account of a great flood that was remarkably similar to the story of Noah and the Ark in the Old Testament. The Mesopotamian account was part of an epic, *Gilgamesh*, which was composed around 2000 B.C.

In 1901 archaeologists discovered a pillar engraved with the Law Code of Hammurabi, the ruler of Babylonia from 1792 to 1750 B.C. Many of the

The stele on the right is typical of Mesopotamian records of ancient stories. On the left is the High Dam near Aswan, Egypt, which controls flooding today.

ACTIVITY

In ancient times, clay tablets, wall paintings, and caves were used to tell stories with pictures. Create a panel of images that depicts the wise saying of Ptah-Hotep: "Good speech is more hidden than the emerald, but it may be found with the maidens at the grindstones."

OPENING THE WORD

Read Proverbs 10:20. How is this similar to the saying of Ptah-Hotep quoted above? What is the meaning of each short saying?

regulations in Hammurabi's code are similar to the laws of the Israelites in the Old Testament Books of Exodus, Leviticus, and Deuteronomy. The ancient Egyptians enjoyed collections of wise sayings, such as the teachings of Ptah-Hotep, the councilor of an Egyptian king who ruled around 2450 B.C. For example, Ptah-Hotep observes, "Good speech is more hidden than the emerald, but it may be found with the maidens at the grindstones." Ptah-Hotep's teachings are echoed in the Old Testament Books of Proverbs, Ecclesiastes, and Sirach (Ecclesiasticus). ■ ▪

AUDIENCE OF THE OLD TESTAMENT

The original audience of the Old Testament was the Israelites. The Israelites believed that their ancestors had entered into a special relationship with God—a covenant, by which they and their descendants had become God's chosen people. The histories, tales, poetry, laws, sermons, proverbs, and other writings that were eventually included in the Old Testament were intended in God's providence to serve as guidance to the Israelites on how to live in order to remain God's people. This story also has a specific relevance for Christians as part of the history of their faith. The values and lessons of the Old Testament provide universal truths of human experience and still apply today to people of all religions and no religion.

This rendition of the Tower of Babel is by the Flemish artist Pieter Brueghel and was painted around 1563. Some other artists have presented much simpler ziggurats or pyramids similar to those dating to ancient Mesopotamia.

OLD TESTAMENT LITERARY FORMS AND TECHNIQUES

The Old Testament contains different types of writing. Some types are basically informational, such as histories, genealogies, and law codes. Other Old Testament works are literary in nature; they have a variety of literary forms and techniques. Literary forms are the different types of literature, such as the forms narrative and poetry. Old Testament narratives include origin stories, short stories, and epics, and Old Testament poetry includes laments, songs of praise, and proverbs. Literary techniques are the artistic methods a writer uses to give meaning and beauty to a work. Those used in the Old Testament include imagery, figures of speech, parallelism, irony, allusions, and puns.

Opening the Word

Read the story of the Tower of Babel (Genesis 11:1–9). What does this origin story explain?

Opening the Word

Read Jonah. Identify the following elements of this story: (1) God's command and Jonah's response, (2) the crisis, (3) the solution. Describe the character of Jonah. How does he change through the course of the story?

Origin Story

An origin story is an explanation of how something came to be. The narrative of Noah and the flood, for example, is in one sense an origin story because it explains the origin and significance of the rainbow. ■

Short Story

A short story is a type of brief narrative in which characters and a plot are fully developed. Ruth, Esther, and Jonah are examples of short stories found in the Old Testament. You will read more about the story of Ruth in Chapter 5. The stories of Esther and Jonah are discussed in Chapter 9. ■

Epic

epic a long, exaggerated, and idealized narrative about a hero or heroine who goes through various trials

An **epic** is the detailed history of a hero who demonstrates both bravery and wisdom and goes through a series of trials. This hero is often a symbolic figure who represents the traits of an entire people. Epics usually are exaggerated and idealized in terms of character or events. An important epic found in the Old Testament is the story of Moses. Moses is an epic hero who represents the people of God. You will read more about the epic form in Chapter 4 of this text.

Imagery

OPENING THE WORD

Read the account of David and Goliath (1 Samuel 17:1–54) and list the concrete details given about each of the two combatants.

Imagery refers to the concrete sensory details that make a literary work vivid and realistic. For example, before David goes out to face the giant Philistine warrior Goliath, the Bible says that "he chose five smooth stones from the wadi, and put them in his shepherd's bag" (1 Samuel 17:40). Concrete details such as these help a reader visually imagine scenes in the Old Testament. ■

Figures of Speech

OPENING THE WORD

Read Psalm 102 and identify several figures of speech. What two things are being compared in each example?

Figures of speech are comparisons that are meant to be taken imaginatively rather than literally. For example, there is a saying: "Tinsel is really snakes' mirrors." We all know that snakes do not possess mirrors, so we recognize the saying as figurative language. Figures of speech are common in Old Testament poetry. The two most common types of figurative comparison are the simile and the metaphor. A simile is a direct comparison, using the words *like* or *as*. For example, the speaker in Psalm 19 says that the sun rising and moving across the sky "comes out like a bridegroom from his wedding canopy, and like a strong man runs its course with joy" (Psalm 19:4–5). Similarly, a metaphor indicates a likeness between two things without directly stating a comparison. For example, the speaker in a love poem such as the Song of Solomon might praise his beloved's beauty in this way: "Your eyes are doves behind your veil" (Song of Solomon 4:1). ■

Parallelism

The most evident feature of Old Testament poetry is parallelism, which can involve the repetition of words and phrases, or the repetition of thought patterns. For example, in the famous passage in Ecclesiastes 3:1–8 on the cyclic nature of life, the parallelism here involves similar phrases being repeated: "a time to weep, and a time to laugh; a time to mourn, and a time to dance." In Psalm 137:5–6, the parallelism involves repeated ideas rather than phrases: "If I forget you, O Jerusalem, let my right hand wither! Let my tongue cling to the roof of my mouth, if I do not remember you."

Irony

Read Genesis 18.

Irony is a literary technique in which what is said or done is contrary to what is expected. For example, "I'd kill for a Nobel Peace Prize." Obviously, a person concerned with world peace would never kill. In the story in Genesis 18, three heavenly visitors announce to Abraham that he and his aged wife Sarah will have a son. Sarah, who is listening, laughs to herself at this improbable event (Sarah is well beyond child-bearing age). There follows a humorous exchange in which the Lord (one of the three) asks why Sarah laughed, she denies it, and the Lord insists that she did. ■

"Sarah Hears and Laughs,"
by James J. Tissot.

ActiviTy

Read Exodus 2:1–10, in which Moses' mother gives him up to save him and ends up being paid to nurse her own child. With other students, role-play the scene, using your delivery of the lines and body language to emphasize the ironic humor of the scene.

For Review

1. What is the Old Testament?

2. What are the four basic divisions of the books of the Old Testament?

3. On what two types of sources were the writings of the Old Testament based?

4. What was the purpose of the Old Testament for its original audience?

For Discussion

One scholar observes that some of the difficulties modern readers have with the Old Testament come from its extensive use of figurative language, so that "we easily attribute to the sacred writers meanings which they never intended to convey." As a modern reader, how is the Old Testament's use of figurative language a help or a hindrance to your understanding of the text?

ActiviTy

Examine Psalm 104 and find examples of imagery, figures of speech, and parallelism. Make a three-column chart, listing the literary technique, the verse or verses in which it appears, and the role it plays in the meaning of the psalm.

The Old Testament narrates a rough historical sequence of events from the creation of the world to the kingdom of the Maccabees. However, the purpose of the Old Testament is to tell the story of God's relationship with his people. God is at work in the history and writings of the Israelites.

Many parts of the Old Testament present real events, but the intent and writings of the authors was not always historical, nor did they have the resources of modern historians. As Thomas Cahill observes in his book *The Gifts of the Jews*, they did not "have access to the card catalogue of the Library of Congress or the resources of the Internet." Some of the Old Testament is based on eyewitness accounts and written records of the events it records, but some parts are based on oral tradition and on written sources compiled centuries after the events. It was also common and useful to use fiction at times to teach a powerful lesson.

THE ANCIENT NEAR EAST

The events of the Old Testament take place against the geographical background of the ancient Near East (see Chapter 2, map on page 33). This area was dominated by two major civilizations—those of Mesopotamia and Egypt. Mesopotamia is the valley of the Tigris and Euphrates rivers in what mainly is now Iraq. It formed one horn of the **Fertile Crescent,** a semicircle of rich farming and grazing land extending from the southeastern corner of the Mediterranean Sea to the head of the Persian Gulf. During the period, a long succession of peoples—Sumerians, Akkadians, Babylonians, Assyrians, and Persians—rose and fell in Mesopotamia. These groups invaded the Fertile Crescent from the surrounding deserts and mountains. ■

Egyptian civilization, on the other hand, developed in the Nile Valley. Although also subject to invasions and periods of disorder, Egyptian civilization was far more stable than that of Mesopotamia. The lands of the Bible—modern Israel, Jordan, Lebanon, and Syria—formed the western horn of the Fertile Crescent. In ancient times, the coastline of this region was known as the "Way of the Sea," and formed the traditional route of armies moving north or south. Modern-day conflicts between the state of Israel and its Arab neighbors form only the most recent chapter in a long history of violence in this region. ■

During the Roman period in Israel, parchment scrolls began to be used for the holy books.

ActiviTy

Research one of the Mesopotamian cultures of ancient times (Sumerians, Akkadians, Babylonians, Assyrians, or Persians). What was life like for these people? Present your findings to the rest of the class.

Fertile Crescent   region of rich farming and grazing land extending in an arc from Mesopotamia to Canaan

ActiviTy

Work in pairs to create short skits set in ancient times. Each skit should be a conversation in which two people discuss their plans for the day. In planning your skit, think about the priorities of an average person in the ancient Middle East (food, shelter, clothing, safety).

According to the story, Abraham's migration from Ur to Canaan involved his entire family. This nineteenth century painting, "The Departure of Abraham," is by the Hungarian artist Josef Molnar.

THE PATRIARCHS

Israelites a people who unified about 1050–1000 B.C. and included Canaanites and peoples called the hapiru, the shasu, Sea Peoples, and the original Hebrews

patriarchs the ancestors of the Israelites, particularly Abraham, Isaac, and Jacob

polytheism the worship of many gods

monotheism the worship of one god

The exact origin of the **Israelites** is unknown; according to the tradition recorded in the Old Testament Book of Genesis, their ancestor Abraham migrated from the city-state of Ur in southern Mesopotamia along the Fertile Crescent to Canaan. This migration of the Israelites to Canaan took place sometime in the second millennium B.C. Abraham, his son Isaac, and grandson Jacob, who are referred to as the **patriarchs,** established themselves in Canaan. The wives of the patriarchs, Abraham's wife Sarah, Isaac's wife Rebecca, and Jacob's wives Rachel and Leah, also play important roles in the Old Testament narratives. They are the matriarchs, or founding mothers, of the people of Israel.

The Canaanites practiced **polytheism,** worshiping many gods; by contrast, the Israelites, led by God himself, practiced **monotheism,** worshiping a single god. The monotheism of the Israelites was a revolutionary concept in ancient times. The history of the Israelites was a long struggle to escape domination by their powerful neighbors and preserve their political and religious freedom. We will learn more in Chapter 4 about the people called the Israelites. ■

OPENING THE WORD

Read the account in Genesis of Abraham's journey from Mesopotamia to Canaan (Genesis 11:31–12:9). Why does God direct Abraham to leave his home?

THE EXODUS

According to the Old Testament, famine in Canaan forced the Israelites (Abraham's grandson Jacob and his sons' families) to migrate to Egypt, where they were eventually enslaved by the Egyptians. Sometime around 1290 B.C. the Israelites escaped from slavery under the leadership of Moses, who responded to a call by God, whose mighty deeds brought about the Exodus. Moses guided the people during a long period of wandering in the Sinai desert that lies between Egypt and Canaan. It was during this period that the Israelites received on Mount Sinai from God through Moses their primary code of laws, including the Ten Commandments. The Israelites' departure from Egypt is referred to as the "**Exodus**," from a Greek word meaning "a going out." ■

Exodus departure of the Israelites from Egypt under Moses, who was led by God

ActiviTy

Work with a partner to compare the story of the enslaved Israelites (Exodus 1–5) to that of African Americans in the early history of the United States. How would being enslaved change your understanding of who you are and from where you come? Participate in a class discussion on the topic or present your findings to the class.

THE CONQUEST OF CANAAN

JourNaL

Write a short paragraph about the importance of having a place of worship. How does the place create a sense of community for the people who go there? How does your place of worship do that for you?

The Old Testament Books of Joshua and Judges give different accounts of the Israelite conquest of Canaan. In Joshua, the Israelites conquer the Canaanite cities in a rapid series of assaults. Judges portrays the conquest as a gradual occupation over many years. Archaeological evidence and other ancient documents indicate that neither book is completely accurate historically. Rather, they are idealized pictures showing the underlying truth of the events—God fulfilled his promise to give the chosen people a land.

The occupation took place under the leadership of a series of charismatic military leaders known as the Judges. The conquest was completed during the reigns of Israel's first three kings, Saul (c. 1020–1000 B.C.), David (c. 1000–962 B.C.), and Solomon (c. 962–922 B.C.). The second king, David—one of Israel's greatest heroes—captured the city of Jerusalem, made it his capital, and relocated there Israel's holiest relic, the **Ark of the Covenant.** Israel was at the height of its power during the reign of David's son, Solomon, who further increased Jerusalem's importance as a religious center by building the first temple there. ■

Ark of the Covenant

an ancient symbol of God's protection and presence; a portable throne in ancient times that included a seat that was believed to be occupied by God

THE DECLINE OF ISRAEL

Under Solomon's successors, the united kingdom of Israel split into northern and southern kingdoms. The northern kingdom (Israel) was larger and stronger, but the southern kingdom (Judah) was more stable. In 722 B.C. the Assyrians conquered the northern kingdom and exiled its people. In 587 B.C. the Babylonians captured Jerusalem, destroyed Solomon's temple, and deported many of the people of Judah to Babylon. It was during the period of the divided kingdoms that the visionary reformers known as the prophets denounced their contemporaries who deserted the pure worship of God and tolerated social injustice.

EXILE AND RETURN

The **Babylonian Exile** (587–539 B.C.) was a watershed period in Old Testament history, during which the Jewish religion was refined and strengthened, and significant portions of the Old Testament were compiled. At the end of this period, in 539 B.C., the Persians, under the leadership of Cyrus the Great, conquered the Babylonians. Cyrus permitted the Jews in Babylon to return to Judah—although many had prospered in Babylon and chose to stay there. In 515 B.C. the rebuilding of the Jerusalem temple was completed.

Around 333 B.C., Alexander the Great conquered the Persian Empire. Alexander's empire split apart after his death, and the Jews were ruled by his successors, first the Egyptian dynasty of the Ptolemies, then the Syrian dynasty of the Seleucids. Under the Seleucid rule, some Jews embraced the Hellenistic Greek culture of Alexander's empire, but the majority continued to worship the God of the Israelites. When the Seleucid ruler, Antiochus IV, forbade the Jews to practice their religion, the family of the Maccabees, a priest and his five sons, started a revolt. In 164 B.C. Judas Maccabeus defeated the Seleucid forces, liberated Jerusalem, and purified and rededicated the temple. Today, this event is memorialized in the feast of Hanukkah.

The Old City of Jerusalem today is home to the Dome of the Rock, seen here from the Mount of Olives.

For Review

1. What role did the Fertile Crescent play in Old Testament history?

2. What different accounts of the Israelite occupation of Canaan are given in the Old Testament Books of Joshua and Judges?

3. How did David and Solomon make Jerusalem the religious center of Israel?

4. How was the united kingdom of Israel divided following the death of Solomon?

For Discussion

Why do you think that the Jewish religion was strengthened by the experience of the Babylonian Exile? In modern times, the watershed experience for Jews has been the Holocaust, which nearly destroyed the Jews of Europe, but also led to the founding of modern Israel. Discuss how these two events are alike and unlike.

The Old Testament can be read, in part, for what it contributes to our historical understanding of the world, and for its beauty as literature. Understanding religious truth, however, should be the primary goal of readers of the Old Testament. The Old Testament is to be read as the inspired story of God at work in human history and in relationship with the people of Israel.

THE HOME OF FAITH

The Old Testament is basic to Christianity and Judaism. This part of the Bible establishes the foundation for the relationship between God and his people. It also sets forth the laws and practices of his people.

For Jews, the Old Testament (Hebrew Scriptures) presents the history of the Israelites and the covenant that God made with them. In Genesis, God made his covenant with Abraham, the early ancestor of the Israelites. Abraham is the father of the Jewish people. The twelve tribes of the Israelites take their names from some of his descendants. The history and laws of the Old Testament continue to have ongoing significance and meaning for the individuals and community of Judaism. Their covenant with God is ongoing.

The roots of Christianity are also found in the Old Testament. Christians cannot fully understand God or their faith without understanding this part of the Bible. The *Torah* (the first five books in the Old Testament) was central to the faith of first-century Jews, including Jesus. The Old Testament stories of God entering into human events are an important part of the history of Jesus' followers and the traditions Jesus practiced. These writings are at the foundation of Jesus' teaching. So for Christians as well as Jews, the Bible is the "home" of faith. ■

THE TEN COMMANDMENTS AND NATURAL MORAL LAW

A fundamental element of the Old Testament is the establishment of God's relationship with his people through a sacred **covenant.** A covenant is an "agreement." At first, God makes promises to his people, but he does not set up any obligations for his people in return. This is evident in God's covenant with Abraham. God promises Abraham a nation and a people, but he asks nothing in return. With Moses, God's covenant includes obligations for the Israelites. God gives the major moral obligations and prescriptions of his Law in the **Ten Commandments.**

This is an example of God's **revelation,** which is more extensively experienced as God acts further in the entire history of the people. In the events and the Law, God gradually reveals himself and his relationship with his people. Through the prophets, God lets the people know what will befall them if they do not keep the Law, if they fail to be his people. For the Israelites, keeping the covenant with God began with following the Ten Commandments.

JOURNAL

Write a prayer that you have memorized and explain why you pray it. Then list the things that are important for you to pray about, and explain why.

covenant a sacred agreement between God and his people; a solemn agreement between two people or groups of people

Ten Commandments the laws given by God to Moses that prescribe moral obligations for the Israelites as part of God's covenant with them

revelation God's deliberate and gradual disclosure to humans of himself—his nature, his plan, his providence, and what he wants from people

NATURAL MORAL LAW

natural moral law the moral order that is part of God's design for creating the law that expresses the original moral sense, enabling people to discern good and evil through the use of reason

The Ten Commandments represent the basic prescriptive moral laws given by God. However, the Ten Commandments are understood to be a natural part of God's design. These laws are "engraved on our hearts." The **natural moral law** is a fundamental part of human nature. It is not outside of us, but within us. It is part of our human makeup and part of God's design.

The natural moral law is the foundation of moral rules and civil laws. The Code of Hammurabi represents one of the earliest developments of laws. The U.S. Declaration of Independence is based on the natural moral law: that people have "inalienable rights" which cannot be taken away. These rights include "life, liberty, and the pursuit of happiness." Respecting these rights is understood to be what is good. ■

Knowing right from wrong is intrinsic to our nature, even though God's revelation is needed to clarify human thinking corrupted by original sin. It is not simply a gift given to those who believe in the Bible. Whenever we are confronted with a difficult decision, we consider right and wrong. We use our ability to reason to search for truth. This is the way we solve problems and respond to God.

ActiviTy

Read the first few sentences of the Declaration of Independence. What principles are derived from the natural moral law?

MORAL PRINCIPLES AND HISTORY

The U.S. Declaration of Independence (1776) was cited as an example of applying the natural moral order to an understanding of human experience. In 1948 the United Nations drafted a declaration of human rights for the world. Among these rights were the right to "life, liberty, and security of person." As the history of the human family progresses, we find ways to apply our moral principles to the challenges of our time. Your school may have a similar challenge in developing and adapting rules to fit the student body at a particular time.

This ever-changing nature of the application of moral principles requires us to use all of our resources when making a decision. In our not-so-distant past, the United States had schools that were segregated—schools for African Americans and schools for whites. During World War II, the U.S. government forced citizens and noncitizens of Japanese ancestry out of their homes and into camps. Discrimination and abuses continue to face many of our citizens—and people in other countries. Our challenge is to maintain a consistent moral wisdom and use our judgment to apply it to the world we both make and have inherited. ■

In this chapter, you have learned that the Bible is many things. It is literature filled with items such as poems and stories. It is the history of God's people. A fundamental value of the Bible is as a guide for moral decisions. The Bible contains the foundation for morals and principles for Jews and Christians. But most of all, the Bible is God's revelation. Through inspiration, the Holy Spirit influenced the writers of Scripture to write the religious truth revealed by God.

ActiviTy

Research present-day violations of human rights in two countries. Express your judgment about these practices for the class.

REVELATION AND INSPIRATION

inspiration divine influence; God flows into and influences the human intellect, will, imagination, memory

To *reveal* is to disclose something that was hidden. In religious terms, revelation means God's deliberate and gradual disclosure of himself to humans—his nature, his plan, his providence, and what he wants from them—as he does in the Old Testament. Much of the Old Testament consists of God's revelations of himself and his relationship to his people. Revelation serves different purposes. On different occasions God revealed different aspects of himself—his love, power, glory, justice, wrath, mercy—that form a complex, evolving picture of his nature. God remains the same, but the human understanding of him develops and deepens because God's gradual revelation in the Old Testament develops and deepens. Sometimes God's revelation deals with his plan of salvation for his people, as in his covenant with Old Testament figures such as Noah and Abraham. Other times, such as when God revealed the Ten Commandments, God asks the Israelites to live in a certain way in order to remain as his people. ■

The Bible is referred to as the inspired "word of God." What does this mean? **Inspiration** is divine influence. Those who wrote and assembled the Scriptures were moved and influenced by God, and these writings therefore are the revealed word of God. Inspiration functions as the guardian of God's revelation.

For over three millennia the Ten Commandments have endured as the basis for moral decisions. "Moses with the Tablets of the Law" is by Rembrandt.

OPENING THE WORD

Read Deuteronomy 29:29. What distinction is made here? What is the purpose of God's revelation in this instance?

For REVIEW

1. What is natural moral law?

2. In terms of the Old Testament, what is meant by revelation?

3. What is the connection between natural moral law and the Ten Commandments?

4. How does God reveal himself to us?

For DISCUSSION

Discuss how the natural moral law depicts humans in a positive way. What does this natural ability assume about human nature?

ActiviTy

Locate your school's student handbook. Create a chart listing the major rules. Make connections to the natural moral law. Post this chart in the classroom.

Mother Teresa

India's Saint

The Old Testament is, in one sense, the story of a family—the family of Abraham and his descendants. In making his covenant with Abraham, God says, "in you all the families of the earth shall be blessed" (Genesis 12:3). Familial love is at the heart of the central relationship of the Old Testament—that between God and his people. Mother Teresa (1910–1997), India's "saint of the gutter," believed that to change the world we must begin with our families: "Peace and war start within one's own home. If we really want peace for the world, let us start by loving one another within our own families."

Born into a working-class family in Skopje (now Macedonia) to Albanian parents, Mother Teresa joined a missionary order and went to teach in the huge city of Calcutta in eastern India. There she saw first-hand the miseries resulting from the breakdown of the family and the inability of the society to provide the support families needed. Moved by the plight of the poor on the city's streets, she received permission in 1946 to leave her convent to study nursing and care for Calcutta's many sick and dying. In 1948, to expand her work, Mother Teresa founded the Catholic Order of the Missionaries of Charity. She became an Indian citizen and her order adopted the sari, the characteristic garb of Indian women, as their habit. Her order opened numerous centers to care for people who are blind, people with disabilities, lepers, abandoned infants and children, older people, and people who were dying. She eventually expanded her missionary order's work to countries throughout the world, and was one of the pioneers in establishing centers to care for victims of AIDS.

Perhaps the most notable aspect of her ministry was her care for the dying. In this work, perhaps the

All of our family histories include examples of suffering and other examples of reaching out to people who are suffering.

saddest cases she encountered were those who were dying and had been abandoned by their own families. With such unfortunates, her concern was to bring them comfort by helping them to forgive those who had deserted them. In 1979 she received the Nobel Peace Prize. As Pope John Paul II observed, "She served all human beings by promoting their dignity and respect, and made those who had been defeated by life feel the tenderness of God."

Our History

At the beginning of this chapter, you were asked to imagine putting together a family history from a variety of materials, such as documents and photographs. As you examined the materials to make your selection, you probably reacted to the documents in a variety of ways. For example, your interest in some documents, such as financial records, would probably be primarily historical and not evoke much emotion. However, other documents, such as letters, diaries, or photographs, might create a much more personal response in you, providing a real link between your life and the lives of family members in the past.

You might also respond to the Old Testament in different ways—approaching it as literature, as history, or as theology. In addition, you can also respond to the Old Testament personally. In reading the Old Testament you will find people struggling with doubt, fear, and loss as we all do. This human dimension of the Old Testament can help illuminate and sustain you in dealing with your own problems. The teachings of the Scriptures have led people such as Mother Teresa to devote their lives to helping others. As believers, we are all part of the family of God.

THE HUMAN CONDITION

Much of the enduring power and value of the Old Testament comes from its vivid and profound depictions of the human condition. When we encounter the first people expelled from paradise, Cain killing his brother Abel, Ruth remaining faithful in her love, David mourning for his son, Job suffering and enduring, we are in touch with timeless human experiences. We identify with the experiences, struggles, and joys of these people. ■

As members of the human family, we experience the sorrows and joys of others as our sorrows and joys.

JOURNAL

How do stories in the Old Testament serve as a guide for you? Which stories help you determine the difference between right and wrong?

THE OLD TESTAMENT IN TODAY'S WORLD

ACTIVITY

As a small group, research and discuss how the Scriptures are important to other religions. How does the religious group demonstrate an understanding of the Scriptures in the way they make decisions? Present your findings to the class.

Many of the materials you would use in creating a family history would be old. What do you first think of when you hear the word *old*? Do you think of wisdom and tradition? Or do you think of dullness and decay? The Jewish sacred writings in the Bible are traditionally referred to by Christians as the Old Testament to distinguish them from the Christian sacred writings of the New Testament. ■

More recently, some Christians have preferred to call these writings the Hebrew Scriptures. The first reason for doing so is to honor these Scriptures in their own right and not just as one part of the Bible used by Christians. If the word *old* is used to mean something that is no longer in use or without value, this sense of *old* certainly doesn't apply to the Old Testament. The Old Testament is sacred to both Jews and Christians and remains a continuing source of inspiration to people of both religions—and, indeed, to many people outside these faiths.

FOR REVIEW

1. Why does the Old Testament continue to inspire Jews and Christians, as well as others, today?

2. Why do some Christians refer to the Old Testament as the Hebrew Scriptures?

FOR DISCUSSION

In your previous reading of the Old Testament, which stories and characters have had the most personal significance for you? Explain their significance for you. What have you studied in this chapter that has given you a different view on any of the stories or characters?

ACTIVITY

In small groups, share stories with one another from your own family histories. Who are your ancestors? What hardships did they face? What joys did they experience? How are your personal stories like the stories in the Old Testament? Discuss among your group the importance of family history.

JOURNAL

How can Scripture help you make good moral decisions?

Summary

The Old Testament is not one book but a collection of books that includes many different types of literature. It is a mixture of genealogies, law codes, narratives, and poetry. Despite these differences, the basic subject of all these books is the same—the revelation of God's nature and God's role in shaping human events. The books of the Old Testament are not history in a modern sense but instead present the story of a people chosen by God.

The Old Testament tells the story of the Israelites, a people of the ancient Middle East. It shows how God is present in the history of his people. It focuses on the individuals who played important roles in the formation of the people of God. The Old Testament conveys God's revelation of himself to his people and his relationship with them. The Ten Commandments are an example of God's revelation concerning right conduct. These laws are rooted in the natural moral law; they are written on people's hearts. By God's design, humans have the natural ability to discern good and evil, even though that ability is weakened by original sin. The Ten Commandments are the written and prescriptive example of God's Law and are consistent with what is good in human nature. The stories of events in the Old Testament help modern readers identify with Scripture's message and apply it to their lives.

> The law of the LORD is perfect,
>   reviving the soul;
> the decrees of the LORD are sure,
>   making wise the simple;
> the precepts of the LORD are right,
>   rejoicing the heart;
> the commandment of the LORD is clear,
>   enlightening the eyes.
>
>   Psalm 19:7—8

All your works shall give thanks to you, O Lord,
    and all your faithful shall bless you.
They shall speak of the glory of your kingdom,
    and tell of your power,
to make known to all people your mighty deeds,
    and the glorious splendor of your kingdom.

Psalm 14:10–12

Events Before Recorded History

18,000 B.C.
Ice Age

2,000,000 B.C.
First use of
stone tools

15,000 B.C.
Lascaux cave paintings

In the Beginning . . . How It All Began

CHAPTER GOALS

Increase the student's knowledge of the composition and meaning of the Pentateuch by studying the following:

- literary forms and elements
- traditions and groups of writers
- prehistoric period
- distinction between a literal reading and a reading for religious truth

CHAPTER OUTLINE

10,000 B.C.	8000 B.C.	5000 B.C.	5000–4000 B.C.	3000 B.C.
Neolithic agricultural revolution	Population estimated to be about 10 million people	Population estimated to be about 66 million people	Artisans in Europe and Asia learning to use copper	Civilizations in river valleys emerge; beginnings of recorded history

The people in your neighborhood are planning the construction of a playground and jungle gym made with wood beams and modeled after castles. The plan also calls for the playground and jungle gym to extend into the existing park and includes the planting of new trees and flowers. Adults, teenagers, and kids in the neighborhood are volunteering their talents and services. An architect in the neighborhood is drafting the blueprint. The people in the neighborhood plan a big block party to kick off the event.

At the party you decide to volunteer as a "carpenter" to help construct the playground. First, plans are made to order the supplies. Two weeks later the supplies arrive. The lumber is delivered on a big flatbed of an eighteen-wheel truck. Tools, nails, and other materials are contributed to get the work started. Some of the supplies are new, and some are brought in from people's homes.

You work with the neighborhood team for two months—during the week and on the weekend. Sometimes the group works into the night to meet the goal of completing the playground before the end of summer. Then

one morning you show up at the playground only to discover that someone has spray painted graffiti on a portion of the wood beams. At a convenience store nearby, you overhear some of your classmates boasting about how they spray painted the beams. You feel very angry.

You can repair the damage, but the jungle gym won't be the same. How do you feel about the fact that someone defaced your work? What will you do?

Keep this story in mind as we further explore the stories in Genesis.

FAITH
SHARING

Write the following this week: three examples of humans keeping God's covenant and three examples of a social sin. Base your examples on your review of newspapers and other forms of media; also include firsthand accounts and experiences from within your community or school.

In the opening story, you read about "a creation" that required a great deal of planning and effort. You probably work for and take care of many things that are valuable to you. As you read this chapter, try to understand how God, as Creator, gave the world to the first humans and how they responded to that gift.

As you read Genesis 1–11, you will learn about beginnings. Everyone has had a first day in a new place—at school, at a job, on a sports team. In fact, you will have many first days in your life because life is full of beginnings. The first stories in the Bible are attempts to explain big ideas—how the world began and the beginning of the relationship between God and his people. These stories are the first steps toward establishing the identity and purpose of God's people: How did the world begin? From where did I come? How do I relate to God? Think about how we respond to God's gifts today. ■

THE ORAL TRADITION

When you think of a story, your first thought may be of a written story. Newspapers are filled with late-breaking stories. Libraries and bookstores circulate your favorite novels and magazines. The Internet is overflowing with narratives. The written word is just one way that we share ideas and information. It is one way that we communicate.

Another popular way to share stories is by *telling* them. Storytelling is an activity that is as simple as a story told from friend to friend. In other cases, storytelling is a major event. Storytelling festivals in the United States, Europe, and other parts of the world attract thousands of people. At such events, people of all ages gather to hear stories told in an entertaining way.

At the Aloha Festival music and dance enhance the storytelling.

In 1947 Hawaiians celebrated their tradition and culture with the first Aloha Festival—an event that continues to be celebrated today. At this festival, storytellers dress as warriors to retell, or relive, Hawaiian history. They perform dance sequences and musical arrangements as a form of theater. They act out their stories for the audience.

Poetry readings (also called "slams") have become very popular in the United States and around the world. Most slams are contests held in small theaters and music venues. Poets stand at a microphone and dramatize their work by playing instruments or calling out to the crowd. The audience participates in choosing a winner. In this way, people share stories and experiences with small groups. This is another example of a modern-day oral tradition.

From 1200 to 1000 B.C. the history and stories of ancient people were handed down orally from generation to generation by storytellers and poets. Thus, these stories were preserved through the **oral tradition.** In ancient times, written language was slow to develop. When it did, very few people could read or write. Groups of people gathered to learn about their history through poetry and storytelling. In a way similar to our festivals and poetry slams, ancient people gathered to tell their history and share experiences. This method of communicating allowed tribes to share a common history and answered questions such as: From where did we come? Why is the world ordered the way it is?

Your family and friends may enjoy telling favorite stories about you! Have you ever heard stories about your first birthday, the day you learned how to ride a bike or swim, or a funny event on a vacation or at home? If you enjoy looking at photo albums, you probably associate certain events with the location and events represented in the photo. Your family and friends might not have a written account of events in your life; however, these oral stories and pictorial recollections contain unique information about who you are. They also may be the only record of such events. ■

Poems

The stories in Genesis express a culture that did not make distinctions between knowledge and belief, science and philosophy, and history and religion. The stories were told in a memorable way and repeated over and over again. To prepare to read Genesis 1–11, consider the genre of the Bible text. Some parts of Genesis 1–11 contain very short poems, which people could easily remember. For example, look at these lines from Genesis:

> By the sweat of your face
>   you shall eat bread
> until you return to the ground,
>   for out of it you were taken;
> you are dust,
>   and to dust you shall return.
>   Genesis 3:19

You will notice that there is repetition in that verse. The writers used a literary device called *parallelism.* This means that parts of sentences and phrases are similar. "You are dust and to dust you shall return" is one example. In your reading of the Genesis stories, look for these similarities. This repetition helped the storytellers and tribes remember their stories. ■

oral tradition   unwritten, memorized accounts of historical events and stories

ActiviTy

Write a one-page memory based on a picture taken at a special event in your life. Gather oral stories of this event from relatives or others who were present.

OpeNiNG THE WoRd

Read Genesis 8:22. This is an example of parallelism. Now read Genesis 1:26–27, Genesis 2:23, and Genesis 8:13–14. Identify examples of parallelism in each reading.

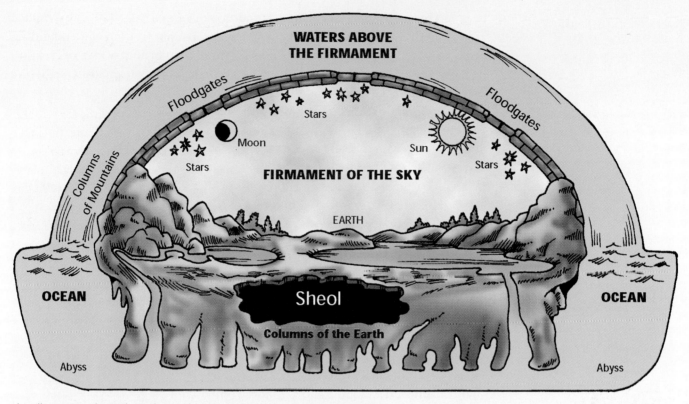

This illustration shows how the world is described in one part of Genesis. Identify the specific Scripture text that matches this illustration.

Myths

myth a symbolic story that gives insight into ultimate questions about beliefs, natural phenomenons, or practices of a particular people

A **myth** is a symbolic story that illustrates views of a particular people regarding the relationship between humans and the divine. You may think that a myth is entirely false, but that is not the case. A myth is a literary form often used by writers for a specific purpose, which is to communicate in symbolic language a reality that transcends experience. The "story" of a myth is universal rather than mainly historical and provides insight into ultimate questions.

Each race and culture has a story about its origin. The Zunis (a Native American people) have a myth that says humans came from the depths of the earth. Roman myths describe how order developed from chaos and describe the creation of flowers, rivers, and rocks.

Genesis contains myths about the origins of the Jewish people. These stories contain the explanation of "from where did we come"—the creation of the world. The most closely related myth to Genesis is a Babylonian epic called *Enuma Elish*. This is a collection of stories with answers to big questions about people and the world in which they live: From where did we come? Why is the world ordered the way it is? *Enuma Elish* is a collection of stories that date from 2000 to 1800 B.C., although the only existing manuscripts date from after 1000 B.C. The myth includes the accounts of many gods competing for power with poison and monsters. The chief god, Marduk, defeats his enemies and establishes his power forever. Then he creates the world—one part to be high as the heavens, the other part to be Earth.

OPENING THE
WORD

Read Genesis
1:1–2:4a, 2:4b–25,
6:5–17, and 11:1–9.
List examples showing
how God gives
identity to things.

ACTIVITY

Read Genesis Chapters 6–8 and
look for similarities between
Gilgamesh, Enuma Elish, and
the story of Noah and the great
flood.

The originators of the first creation story in Genesis knew the *Enuma Elish* myth, but they told their story with details that fit their understanding of the world and God. The storytellers wanted to explain the idea of creation differently. They focused on the God of order—not on chaos. God is the being who makes everything that is good: God commands and gives things their identity. ◼

Those who told and wrote the stories in Genesis 1–11 also would have been familiar with the famous epic *Gilgamesh*. This is one of the oldest and greatest epics in literature. The first records of this story were found on stone tablets, and copies of the story have been found in Syria, Turkey, and the Near East. The hero of the story is Gilgamesh, who was thought to be the king of Uruk, a city.

Gilgamesh is a story that chronicles serious life-and-death problems of the hero. In the course of the story, Gilgamesh and his friend Enkidu (who is made from clay) triumph over the forces of evil—and often encounter dragons and monsters. In one section of the epic, the gods try to destroy human-kind with a flood. The god of wisdom tells one of the characters, Utnapishtim, to build a large boat with which to carry the seed of all living things. ◼

For Review

1. How did ancient people learn the history of their people?

2. What literary forms are used in Genesis 1–11?

3. How is the literary style of Genesis 1–11 similar to other myths and ancient stories?

For Discussion

How is the modern-day understanding of the order of the universe—Earth and space—different or similar to that described in Genesis?

Activity

Write the lyrics to a song that you have memorized. What helps you remember the song? Is it like a poem or is it told in a story format?

Who Wrote the Pentateuch?

The oral tradition of the Bible is the first evidence of efforts to preserve and keep the stories of the Israelites alive. For many centuries, oral traditions continued to be passed down simultaneously with the drafting of written versions. Many ancient people could not read or write—and making copies of the texts was very expensive and difficult. The written and oral traditions influenced each other and resulted in the interwoven text we have today. Our Bible text represents the events and stories of the Israelites throughout several generations.

If you were to follow the written path of the Old Testament, you would need a time machine to take you back and forth through different periods in history. The written history of the Old Testament is not linear. No single person sat down and wrote the Old Testament from start to finish. Different books and parts of the Bible were written at different times. Some of Genesis (the first book of the Bible) may have been written about 550 B.C., whereas parts of Exodus (the second book) were probably recorded much earlier, in about 950 B.C. Biblical scholars debate about these dates; no one is certain. ■

THE FOUR TRADITIONS

It was very important to the Israelites to record events and deeds. Recognizing God's work in their history was central to the Israelites' identity. Their belief in one God set them apart from many people in the ancient Near East who practiced polytheism; the Israelites practiced monotheism. *Gilgamesh* and *Enuma Elish* are stories with many different gods.

The first five books of the Bible are called the **Pentateuch**, which in Greek means "five scrolls." The Hebrew word for this is *Torah,* which means "the law." These books are Genesis, Exodus, Leviticus, Numbers, and Deuteronomy. These stories were once thought to be written by Moses, but biblical scholarship shows that many authors wrote these books. The Pentateuch gives the religious history of humankind, particularly the chosen people, from the creation of the world to the death of Moses. The Pentateuch is often referred to in the New Testament as "the book of the Law" (Galatians 3:10) or simply "the Law" (Romans 3:21).

God spoke through or inspired the human authors to compose these stories, so the Bible includes many different writing styles and forms. Scholars believe that the Torah is a single work of many different writers and was composed over a period of several centuries. (Scholars debate about many details of the composition of the Pentateuch.) Each writer or school of writers contributed a piece or pieces in order to produce the story of God's people. As you know, Genesis contains myths and poems, but it also contains other writing styles—narratives, speeches, hymns, parables, and historical accounts. Historians and Scripture scholars continue to study the early texts today—like detectives trying to solve the mystery of authorship. Most historians settle on four different traditions in the writing in the Pentateuch, but each of these traditions included many writers. Evidence of these four traditions can be seen in the other historical books, but the greatest influence is from the Priestly tradition, the final editors of the historical books. ■

JOURNAL

Consider the way the parts of the Bible were constructed at different times. Then consider how your message might change if you were to write a letter or E-mail to a friend at three different times in a week—at the beginning of the week, middle of the week, and end of the week. Write a few sentences describing how your message might change throughout the week.

Pentateuch   the first five books of the Bible; the *Torah*

OPENING THE WORD

Read Joshua 22:2–5; Psalm 117; Ezekiel 18:2–3; and 1 Samuel 8:1–9. Match the following writing styles to each reading: hymn, proverb, historical account, and speech.

The Four Traditions

Tradition	Abbreviation	Period of Writing
Yahwist	J	up to c. 950 B.C.
Elohist	E	up to c. 850 B.C.
Deuteronomic	D	up to c. 650 B.C. and later
Priestly	P	up to c. 550 B.C. and later

Biblical scholars continue to debate about the traditions (sources) of the Pentateuch and when they were written. The "E" and "J" traditions are thought to have merged about 721 B.C. Some scholars believe the Priestly tradition was recorded about 587 B.C. What might cause archaeologists and scholars to continue to debate the sources of authorship?

The "J" Yahwist Tradition (fixed about 950 B.C. or later)

 The chart on this page shows how the different traditions, or sources, comprise the Pentateuch. You can refer back to this chart as you read the Pentateuch; however, remember that there is much disagreement among biblical scholars about the dates of different parts of these books. The dates given here are for your general reference.

To understand the text, scholars and historians study vocabulary, styles of writing, and common subjects or themes in the original writings. The Yahwist or "J" tradition source is notable for its use of the Hebrew name *Yahweh* for God. (This tradition is called the "J" tradition after the German spelling of *Yahweh*, which is *Jahweh*.) This name, *Yahweh*, has been thought to be too sacred to be spoken. At one time it was spelled as "YHWH," without any vowels, since this is how the original Hebrew Torah was written. Centuries later, vowels were added. By this time, in speaking of God, people were substituting *"Adonai,"* meaning "Lord," for the name of God, so the vowels of the word *Adonai* were inserted in YHWH. Your Bible probably uses the word *Lord* throughout the Yahwist writing and in many other sections of the Pentateuch. (Your Bible also probably uses the word *God* in some sections of the Pentateuch.)

Historians believe that the main "J" writer lived in the tenth century B.C., during the period of the United Kingdom of Israel, which was a proud time in Israel's history. People wanted a history written to show their national pride and national identity. The Israelites were God's special people. This writer created a foundational epic from earlier oral and written stories in order to express a national unity. The Yahwist writing includes the mythical stories of sin and God's promise.

Often, the "J" writers used **anthropomorphism** in describing God. For example, God speaks to the first man, the first woman, and the serpent. God also plants the garden in Eden. In the "J" tradition, God deals directly with humans in stories that are imaginative and dramatic. ■

OPENING THE WORD

Reflect on the cycle of divine blessing, sin, punishment, sign of YHWH—blessing or grace. Give details of this Yahwist cycle, or pattern, in the following Scripture passages: Genesis 2–3, the garden; Genesis 4, Cain and Abel; Genesis 5–8, the Flood; Genesis 9–10, Noah; Genesis 11, The Tower of Babel.

anthropomorphism
the attributing of human characteristics to nonhuman realities

ActiviTy

Role-play the relationships depicted in the following Scripture readings: Genesis 22:1–9, Isaac; Genesis 28:10–17, Jacob's vision; Genesis 35:2–4, Exodus 20:4–6, other gods; Exodus 19:15, covenant.

OpeNiNG THE WoRD

Find examples of the Deuteronomic writers' style (long sentences) and the writers' focus on law in Deuteronomy 12–26; Judges 2:6–20.

JoUrNaL

Write a few sentences to explain when it is important to have written laws rather than verbal laws. When might you have trouble following laws that are only spoken laws? Explain why.

The "E" Elohist Tradition (fixed about 850 B.C.)

In this tradition, the writers refer to God as *Elohim*. This history was written during the time of the divided kingdom (c. 850 B.C.), and is thought to have been created in the northern kingdom of Israel. After the northern tribes split from Judah in the ninth century B.C., the Elohist writers rewrote the traditional stories by focusing on the heroes from the northern tribes. The writers also included information about the covenant relationship or pact that God had made with his people. God is a God of love, but also a God to be feared. He demands righteousness and justice, and his demands are not to be taken lightly. The Elohist writers emphasize human responsibility, service, and faithfulness and obedience to God, and often include dreams or messengers. For the Elohist, God deals with humans indirectly and sends messages through angels and other means. ■

The "D" Deuteronomic Tradition (fixed about 650 B.C.)

This tradition of writings includes updates to the religious laws from Moses' time. This was called the second giving of the Law—*deuteros* means "second"; *nomos* means "law." This tradition of writers encourages people to obey laws out of love and not just out of duty. The success or failure of Israel depends upon Israel's observance of the Law. These writings began around the eighth century B.C. and are noted for their long sentences. ■

Most of the subject matter is about the covenant with God. For example, Moses gives speeches to urge Israel to follow the Torah. Other than the Book of Deuteronomy, there is not a great deal of the Deuteronomic style in the Pentateuch. However, the Deuteronomic writers did work with the Books of Joshua, Judges, Samuel, and Kings.

The "P" Priestly Tradition (fixed about 520 B.C.)

This tradition is present in the Book of Genesis and in other places in the Old Testament. These authors (actually a school of priests) write about God calling things into existence, and they give other examples of the power of God's word. Many Scripture scholars believe that in about 587 B.C. these writers developed the final version of the Pentateuch. They sought to unify the people by documenting the laws of the cult (the religious practices during the time of Moses and the Tribal Confederacy). ■

The final version of the Pentateuch was written after the Israelites' return from the Babylonian Exile, during the period of resettlement and rebuilding. The priestly writers believed that the religious concepts needed to be purified and that basic religious practices needed to be revived because the people had lost touch with their past. The stories in this tradition reteach the beliefs and practices that were lost while the people were separated and divided or exiled. The writers give special emphasis to subjects important to priests. For example, the Priestly tradition mentions special religious ceremonies and cultic rituals, such as circumcision.

In some cases, writers from two different traditions cover the same content or story. For example, in the first chapter of Genesis, we learn that man and woman were God's final creation. In the second chapter, we learn that God created trees and plants *after* creating man and woman. It is understood that there are two creation stories in Genesis. When the writers and editors put them together, they chose to preserve material from both sources concerning the same story. The two accounts of the creation present different views, but the theology remains constant: God created the world. (In parts of Genesis, the "J" and "E" traditions overlap; some scholars consider "J" and "E" traditions one tradition, "JE." Another group of scholars believes that there was never an Elohist tradition, since that tradition is difficult to distinguish from the Yahwist or Priestly tradition.)

"And the LORD God planted a garden in Eden, in the east; and there he put the man whom he had formed."

Genesis 2:8

For Review

1. List the four traditions of writing in the Pentateuch.

2. Which tradition captures a proud period in Israel's history?

3. List two characteristics that mark the Elohist tradition.

4. What were the main goals of the Priestly writers?

5. What is the meaning of the word *Deuteronomy*?

For Discussion

Review the four traditions of the Pentateuch. Imagine finding a part of the original text that shows great ingenuity by the writer. To which tradition would you assign the writer?

Activity

Imagine you are given the assignment of writing or otherwise creating a short autobiography of your childhood. You may use photos, videotape, and interviews from family and friends. Write a one- to two-page description or create a presentation (perhaps using various media) explaining how you might use each source to produce your story.

Journal

Choose a story told in the Pentateuch and relate it to your understanding of who God is.

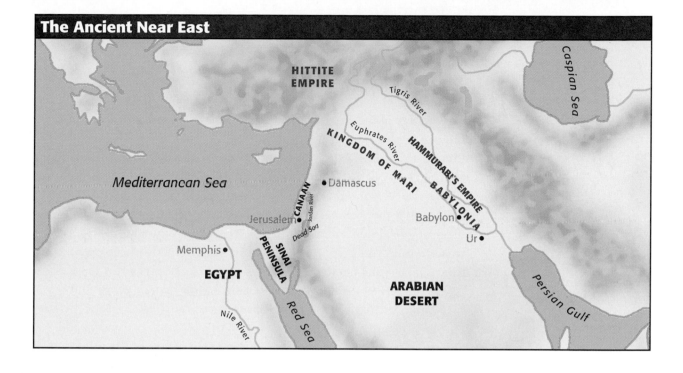

The Ancient Near East

Caspian Sea

HITTITE EMPIRE

Tigris River

Euphrates River

HAMMURABI'S EMPIRE

KINGDOM OF MARI

BABYLONIA

Mediterranean Sea

• Damascus

CANAAN

Jordan River

Jerusalem •

Dead Sea

Babylon •

Ur •

Memphis •

SINAI PENINSULA

EGYPT

Red Sea

ARABIAN DESERT

Persian Gulf

Nile River

The ancient Near East, particularly the Fertile Crescent area, is the setting of the Old Testament.

PRIMEVAL HISTORY

The stories presented in Genesis 1–11 are not history in the modern sense. This part of Genesis is written about a period of time that is called primeval history, which means before historical dates, facts, and events were recorded. The stories are not tied to any specific dates or periods. Primeval history, or prehistory, is the record of human events before the invention of writing. Historians believe that while events were not recorded, many great accomplishments took place in ancient times. Archaeologists and scientists have found tools, paintings, fossils—even jewelry—from these ancient times. These historical artifacts represent evidence of this time period and help us piece together parts of early human history.

The rose limestone stele depicts a king and his soldiers approaching a mountain summit. The sculpture originated in Mesopotamia over 4000 years ago and was discovered in Susa, Iran.

EXPLORING GENESIS 1–11

Genesis 1–11 contains the primeval stories or myths about the creation, the fall, and its aftermath.

Creation

The writers of the first chapters of Genesis accepted an enormous responsibility when they attempted to craft and document the origins of the world. Imagine yourself in their position: How do I explain the beginnings of the world? How will my reader understand the first humans and their actions? These writers worked to craft the centuries-old oral traditions into a written format that their readers could understand. If you were given the responsibility of explaining something that exists in the natural and historical world, where would you begin? For example, imagine writing an essay explaining what makes your family a family—is it the experiences you have, the home you maintain, or the emotions you share? How do you prove that you have a true family or that you truly love another person? Abstract concepts are difficult to explain.

Read Genesis 1–2:4a.

The first story in Genesis describes the creation of the universe, a world that is all good. The writers of this story present a naive explanation of the universe that is not based on historical events nor on facts of natural science. The writers present a religious truth, but not a literal truth, because the writers' focus is God, not cultures and peoples—and not nature or science. God creates the first man and woman in the image of God as beings with dignity and free will who share in creation through their own work. This creation story describes how humans entered the world in the image of God and how they have a special role to protect that world. For us, the religious truths presented here are more important than the literal accuracy of the details of the stories: God created the world and all that is in it; how he made it is not as important. ■

This story also sets up the relationship between God and his people. Human life is lived in relation to God and in relation to other people and nature. This is often described as right relationship with God. Right relationship is an acknowledgment of the covenant and its giver. It is the way to live as prescribed by God—as first revealed when God spoke to the first humans (according to the first creation story). God chose to have a special people and made a covenant with or promise to them. These were God's plans arising from his loving goodness.

Evolution and Creationism

The stories of creation are included in an ongoing debate about how to interpret the Bible. Creationism is the teaching of the origins of the world through a literal interpretation of the creation stories in the Bible.

Activity

Imagine that you are an archaeologist and find the text about the first humans and God's creation, along the lines of the first creation story. Write a paragraph interpreting the meaning of the text.

"God saw everything that he had made and indeed, it was very good."

Genesis 1:31

The Bible is the written record of God's revelation. The important truth in the Bible is religious truth. It is important to know that God made the world and all that is in it. It is less important from a religious point of view to know how he made it. Evolution seeks to explain the origins of humans through science. This understanding of the world and the origins of humans relics on science, but it neither excludes nor contradicts religious belief in a Creator, in God.

In this chapter, you have learned about literal truth and religious truth in the Bible. In the story of the creation, you read that the writers presented religious truth, but that the details of the creation stories are not to be interpreted literally. In reading them, we need to consider the culture, literary forms, and the author's purpose in telling or writing the story. Our scientific knowledge was unknown and unimportant to the writers. Today, the natural sciences enrich our knowledge of the development of life on earth, the appearance of humans, and the structure of the world. For us, the physical origins of life on earth (which are explained by the natural sciences) are important, as is the religious meaning underlying the stories in Genesis. Who created the world? Why did God create humans? Who is responsible for the world? These are questions that are central to religious truth and the faith community, and the answers in Genesis tell us a great deal about God, human nature, and the relationship between God and humans.

The Fall

In the highly symbolic story of the fall, the first humans eat the forbidden fruit, and in this act they disobey God. They choose to replace God with themselves. After they sin, they feel naked and ashamed, and they hide. This first sin has effects for the remainder of human history.

What is sin? Sin is something spoken, a deed, an attitude, or a desire contrary to God's law. Sin is an offense against reason, truth, and right conscience; it is failure in genuine love for God and neighbor. In this story, sin is the act of the will in revolt against God. The first humans break their relationship with God by disobeying him and by acting contrary to his law. The fall is the first sin of human history, or the **original sin.** This initial sin is an act of arrogance that leads to other sins. But God does not abandon his creatures; rather, he offers them the promise of salvation after the fall from grace. ■

OPENING THE WORD

Read the story of the fall in Genesis 3. Why do you think the first woman and man acted on the serpent's words? What do you think of their responses to God? What human conditions are explained in their punishment? In what way is this an "origin story"?

original sin the human condition of the need for salvation based on the first humans' choice to disobey God

Cain and Abel

Read Genesis 4:1–16.

Chapter 4 of Genesis introduces the reader to a second story about sin. Cain and Abel, two brothers, are the sons of the first humans. The brothers represent the two major occupations, farming and herding. (Cain works in the fields. Abel is a shepherd.) They make sacrificial offerings to God, but Abel offers the finest and fattest of his flock, while Cain offers less than the best produce. God is pleased with Abel's offering. This angers Cain and he murders Abel. Cain's sin is a **personal sin.** This story presents an important point: The first sin is followed by a continuation of sin, and within a short time, other forms of personal sin enter the world—the murder of a brother being one of the worst. The original sin affects the children of the first humans and indeed of all the human family. ■

personal sin the free choice to disobey God; to do something that is the opposite of the good

Journal

Why do you think the writers chose to include sin in the stories about the first humans? Describe the way the writers set up the relationship between God and his people in Genesis 1–11. How would you describe your relationship with God?

Noah and the Great Flood

As the descendants of the first humans grew in number and disseminated into other regions, the sins of humankind continued. God saw the evil humans had done and was sorry that he had created humankind. In the story of Noah, God chooses a good and honest man. God intends to destroy every living thing he has made, but will save Noah and his family. He gives Noah instructions for building a giant ark, stocking it, and otherwise preparing for the flood. Noah's acceptance of God's instructions is an act of faith, and in this he becomes an example for all of us.

After forty days and nights of rain, every living thing on earth is destroyed, all except Noah and the others on his ark. Noah builds an altar in thanksgiving to God. God's covenant with Noah foreshadows God's covenant with the Israelites through Abraham. As events transpire in the Bible, the Israelites experience God's covenant over and over again. Christians believe God's covenant with his chosen people was fulfilled in Jesus and extended to all people.

From babies' rooms to art museums, we see evidence that the story of Noah has captured the imagination of every generation. This painting of "Noah's Ark" by Malcah Zeldis resides in the Jewish Museum in New York City.

In the creation, fall, and flood stories, the reader may notice that God punishes sinners justly, yet continues to love and care for them. The first humans must leave the garden, but God provides clothes when they find they are naked. Cain is forced to wander, but God marks him to keep him from harm. God gives Noah instructions for building the ark, thus ensuring that not all humans will die. These are all examples of God's mercy. God enters human history and saves them through his mighty deeds. These occurrences of divine intervention make up **salvation history.**

salvation history   historical events through which God saves; how God enters into history to bring the salvation he has promised; God's saving actions in human history

Read Genesis 11:1–9.

social sin   a collective, societal act or sign that society has distanced itself from God

The Tower of Babel

The last story in primeval history (Genesis 1–11) is the story of the Tower of Babel. The descendants of Noah multiply and settle in a plain. Once again, humans commit personal sins and the effects of the original sin continue. According to the story, the people of the different nations try to build a tower to the heavens—a tower that will make them famous. But because of their sins, these people seek power without recognizing or remembering their relationship with God. God sees that this is not good and can see that there will be no limit to what the people will want. God halts the efforts of the people of different nations by confusing their speech.

The building of the Tower of Babel is a **social sin.** The people build a tower independent of God. Babel is similar to the word "babble" in English, which you may know means to talk nonsense or to make no sense. In the end, then, the story gives the people an explanation for the many languages they hear and the inability of different nations to work together because of their language differences.

For Review

1. What is primeval history, and why is it important to consider this when reading Genesis?

2. What big questions do the stories of the first humans address?

3. Who is Cain, and what does his story signify?

4. Explain how God treats sinners in the stories in Genesis 1–11.

For Discussion

How would you instruct a new reader of the Bible to interpret the stories in Genesis 1–11 in order to arrive at the religious truth? What advice or guidelines would help the reader understand the stories?

Activity

Use a library or the Internet to research examples of fine art depicting some of the stories in Genesis 1–11. The Renaissance period includes many examples. Create an oral presentation or write a brief essay describing a painting and how the artist conveyed the emotions or actions of the figures in the art.

Francis of Assisi

Patron of Environmentalists

Francis of Assisi (1182–1226) was a man who had a profound love for God's creatures. He is often depicted artistically with arms outstretched preaching to the birds and beasts of the forest. Stories about Francis show him on friendly terms with horses, donkeys, deer, pigs, sheep, rabbits, cats, bees, worms, and other animals. Tradition has it that Francis communicated with a wolf near Gubbio in Italy and persuaded him not to attack the villagers.

Francis spent a great deal of time out of doors as a result of his chosen lifestyle of poverty. A passage from Scripture that inspired him was "Consider the lilies of the field, how they grow; they neither toil nor spin, yet I tell you, even Solomon in all his glory was not clothed like one of these" (Matthew 6:28–29). A song calling the sun his brother and the moon his sister is attributed to St. Francis. He respected water because it was used in Baptism, rock because God was called The Rock, and trees because Christ was crucified on the wood of a tree. Indeed, Francis regarded both animate and inanimate realms of creation as members of his family.

> All praise be yours, my Lord, through all
>   that you have made,
> And first my lord Brother Sun,
> Who brings the day; and light you give to
>   us through him.
> How beautiful is he, how radiant in all his
>   splendor!
> Of you, Most High, he bears the likeness.

The use of nativity sets in churches and homes at Christmas is attributed to Francis, who built a manger scene in an outdoor cave and included live animals in the scene.

Francis was born in Assisi in central Italy and was christened John (Giovanni). His name was changed later to Francis (Francesco) to acknowledge his mother's French background. His father was a rich cloth merchant. As a young man, Francis enjoyed life and had many privileges. However, a series of

Saint Francis was a good steward of God's creation. Modern-day environmentalists find inspiration in his respect for all creation.

experiences—being a prisoner of war, becoming ill, and encountering a leper—led him to question his values. At San Damiano church, Francis experienced a call from God to repair his Church. Misunderstanding the call, Francis first removed and sold goods from his father's warehouse to finance the renovation of the church of San Damiano. When brought to trial for the theft, Francis publicly disrobed and returned his clothes to his father, understanding at last that God was calling him to reform God's Church, which was caught up in the wealth of many city-states.

This was the beginning of Francis's commitment to poverty, as he, and eventually his many followers, left town wearing rough brown peasant garments to live in the hills, help those who were destitute and sick, and witness to the gospel. In 1210 his little community journeyed to Rome to seek the approval of Pope Innocent III for its religious rule and order. In an age of wealth, Francis favored the poor; in an age of crusades and battles, he stood for nonviolence; in an age of male domination, he formed a religious community for women. At the end of Francis's life, after being pierced with the wounds of Christ and suffering multiple illnesses, he welcomed "Sister Death."

Making Choices

Genesis illustrates the three theological virtues: faith, hope, and charity. These virtues inform all the moral virtues and give life to them. But how can you make these virtues a part of your life?

You make decisions every day that govern what you say and what you do. Treating family members and friends with respect is one way that you follow God's word. Like Saint Francis, your respect for life on earth may show itself in other ways. Read the following text from Genesis:

> Then God said, "Let us make humankind in our image, according to our likeness; and let them have dominion over the fish of the sea, and over the birds of the air, and over the cattle, and over all the wild animals of the earth, and over every creeping thing that creeps upon the earth."
>
> Genesis 1:26

> The Lord God took the man and put him in the garden of Eden to till it and keep it.
>
> Genesis 2:15

According to the Genesis story, humans were given dominion over all the animals of the earth. Further, they were expected to take care of the garden in which they were placed by God. From earliest times, the earth's resources have seemed unlimited and there for the taking by humankind. Having dominion has been interpreted to mean control and consumption. Today we have a different picture. Nature deserves respect as God's creation. Natural resources—animal, vegetable, and mineral—are limited and many are nonrenewable. Many animal and plant species are endangered and many have become extinct. Fossil fuels are being exhausted. Air and water are polluted. Natural cycles have been disturbed. In many regions environmental deterioration has resulted in poverty, hunger and thirst, illness and death.

Today's environmental concerns include open-pit mining and the destruction of rainforests. Consequences are both local and worldwide.

Each of us should accept responsibility for life, respect the environment, and be caretakers of the world that God created. The choices made by our parents and grandparents have affected our present. The choices we make today will affect the future. Every time we are involved in a give-and-take with the environment, there is an effect. Actions have consequences; some consequences are good and some not so good.

GOD

Some of us mumble or recite a familiar prayer of thanks before eating a meal. With thought, however, our words praise and thank God for our food and the people who raised it and prepared it. Think of a way to pray these thoughts using only gestures and no words. Use it as your family prayer during the week.

NEIGHBOR

Research the U.S. Catholic Bishops' statement *Renewing the Earth: An Invitation to Reflection and Action on Environment in Light of Catholic Social Teaching* (1992). What does this document teach about how attention to environmental issues affects our neighbors in our community and the world? If the bishops' statement were being written today, how might it be different? Explain your answer.

SELF

Using flyers or promotional material from an environmental group, note what their purpose is and how they hope to achieve it. Do you agree that their purpose is important? Do you agree with their approach? If you agree, prepare a plan for supporting their goals that you can do as an individual without joining the group or giving them a financial contribution.

For REVIEW

1. Describe the present state of the environment and the earth's resources.

2. What can you do to show your respect for the earth and God's creation?

For DISCUSSION

Scientists have developed creative solutions to the energy needs of the human population. Some exciting innovations produce electricity using ocean currents and wind farms that should generate clean, renewable energy sources. Discuss some other developments that humans have made in relation to God's gifts. How have humans performed? What are some future possibilities?

ACTIVITY

Compare the story about the construction project at the beginning of this chapter to Genesis. How did God respond after the first humans disobeyed? What might you have done? Write a short essay describing your response.

Many cultures have creation myths as a way of explaining the origins of the universe and the practices of different peoples. The opening chapters of the Bible include such stories about the world God created. When we read the stories, we need to consider the literary forms, the history, and the cultural elements employed by the writers. All of these factors make the stories rich with meaning for God's people. The authors had a specific purpose in writing the stories. Our scientific knowledge was unknown and unimportant to them. What is important in the Bible is what the facts represent, the religious meaning conveyed by the stories.

The stories tell us something about human nature and the human relationship with God. The creation stories illustrate in a dramatic style the sin of the first man and woman. The writers call attention to this point to explain how God's people are to live and not live in the world he created. The stories of Cain and Abel, Noah, and the Tower of Babel introduce a common theme throughout the Bible—the continuation of sin and the mercy God shows sinners.

Lord, you have been our dwelling place
    in all generations.
Before the mountains were brought forth,
    or ever you had formed the earth and the world,
    from everlasting to everlasting you are God.

Psalm 90:1–2

Seek the LORD and his strength;
   seek his presence continually.
Remember the wonderful works he has done,
   his miracles, and the judgments he uttered,
O offspring of his servant Abraham,
   children of Jacob, his chosen ones.

Psalm 105:4–6

Events in Old Testament History

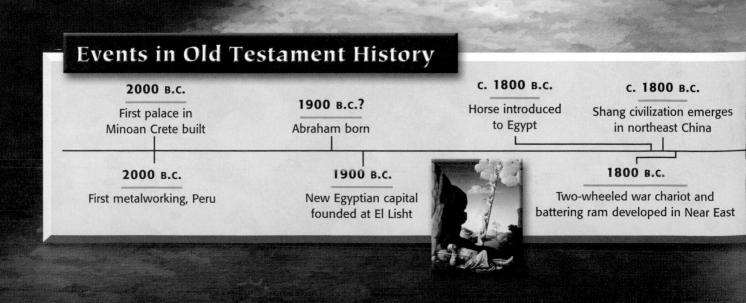

2000 B.C.
First palace in
Minoan Crete built

1900 B.C.?
Abraham born

C. 1800 B.C.
Horse introduced
to Egypt

C. 1800 B.C.
Shang civilization emerges
in northeast China

2000 B.C.
First metalworking, Peru

1900 B.C.
New Egyptian capital
founded at El Lisht

1800 B.C.
Two-wheeled war chariot and
battering ram developed in Near East

Ancestors and Their Journey of Faith

CHAPTER GOALS

Increase knowledge of the meaning of the Old Testament and deepen understanding of its value by studying the following:

- Literary characteristics of Genesis 11:27–50:26
- Genesis 11:27–50:26 and its connection to recorded history
- Laws, codes, and ways of life as they influenced the patriarchal stories
- Ancestral history of God's people

CHAPTER OUTLINE

Literary Interpretation: Genealogies and Narratives

Historical Interpretation: Life in the Fertile Crescent

Theological Interpretation: The Story of the Patriarchs

Witness: Louis Martin and Azélie-Marie Guérin

Personal Challenge: Family and Community

Summary

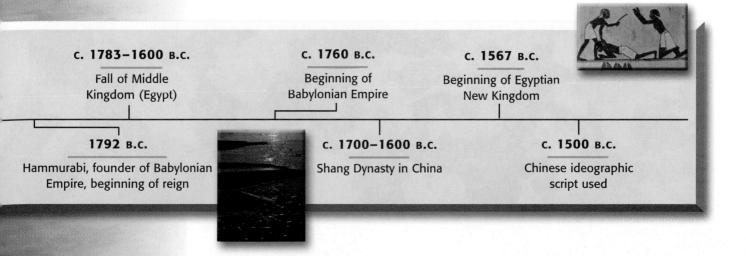

c. 1783–1600 B.C.	c. 1760 B.C.	c. 1567 B.C.
Fall of Middle Kingdom (Egypt)	Beginning of Babylonian Empire	Beginning of Egyptian New Kingdom

1792 B.C.	c. 1700–1600 B.C.	c. 1500 B.C.
Hammurabi, founder of Babylonian Empire, beginning of reign	Shang Dynasty in China	Chinese ideographic script used

Imagine the school year has just begun. As usual, you feel excited to start a new year, but you also feel nervous about it. You see friends you haven't seen in several weeks, and you visit with the friends you spent time with over the summer. You easily begin laughing at the same jokes. You enjoy sharing common interests and talking about the upcoming year—sports events, school clubs, and class activities. You compare schedules and discover that you share some of the same courses and teachers. Being with your old friends feels comfortable and easy.

Within the first week, you meet new people in your classes. A new friend hands you a flyer for a party next weekend. As the date gets closer, you talk about it with your old friends and learn that they will not be attending the party. You decide that it is a good idea to meet new people and do new things. You decide to go to the party on your own.

When you arrive at the party, you learn that the student's parents are not home. Very quickly you learn that your new friends are interested in some things that you have avoided in the past. After you decide to stay, it strikes you—you are in the middle of making some tough choices. The topics of conversation and all of the jokes seem foreign to you. You struggle to find something to say to contribute to the conversation, but you can think of nothing. Your mind and speech are frozen. You feel lost and isolated—as if you were on an island.

You decide to step outside for a moment to catch a breath of fresh air. In front of a group of her friends, your new friend offers you a drug. You do not want to accept it. What do you do? Do you agree to please your new friend? Do you say no? How much do you know about yourself to make the right decision for you? Does the offer feel like a test of your new friendship?

How do you know what is the right thing to do?

Literary Interpretation

FAITH SHARING

Three times this week consider how your friends, family, and community affect your daily life.

Think about these questions:

- Do I make decisions on my own—or do I wait to see what my friends do first?
- Who affects my life more—my friends or my family? Why?
- How do each of the following influences affect my values—family, friends, community (school, Church, social group)?

genealogy an account of ancestry

providence divine guidance and care

narrative prose or poetry story

Many events described in the Old Testament seem unbelievable to us because they are unlike anything that occurs in our present-day surroundings. It is important to remember that what the Old Testament's stories are designed to teach us can be found at the heart of each story, not in the literal interpretation of the details. When we look closely, we see that while the circumstances may be different, the issues faced by humanity remain the same. Problems faced by our biblical ancestors are in fact very similar to modern-day issues. An example is the difficult choices related to the teen party in the opening story. ■

TRACING THE STORY OF OUR BIBLICAL FAMILY

The Book of Genesis provides stories of important figures in the early stages of our religious history. This biblical **genealogy,** or account of our ancestry, shows the succession of generations and illustrates that we are descendants of many faithful followers of God. The genealogies found in Scripture show how the Israelites saw themselves as being related to the surrounding peoples. They gave the Israelites a stronger sense of God's **providence** and their rootedness, which was important during the Exile when the Pentateuch was probably written. The combination of genealogies and **narratives,** or prose or poetry stories, provides a well-rounded picture of our religious history— salvation history. A narrative, which can be either fictional or true, can illuminate a detail within a genealogy that might otherwise be overlooked. Some narratives begin or end with a genealogy. Narratives can also be stylistically framed by placing genealogies at the beginning and the ending of a story.

We sometimes describe ourselves in terms of when we were born and who our parents and other family members are. Our personal narratives include a type of simplified genealogy. Understanding the personal background of an individual can help others better understand that person. Recounting genealogies and personal narratives also helps us maintain our sense of heritage and community.

Genealogies and family histories help us celebrate the present while rooting us in the family story.

Patriarchs

patriarch male leader of a family or tribe

OPENING THE WORD

In pairs or small groups, read the following passages: Genesis 11:27–12:3, 13:14–17, and 17:1–8. Identify the important figures and their roles in salvation history.

One of the prominent figures in our biblical genealogy is Abraham. He was the first great leader, or **patriarch,** of the people of Israel. Leadership passed from Abraham to his son, Isaac, to Isaac's son, Jacob, and then to Jacob's sons and grandsons. The heads of the twelve tribes of Israel, twelve male descendants of Abraham, are also considered patriarchs. The female ancestors of Israel, such as Sarah, Rebekah, Leah, and Rachel, are called matriarchs. Studying the narrative of Abraham and his family provides us with a sense of our spiritual ancestry and an example of the power of faith. ■ ■

ActiviTy

Gather information from members of your family to compile a family tree, or an illustrative chart, of your ancestry (or, if you are adopted, of your adoptive family's ancestry). Try to chart four or five generations of your family. Remember, you and your siblings count as one generation.

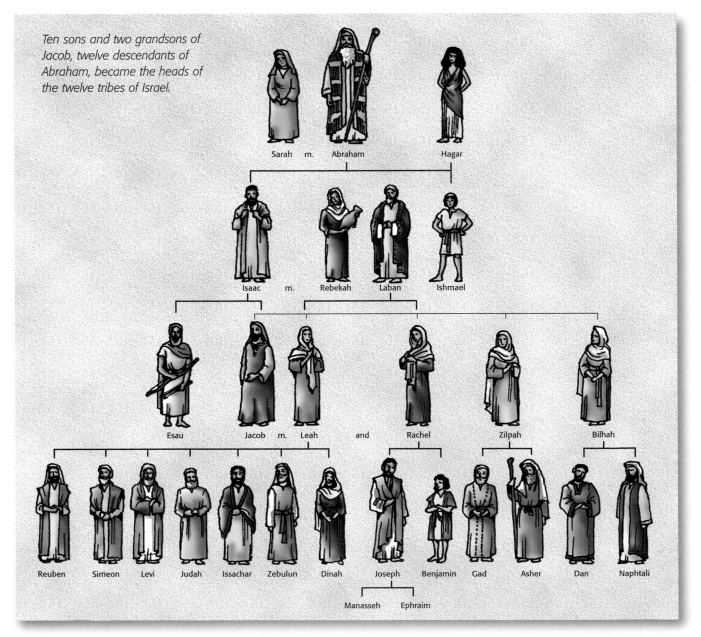

Ten sons and two grandsons of Jacob, twelve descendants of Abraham, became the heads of the twelve tribes of Israel.

Sarah   m.   Abraham   Hagar

Isaac   m.   Rebekah   Laban   Ishmael

Esau   Jacob   m.   Leah   and   Rachel   Zilpah   Bilhah

Reuben   Simeon   Levi   Judah   Issachar   Zebulun   Dinah   Joseph   Benjamin   Gad   Asher   Dan   Naphtali

Manasseh   Ephraim

Esau returned from the hunt to find that Jacob had tricked Isaac into giving him the blessing meant for the elder Esau. This rendition is in the baptistry of the cathedral in Padua, Italy.

FOLKLORE

folklore composite of traditional customs, art forms, tales, and sayings preserved among a people

Various elements of **folklore** also contribute to the narratives within the Book of Genesis. The term *folklore* refers to the composite of traditional customs, art forms, tales, and sayings preserved among a people—in this case, the people of Israel. An example of folklore is found in the story of Jacob and Esau in Genesis 27. Isaac intended to give his blessing to his oldest son, Esau, but was tricked into giving it to Jacob instead. Due to traditional customs that were part of Israel's folklore, Isaac was not able to take back the blessing bestowed upon Jacob, his younger son. A spoken blessing, much like an arrow that has been shot toward its target, was believed to release a power that determined the destiny of the recipient and, therefore, could not be retracted. Isaac's blessing of Jacob is given in a traditional poetic form, which illustrates the importance attached to the ritual. ■

Read Genesis 27.

OPENING THE WORD

Connections to the narrative of Jacob within the narrative of Joseph form a stylistic framework by which Joseph's life is shown to be a continuation of his ancestral history. Working in small groups, review Genesis 27 and read 37:1–20. Then compare the two stories.

"Ah, the smell of my son
    is like the smell of a field that the LORD has blessed.
May God give you of the dew of heaven,
    and of the fatness of the earth,
    and plenty of grain and wine.
Let peoples serve you,
    and nations bow down to you.
Be lord over your brothers,
    and may your mother's sons bow down to you.
Cursed be everyone who curses you,
    and blessed be everyone who blesses you! "

Genesis 27:27–29

The dreams of the pharaoh functioned as parables of what was to come. This stitched art of the fat and lean cattle/years was created by Sister Helena Steffensmeier SSSF.

PARABLES

parable story with a moral or religious lesson

Read Genesis 41:1–8, 14–36.

JOURNAL

Dreams are often a collection of our private thoughts and real events. Recall a dream that you had recently that was particularly vivid. Write a sentence or two explaining this dream. Compare your interpretation of dreams to that of Joseph in his work for the pharaoh.

A **parable** is a literary device by which an analogy refers to a similar but different circumstance. It is a short, illustrative story that teaches a moral or religious lesson, often through the use of comparisons. In the Old Testament, a parable can be a proverb, riddle, or allegory. Parables differ from fables in that a parable is told in response to a specific situation. A parable can often prove to be more memorable than other types of stories due to its accessible narrative style.

A dream can sometimes function as a parable. In Genesis 41, the pharaoh has a series of vivid dreams. When Joseph is able to interpret the dreams for the pharaoh through divine inspiration, thereby solving the riddle, he is able to tell the pharaoh that the dreams are parables about what is to come. The dreams, when combined with Joseph's interpretation of them, teach the pharaoh what he must do to preserve the land and his people. ■

As you continue to read from Genesis, consider how the storytellers used the literary devices to build their stories and teach religious truths.

For REVIEW

1. What is genealogy, and why is it important in the story of the patriarchs?

2. How does folklore come into play in the story of Isaac blessing Jacob?

3. Why did Scripture storytellers use parables?

For DISCUSSION

Consider a time when you moved to a new place—or started at a new school. What challenges did you face? What things did you miss most about the life you left behind?

ACTIVITY

Think of a formal ceremony that is performed in modern culture, such as an initiation or coronation. List the standard characteristics of that ceremony. How does the formality of this ceremony relate to the formality of giving a blessing?

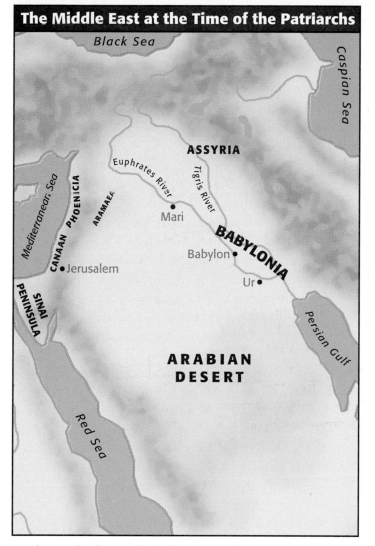

The Middle East at the Time of the Patriarchs

Black Sea

Caspian Sea

ASSYRIA

Euphrates River

Tigris River

Mediterranean Sea

PHOENICIA

ARAMAEA

CANAAN

Mari

BABYLONIA

Babylon

Jerusalem

Ur

SINAI PENINSULA

Persian Gulf

ARABIAN DESERT

Red Sea

For thousands of years the Fertile Crescent has been home to a myriad of important cultures.

The Genesis storytellers included many details that are based in historical fact. Ancient ways of life, laws, and some events are similar to those in the stories of the patriarchs. It was later during the monarchy and exile that the stories were written down and compiled. A major concern of this later time was God's promise of a land, and this too is reflected in the stories.

The story of Israel's patriarchs begins in earnest with Abraham and includes his son and grandson, Isaac and Jacob, and Jacob's sons and grandsons. Twelve of Jacob's male descendants (ten sons and two grandsons) were the basis for the twelve tribes of Israel. These tribes were more like clans than political units. These tribes, and other peoples that populated the ancient Middle East, are known ethnically as Semites. This group included many different peoples—Arameans, Assyrians, Babylonians, Canaanites, and Phoenicians.

In Chapter 2, you learned that Genesis 1–11 is rooted in prehistory—a time before events were recorded. Genesis 12–50 has a more historical basis in the sense of being related to the known history of the ancient Middle East. Unlike the primeval history in Genesis, considerable archeological evidence exists that, in part, connects the history of the ancient Middle East to the time of the patriarchs. The geography of the ancient Middle East contains an area known as the Fertile Crescent that stretches roughly from modern-day Iraq into Egypt and contains the Tigris, Euphrates, and Nile rivers. These rivers provided a source for agriculture and trade, which enabled cities to grow and civilizations to flourish. Remains of these cities exist today. Customs and laws of the ancient Middle East are evident in the story of the patriarchs. ■

The city of Ur is the birthplace of Abraham. Ur was in Sumeria in the far eastern fertile plain between the Tigris and Euphrates rivers. The kingdom of Ur collapsed when the people who dwelled in the mountains above the Mesopotamian plain, the Elamites, attacked. For 200 years, struggles persisted among the smaller city-states in Mesopotamia, and then the Amorites, a semi-nomadic Semitic group, came into power. During this period, known as the First Babylonian Dynasty, the center of power transferred from the northern city of Mari to Babylonia.

Activity

Find a current article about political, ethnic, or religious tensions in the Middle East by looking in a newspaper or a magazine or searching the Internet. Write an essay describing one conflict in the area. Include a description of the groups involved in this conflict.

Hammurabi, this dynasty's greatest king, reigned from 1792 to 1750 B.C. Around this time, the epics *Enuma Elish* and *Gilgamesh* were written. The Code of Hammurabi—a collection of laws that encompass economic, family, and criminal and civil matters—was also compiled. The Code of Hammurabi was based on laws and customs that had existed in Sumerian communities for centuries. As has been noted, it is likely that this code provided the basis for parts of the Israelite law codes.

Ancient inheritance laws and the custom of sacrifice are crucial in the stories of the patriarchs. Ritual sacrifice was an integral part of the Sumerians' religion, and they would offer sacrifices of grain, animals, or wine to the god or goddess particular to their city-state. For the patriarchs, sacrifices intended for God were considered an act of petition or thanksgiving and had the power to bring two parties together.

In order to ensure the survival of the tribe, it was not an unusual custom in the ancient Middle East for a man to take a second wife, or a female servant—a concubine—to bear children. The Code of Hammurabi states that a wife may give her husband "a maid-servant as wife." The writers used these details for the story of Abraham, Sarah, and Hagar (Genesis 16:1–4).

When Abraham's wife, Sarah, is unable to conceive, she offers her slave, Hagar, to Abraham. Hagar gives birth to Ishmael, who is loved by Abraham. Later, when Abraham learns from God that Sarah will also bear a son, God assures Abraham that he will bless Ishmael as well as Sarah's son, Isaac.

After the birth of Isaac, Sarah asks Abraham to send Hagar and Ishmael away. Abraham does so, thereby placing Isaac in his predetermined role in salvation history and giving him the privileges of the firstborn. Hagar, in her distress at having been cast out, is prepared to abandon her child. However, an angel of God speaks to her and promises that God will make of Ishmael a great nation. Muslims believe that they are the descendants of Ishmael and, therefore, believe themselves to be children of Abraham and the great nation promised by God.

Mesopotamian law codes gave protection to children born of a female servant. Hammurabi's code states that if a man's wife bears children, yet the man "adopts the slave's children, then his household shall be divided evenly between the children of both." Another ancient custom and law present in the story of the patriarchs is that the firstborn son of a man's first wife would be the principal heir. Hammurabi's code states that the household will be evenly divided among children after the "firstborn son receives the preferential share." This custom has been known to cause conflict. (The Old Testament writers dramatize such a conflict when Isaac's intentions for blessing his firstborn son (Esau) are upset by Jacob's trickery.

According to the Abraham story, Hagar and Ishmael were abandoned once Sarah gave birth to a son. Muslims trace their origins to Abraham through Ishmael.

Read Genesis 25:30–34.

Chapter 3

This wallpainting of the beating of a slave in Egypt was created sometime between the sixteenth and the fourteenth century B.C. It was found in the tomb of a prominent scribe.

Genesis tells the stories of Abraham. Sometime in the second millennium B.C., Abraham led his people westward out of Ur in Sumeria and eventually settled in Canaan, later called Palestine. The Hyksos people who came from Palestine were a predominantly Semitic people who entered Egypt around 1720 B.C. This immigration occurred after the Thirteenth Dynasty, during which there had been civil unrest in Egypt while provincial governors vied for the pharaoh's throne. The immigrants took control and the Egyptians eventually became subject to the Hyksos. Slavery was common in the ancient Middle East. In fact the Code of Hammurabi has a section of laws dedicated to stealing or housing others' slaves, the consequence for runaway slaves (death), and the reward for returning slaves.

The writers of the Old Testament included historical details and were influenced by existing laws and codes. Floods, drought, and irrigation were ever-present factors in the way of life in the ancient Middle East. When the seven-year famine occurred in Egypt, the Egyptians fared well, as did the Hebrews. However, some historians say that the pharaohs of the Eighteenth Dynasty expelled the Hyksos and enslaved the Hebrews. ■

Opening the Word

Read Genesis 37–50. Find three examples of the writers using famine and slavery to add drama to the stories of Joseph.

For Review

1. What is the major difference between Genesis 1–11 and Genesis 12–50?

2. What do the twelve sons of Jacob represent? What do ten sons and two grandsons of Jacob represent?

3. What is the Code of Hammurabi? How is it related to the Old Testament?

4. What climatic features contribute to the details of the story of Joseph?

For Discussion

Discuss the purpose of a will. Why do you think it is important to have the details of a will in writing?

Journal

If you were to write your own will, what would you include? What would you leave to whom? Explain the importance to you of each item listed, and explain your reasons for leaving it to that particular person.

Activity

Compile your own research on the Hyksos people using the Internet and other resources. Prepare a brief report of the details you find that go beyond the information provided in this text.

There is a connection between the history of Israel's descendants and the history of the ancient Near East. Details of ways of life, laws, and descriptions of a nomadic people are woven throughout these stories. The Old Testament writers' intentions were to present the story of God at work in the history of a people.

I can write with [handwritten annotation]

THE STORY OF THE PATRIARCHS

The Pentateuch addresses the concerns of the time in which it was written—the years of exile. The covenant was understood as a solemn promise by God to give the people a land and a strong nation. The delays and obstacles in the stories are somewhat like the experiences of their descendants in exile who did not know if their nation and religion would survive.

Genesis 11:27–50:26 establishes critical foundations about the ancestors of Israel and the dynamic relationship between God and his people. In these stories, God makes a covenant with Abraham in which he promises a home for his people—the promised land. Although God's people struggle with their faith, the obligation of the covenant is with God alone. God puts no obligations on the people, and Abraham does nothing to merit God's promises. God will make Abraham's descendants a great nation, even if they don't deserve it.

Abraham

The first story of Abraham illustrates promise and faith (Genesis 12–15). This story represents the cycle that is common to all of the Abraham stories. In all circumstances, even when people fail, God is always faithful to his promise. As you read, follow the events as God fulfills his promises to Abraham and then to Abraham and Sarah. ■

You will note that names are very important and significant. *Abram* is changed to *Abraham* when he is assigned a mission—to be "the father of a host of nations." *Sarai* too receives a change of name—to *Sarah*.

Abraham and his wife Sarah do not have any children. Among these nomadic people, barrenness was considered a terrible curse. Children were a sign of God's blessing. God visited Abraham and told him to move to a place where God would bless him and make of him a great nation. This is an example of God's covenant with his people, his promise to give them land—a home and a great nation. Abraham responded to the covenant with faith and obedience to God's commands and promises. He shows his trust in God by leaving his home and setting out for the unknown, relying on God to be faithful to his promises to him. ■

OPENING THE WORD

Read Genesis 15, the story of God's covenant with Abram. What were the terms of the covenant?

OPENING THE WORD

Read Genesis 17:3–6 and 17:15–16. Note how the authors describe the change in names and how the new names assign a role or importance to the people. Then in pairs or small groups discuss the importance and meaning of some names, such as your confirmation name or the meaning of Jr. for Junior.

Read Genesis 13:14–18.

Read Genesis 15.

ActiviTy

Read the story of Sodom and Gomorrah in Genesis 18:16–19:29. With a partner, role-play the debate between Abraham and God about the destruction of the righteous among sinners. Model your debate on the dialogue found in Genesis 18:16–32. As a class, vote on the best presentation of debates.

Read Genesis 17:4–22.

Read Genesis 22:1–19.

JournaL

Write a paragraph about a situation in which you had to sacrifice something very important to you. What factors helped you make your decision? Why was it important for you to make this sacrifice?

When Abraham and Lot decide to part, their choices for land in Negeb influence their individual futures. Abraham and his people ventured into the land of Canaan while Lot settled in the city Sodom—a place we associate with many sinners. Lot did not choose the promised land.

God and Abraham renew their covenant in a sacrificial ceremony. Abraham takes a cow, a female goat, and a ram and cuts them in half. He then kills a turtledove and a pigeon—leaving them whole. These acts were ritual demonstrations of Abraham's obedience to God. After Abraham made his sacrifices, God restates his promise to Abraham.

The Sons of Abraham

Sarah believed that she was too old and therefore unable to bear children. Following the custom of the time, she gives her servant Hagar to Abraham and tells him to treat Hagar as his wife. Hagar bears Abraham a son, named Ishmael, who eventually had many descendants. This son is not the child of the promised land, however. God promises a son for Abraham and Sarah. God continues to make this promise to them even though they deny the possibility that it will happen. Sarah's harsh treatment of Hagar raises an important point for later generations. Even though the nearby Arabic tribes are closely related to the Israelites, they have not received the same promise. God does protect and bless them, however, which illustrates a part of the promise to Abraham: Through him all nations will be blessed. ■

The history of God's promise continues in the event of Isaac's birth when, against all odds, Sarah and Abraham have a child. Their God is indeed powerful. But in the very next chapter of Genesis (22), another important story is told. Abraham's faith is tested when he believes God is commanding him to sacrifice his son by Sarah. This was to be the promised son, but Abraham prepares to sacrifice him. The storytellers fill the story with great tension by emphasizing the lengths to which Abraham is asked to go to show his devotion. At the last moment, God intervenes and stops Abraham. Abraham proved his faith in God by his willingness to sacrifice his only son. This story also presents a strong statement against human sacrifice, which was practiced by some groups in the Middle East. Abraham's unselfish faith in God—his willingness to give up his son of the promise at God's command—is a sacrifice in itself. ■

For Review

1. Describe two examples of how the covenant between God and Abraham was lived out.

2. Why does Sarah give Hagar to Abraham?

3. What does the story of Abraham and Isaac say about human sacrifice?

For Discussion

Discuss the moving story about Abraham's willingness to sacrifice Isaac. Why is this considered the ultimate test of a person's faith in God?

Read Genesis 27:1–45.

The reconciliation of Jacob and Esau is recounted in Genesis 33. This painting by Tissot captures the moment.

OPENING THE WORD

In Genesis 26:6–11, Isaac asks Rebekah to call herself his sister, not his wife, while they are in Gerar. This parallels his father's request of Sarah in Genesis 12:10–20. Compare the two passages. What might be the significance of this parallelism?

Isaac's Wife and Sons

God guides a servant's journey to find the right woman for Isaac. The search leads the servant to Rebekah. Rebekah gives birth to Jacob and Esau, who were known to constantly battle with each other. Even in the womb they struggle with one another. The storytellers included this to foretell the struggle between the nations in later stories. In Genesis 32, you will see that Jacob is given the name *Israel*. In Genesis 36, Esau is Edom—the enemy of Israel. The descendants of Jacob represent God's plan to create a people great in number, such as that of a nation. ■

The Birthright and the Blessing

You have read about the importance of inheritance laws and the rights of sons. In Genesis, Jacob manipulates his brother Esau, who is the elder of the two sons, out of his birthright. Then their father Isaac is fooled and gives his blessing to Jacob—instead of Esau.

These are the first of many examples of Jacob's trickery. Remember the overall purpose in these stories is to show God's promise despite all obstacles. In Chapter 2, you learned about how the oral tradition presented the stories verbally. Try to imagine Israel's ancestors telling these stories around a campfire. They probably presented Jacob as someone who outsmarted the others. He wins! The younger son obtains the privileges meant for the older son. The writers present exciting events to keep the stories lively and to show God at work in human history, unhampered by the customs of the time.

The story of the struggle between Jacob and Esau is one of many elder son/younger son stories in the Old Testament (Isaac in Genesis 21, David in 1 Samuel 16). The Israelites saw themselves as a "younger son" people. (Remember Ishmael?) They had few natural advantages compared to the nations around them, and they became successful only because of God's blessings. The trickery of Jacob is also a reminder that the chosen people are not blessed because they are better people than their neighbors are. They are blessed because God has chosen them.

As the situation develops, Isaac cannot take back his blessing, but he does give Esau another blessing. The storytellers portray Rebekah as being aware of the continuing struggle between her two sons and of God's plan for Jacob. Her actions on behalf of Jacob point to her willingness to be a part of God's plan to fulfill his promise. ■

On his journey to Haran as he escapes his brother's fury, Jacob has a dream and is visited by God. God restates the covenant he made with Abraham: "I am the LORD, the God of Abraham your father and the God of Isaac; the land on which you lie I will give to you and to your offspring" (Genesis 28:13). Repeatedly in the stories of the patriarchs, the writers remind the reader of God's promise in the midst of struggle. The faith of each patriarch in turn is tested.

After Jacob marries and becomes quite wealthy, he decides to leave Haran. He sends a message to Esau that he is on his way home and that he hopes to reunite with him, but he still worries that Esau will kill him. On his journey, he meets a man (angel?) and wrestles with him until daybreak. In this struggle, Jacob demands that the man bless him. Through his blessing, it becomes clear that Jacob has been struggling against God. The man gives him the name *Israel*, and Jacob walks away from this struggle limping. The name change marks Jacob's prevailing in his struggle; so too will the people of Israel prevail in their struggles.

The writers included several details in this story that call forth different interpretations. God is a mystery, even when he reveals himself to humans. Jacob has two struggles—one with his brother and one with God. Jacob had been away for fourteen years and did not know what he would find upon his return. He returns to the promise that was given to his father and his grandfather a long time ago—the promised land and a great people, God's chosen people.

OPENING THE WORD

Read Genesis 27:5–17. Was Rebekah dishonest or was she clever and wise like Jacob? Support your viewpoint.

Read Genesis 28:10–17.

Read Genesis 32:24–31.

"Then [Jacob] had a dream: a stairway rested on the ground with its top reaching to the heavens; and God's messengers were going up and down on it."

Genesis 28:12

Joseph

Joseph, the favored son of Jacob, endures mistreatment at the hands of his brothers and, in Egypt, by Potiphar's wife. These are difficult challenges, but God is with him and ensures his favor with the chief jailer. Inspired by God's support, Joseph shows great courage, honor, and integrity. The stories of Jacob that conclude the Book of Genesis illustrate the truth that despite evil acts on the part of humans, God is present to them with loving goodness. He works for the good in all things. Joseph gains the favor of the pharaoh by his good deeds in prison and by interpreting the pharaoh's dreams, and he becomes the governor of Egypt.

Review Genesis 39–41.

In Egypt, Joseph's brothers are brought in to see the governor. Joseph knows them, but they do not recognize him grown up and in a position of power. Joseph puts one brother, Simeon, in jail and tells the brothers that they must return home to get their youngest brother. Upon hearing this story, Jacob is distraught over the loss of yet another son. Jacob reluctantly sends his other favorite son, Benjamin, as a sort of sacrifice to save Simeon. This story recalls the sacrifice Abraham attempted to make of his son Isaac.

Review Genesis 45.

Finally, when all of his brothers are together, Joseph reveals his identity and tells them that God has drawn good out of their horrible acts against him. This is a tale of reconciliation as Joseph reunites with his family. Joseph interprets their past actions (just as he interpreted dreams)—all the past events were part of God's plan to save his people from famine. In this story Joseph also brings security and prosperity to his people. The blessing of God is shown through the perseverance and strength of Joseph. Despite the acts against him, he obeys God and keeps the covenant.

The stories of the patriarchs remind us that God is our ultimate goal and that our faith in God is well-placed because he is Truth and Love. The generations described in the stories in Genesis are examples of how God perpetuates the covenant with every generation. God gifts us with faith to respond to him.

For Review

1. Which son eventually receives the birthright and Isaac's blessing? How does he do this?

2. How is Jacob given the name *Israel?*

3. How are we to understand the overall purpose for the events of Joseph's life?

For Discussion

What are some ways that we, in response to God's call, can be self-sacrificing in our own lives? How can our unselfish attitudes benefit other people?

Activity

Listen to a recording or watch the video of *Joseph and the Amazing Technicolor Dreamcoat* and correlate each song with the story in Genesis.

Louis Martin and Azélie-Marie Guérin

Louis Martin was born in Bordeaux, France, in 1823. When he was twenty-two years old he sought to enter the religious life at St. Bernard Monastery. Unfortunately, he was not accepted because he did not know Latin, a requirement at the time. In 1850 he began working as a watchmaker, and for the next eight years, he led a life of hard work and worship of God. Though refused admission to the monastery, Louis did not waver in his faith.

Azélie was born in Gandelain, France, in 1831. Her faith in God also was tested, because she had an unhappy childhood. Writing to her brother, she expressed the frustrations of many young people:

The family of Louis Martin and Azélie-Marie Guérin was a testament to their faithful response to God and each other.

> My childhood, my youth, were as sad as a shroud, for if my mother spoilt you she was, as you know, too strict with me. Although she was so good herself she did not understand me and I suffered from this very much.

Azélie did have an unusually tough childhood, but her faith was a source of strength. Like Louis Martin, she attempted to enter the religious life, at Hotel-Dieu, and she too was turned away. In an attempt to get past this disappointment, she learned the craft of lace-making. At the age of twenty-two, she set up her own business. Shortly after this she endured more hardship when the sister to whom she was closest, Marie-Louise, died unexpectedly.

In 1858 Louis and Azélie met. Within three months they exchanged wedding vows. Over a span of ten years the couple had nine children, seven girls and two boys. As had been the pattern of their lives, however, Louis and Azélie's faith was tested again. Two of their daughters and their two sons died as infants or young children.

By the time her next and last daughter was born, Azélie said, "I have already suffered so much in my life." Her suffering was also physical, in that for seven years she endured a tumor that became progressively worse. Pregnant with her last child and suffering from cancer, Azélie's faith persisted: "If God gives me the grace to nurse this child, it would only be a pleasure to rear it." Marie Françoise Thérèse, who would later become a saint, was born on January 2, 1873.

Louis Martin had his faith challenged yet again when Azélie died of breast cancer in 1877 at the age of forty-six. Left with five daughters and no wife, he gave up his watchmaking business and moved the family to Lisieux, Normandy, where Azélie's brother lived with his wife and family. Eventually, all of Louis and Azélie's daughters became nuns, carrying on the strong relationship with God learned from their parents. Thérèse, the youngest, entered the convent at age fifteen and touched many lives with her deep devotion to Jesus. Called Thérèse of the Child Jesus or "The Little Flower," she died at the age of twenty-four and was canonized a saint by Pope Pius XI in 1925.

Louis Martin and Azélie-Marie Guérin faced many difficult times in their lives, and their faith was often tested. Ultimately, however, their strong faith influenced the lives of their surviving children—who devoted their lives in turn to God.

Conflicts within families do not have to result in broken relationships. Rather, conflicts can lead to reconciliation and stronger relationships.

Family and Community

The stories of the patriarchs contain many examples of faith being tested by the trials of life. By prevailing through these hardships, each of the men and women in the stories fulfilled a specific role in their families and communities. Abraham was the father of a people, Sarah was the mother of Isaac—the child of the promise, and Rebekah helped Jacob gain his father's blessing and escape to Haran. God chose these people, communicated to them, and made a covenant with them. His promise and covenant with them continued through the ages because God is faithful even when people fail. He always calls them back to a covenant relationship. ■

Who makes promises to you? Your family members, for example, make a promise to love and care for you. To whom do you make promises? You have an obligation to care for and love your family as well. If you contribute to your household by completing chores or by simply bringing laughter—you are building up your family. Small sacrifices might come in the form of giving up something that you would enjoy in order to help someone in your family. In such ways you live in faith.

Like the patriarchs, you face small and sometimes large tests of your faith every day. If someone hurts you verbally or physically, you face a decision. You can respond in a hurtful way, or you can find a peaceful way to end the conflict. At these times, it may be difficult to see how to maintain *right* relationships with God and other people. Remember the example of those who have gone before you. Abraham trusted God and was blessed with a destiny beyond his wildest dreams. Joseph was faced with the misdeeds of his brothers and Potiphar's wife. He showed strength and integrity and persevered on a path that put him in the position of saving his family. Louis Martin and Azélie-Marie Guérin chose to put their faith in God despite many trials and difficulties. They and their surviving children became saintly people, made holy through the ordinary decisions of everyday life. ■

JOURNAL

Think of a time in your life during which something bad happened that later worked out for the best. What did that experience teach you about the reliability of your initial perception of events?

JOURNAL

What did you do in the last two years that benefited your family or community?

People in your school and community make promises to you, but sometimes the fulfillment of these promises is difficult to notice. More often you may simply neglect to acknowledge how well people keep their promises. Teachers make a commitment to you and to your education. Firefighters, police officers, and hospital workers make commitments to care for the community within which they work. You might have neighbors who help you when you forget your house key or pick up your mail when your family is out of town. Maybe your friends do special things for you when you have a tough day. When you live within the laws and customs of your community and help other people become their best, you are living the commitment to which you are called. You are being faithful.

THE RELIGIOUS COMMUNITY

The stories of the patriarchs represent a structured presentation of the people of Israel. The characters in the stories are identified as "the son of Abraham" and "the daughter of Laban." These identifications set ethnic roots for God's people. This history in the Old Testament sets important foundations for the relationships among people in the human family.

The Old Testament, as a part of Sacred Scripture, holds a place of high honor in Judaism and Christianity—it is God's revelation and the story of salvation. The storytellers show us how God's promises to Abraham are later fulfilled in the time of David and Solomon. Israel's history is also integral to the identity of Jews and Christians.

In biblical times and texts, neither *Jews* nor *Christians* were terms that were used as they are understood today. Yet Jews and Christians today share the common history found in the Old Testament, which is also referred to as the Hebrew Bible. The stories of the patriarchs help people of faith understand God's commands and implement them in their lives and communities.

Storytelling has been part of all cultures, probably from the beginning of human society. Many religious experiences have been passed on in this way.

The Old Testament is sacred to Jews and to Christians. It is the story of God at work in the history of the Israelites.

Jews and Christians are called into a reconciliation after many centuries of separation. The Second Vatican Council set forth the challenge of reversing centuries of hostile Christian teaching about Jews and Judaism. Since then, Jewish-Catholic relations have been based on a respectful exchange among people who share a faith in the same God and recognize the faith commitment of the other group. Within the Catholic Church, the Catechism (teachings of the Catholic faith) strives to educate Catholics about the faith of Jewish people. For instance, an understanding of this living religion can help us to better understand Christian liturgy. In other words, an understanding of the Jewish roots and practices will help us to better understand Christian beliefs and practices. Like Joseph who reconciled with his brothers, Jews and Catholics are called to a sincere reconciliation. God has never revoked his covenant with the Jewish people, and for this Christians are grateful.

For Review

1. What obligations do you have to your family?

2. What can you do in your community to model your faith?

3. Explain the steps that have led to a Jewish-Catholic reconciliation.

For Discussion

Compare major events in the practice of Judaism—such as Passover or Hanukkah—to major events in the calendar year for Christians. How do these events differ? How are they similar?

Activity

Working together as a class, create a newspaper based on the Book of Genesis. Your newspaper should include all the components of a regular newspaper: news articles, editorials, cartoons, weather reports, advice columns, undercover investigations, and eye-catching headlines. Be creative in your approach to the material.

Chapter 3

Genesis 11:27–50 contains early stories of the Israelites who understood that God was at work in their history and even in prehistory. These inspired writings evolve around some of the most dramatic elements in the Old Testament: infertility, the willingness to sacrifice a child, deceit, slavery, and victory. The stories are presented in a cycle: God makes promises and his people face a decision to be faithful or not. Often, God's people fail to trust God, but God always keeps his promises. The stories are framed by real historical events: political tensions in Egypt and the laws, codes, and customs of ancient people.

The writers of Genesis present the ancestors as people who face great challenges and show that they do not always make the best choices. The challenge is to continue to strive to be faithful. The world of the Israelites was not all that different from our world—as we face challenges of our own time and the call to be faithful to God's covenant with us. Being placed in a difficult situation, such as in the story at the beginning of this chapter, can be a test of your faith.

Love the LORD, all you his saints.
  The LORD preserves the faithful,
    but abundantly repays the one who acts haughtily.
Be strong, and let your heart take courage,
  all you who wait for the LORD.

Psalm 31:23–24

For you, O God, have tested us;
   you have tried us as silver is tried.
You brought us into the net;
   you laid burdens on our backs;
   you let people ride over our heads;
   we went through fire and through water;
   yet you have brought us out to a spacious place.

Psalm 66:10–12

Events in Old Testament History

c. 1792–1750 B.C.

Hammurabi rules;
Hammurabi's Code produced

c. 1550–1200 B.C.

Egyptian rule over Canaan

c. 1552–1527 B.C.

Egyptian war of liberation from the Hyksos under leadership of Amosis (Ahmose)

c. 1850–1700 B.C.?

Famine drives Israelites to Egypt

c. 1600 B.C.

Semites invent an alphabet

1527 B.C.

End of reign of Amosis (Ahmose)

CHAPTER 4

Moses and the Formation of God's People

CHAPTER GOALS

Increase knowledge of the meaning of the Old Testament and deepen understanding of its value by studying the following:

- literary characteristics of the epic, archetypes, and symbols
- historical events that shaped the Old Testament
- significance of the remaining books of the Pentateuch

CHAPTER OUTLINE

Literary Interpretation: Epic and Archetype

Historical Interpretation: The Israelite People

Theological Interpretation: Exodus and Sinai

Witness: Stephen Bantu Biko

Personal Challenge: Isolation and Oppression

Summary

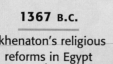

1367 B.C.
Akhenaton's religious reforms in Egypt

1333–1323 B.C.
King Tutankhamen rules

c. 1290–1224 B.C.
Reign of Ramses II; expansion of Egyptian territory

c. 1472 B.C.
Hatshepsut declared herself pharaoh of Egypt (only woman to rule Egypt)

1305–1290 B.C.
Reign of Seti I

c. 1290–1250 B.C.
The Exodus: Moses leads the Israelites back to Canaan

magine that you are about to embark on a journey that will take you from a life in your homeland to a new life in another country. You hope to cultivate an incredible life in this new land. You wonder what the people will be like. Will people your age like the same kind of food, clothes, and music you do? You find you are as excited about your upcoming adventure as you are nervous.

Once you arrive, you find that life is very different from that to which you are accustomed. The popular food, clothes, and music are different. People even act toward one another in ways that people from your native country never would. How are you feeling about your adventure at this point? Comfortable? Homesick? Lost? You discover that some people even stare at you because you look, speak, and dress differently.

Little by little, you begin to like some of the new things to which you have been introduced. You change the way you dress, and even your musical tastes begin to change. A relative comments that she hardly recognizes you and is shocked at some of your behavior, which is perfectly normal among your new friends. You like your new friends. Should your relative be shocked? You think to yourself, what is different anyway? What's on the inside or the outside?

Keep this story in mind as you read about the formation of the people of God—their Exodus from Egypt, their wanderings in the wilderness, and their return to Canaan.

Literary Interpretation

FAITH SHARING

Create a chart with two columns: Responsibility and Response. Over the next few weeks, note occasions when you are asked to be responsible for something at home, school, or through your religious faith. Record your response, noting whether or not you were able to fulfill this role or answer these "calls."

The remaining four books of the Pentateuch have great focus on cultic material such as genealogies and laws. They tell the story of how the people of Israel became an independent nation, and the gradual development of their faith in God. These adjustments were not always easy to make, just as adjusting to life in a new culture would be challenging. But God was present in the formation of the people of Israel, helping to guide them along the way. ■

In Chapter 2, you learned about the Deuteronomic style in which these laws were written. One characteristic of this style, found primarily in the Book of Deuteronomy, is very long sentences. For example, Deuteronomy 17:2 begins with a sentence that is 127 words long! If you are asked to read any passages of Deuteronomy out loud, take a deep breath first!

These books pack in much more than laws and occasional long sentences. You will find great drama, a hero, and the real goal of God's people—to keep their part of the covenant so that they will reach and occupy the Promised Land.

This text also includes richly detailed stories (some taken from Egyptian and Palestinian folklore): a rod changes into a serpent, bread falls from the heavens, and other signs of God's action.

AUTHORSHIP OF THE PENTATEUCH

Genesis is the first book of the Pentateuch; Exodus, Leviticus, Numbers, and Deuteronomy are the other books. The dominant theory of biblical scholars is that the Pentateuch is a composite record of many generations of oral narrators and that it was written by many people. Each writer provided a different link in the chain that would become the record of the spiritual history of Israel. The different schools or traditions—Yahwist (J), Elohist (E), Priestly (P), and Deuteronomic (D)—were discussed in depth in Chapter 2.

OPENING THE WORD

Working in a small group, read Exodus 20 and Deuteronomy 5, and compare the two versions of the Ten Commandments. Explain how such a comparison provides support for different sources and many authors.

At one point, Moses was thought to be the sole author of the Pentateuch. But scholars and historians then pointed out parts of the narrative that speak of Moses in the third person, as *he* or *Moses,* and the fact that some of the events in the Pentateuch occur after the death of Moses. When scholars were able to isolate sections and verses that come from the four sources, they provided an explanation for why there are two versions of a number of items within the Pentateuch. For instance, there are two versions of the Ten Commandments, found in Exodus 20 and in Deuteronomy 5. Overall, however, regardless of the source, Moses is at the heart of the Pentateuch. Thus, the books are considered the "five books of Moses." ■

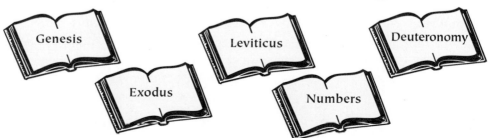

This stele from Babylon portrays Hammurabi before the sun-god Shamash.

LEGAL DOCUMENTS

The Pentateuch is a combination of narratives and law codes, which cover time from the creation of the universe to just after the death of Moses. Some of the laws outlined in the Pentateuch are general laws, such as the seventh commandment: "You shall not steal" (Exodus 20:15). Other laws describe how specific situations are to be handled, such as "You shall not see your neighbor's donkey or ox fallen on the road and ignore it; you shall help to lift it up" (Deuteronomy 22:4). The Pentateuch also provides instructions regarding the punishments for certain crimes.

In a religious society, religious laws also include *civil laws.* Civil laws relate to private citizens and are mandated by the nation or state. People who do not obey the laws are punished accordingly. It was once believed that the laws found within the Old Testament were unique in ancient times. However, the discovery of such legal documents as the Code of Hammurabi and Hittite laws proves that law codes were not uncommon during that time.

The Hittites were one of the dominant powers in the Middle East from around 1600 to 1200 B.C. The *Edict of Telipinus,* a set of Hittite laws written around 1500 B.C. and followed by many generations, sets forth guidelines for social behavior that are similar to those we find in the Old Testament.

You will read about the covenant between God and the Israelites under the leadership of Moses in the Book of Exodus. This covenant recalls God's covenant with Abraham, which you read about in Chapter 3, but this time certain obligations are placed upon the people, and threats of punishment if they fail to keep the covenant are added. Historians have found a record of a Hittite covenant between a king and his subjects that has similar language to the words of God's covenant with Israel. Both covenants reflect the value that the people of that time placed on loyalty. You can see this in the following excerpt from the Hittite covenant:

> When I, the Sun, sought after you in accordance with your father's word and put you in your father's place, I took you in oath for the king of the Hatti land, and for my sons and grandsons. So honor the oath . . . And I, the king, will be loyal toward you . . . And just as I shall be loyal toward you, even so shall I be loyal toward your son. . . . Do not turn your eyes to anyone else!
>
> Akkadian-Hittite Treaty

The discovery of this Hittite covenant and others like it help us place the covenant between God and the Israelites under Moses in its historical context. The writers of the Old Testament would have been familiar with the language used in other covenants. As you read Exodus, recall the language of this Hittite covenant. ■

OPENING THE WORD

Read Exodus 34:4–11, in which the covenant is made, and Deuteronomy 30:15–20, in which the covenant is renewed. Compare the description of the covenant in each passage and the obligations it places upon the people of Israel.

EPIC

As we learned in Chapter 1, an epic is a sprawling history of a hero or heroine who goes through various trials. The hero or heroine (main character) often embodies the traits of a people and is therefore a symbolic figure. An epic hero or heroine is a person of great historical, mythical, or religious significance who demonstrates both bravery and wisdom. This hero or heroine performs noble, even superhuman, actions. He or she also has direct involvement with a supernatural being and often gives powerful speeches throughout the epic. The hero's or heroine's story takes place in a vast setting, often extending throughout the known world of that time.

Traditional Epic

A traditional epic generally began as an oral tradition and often tells the story of a historical figure. Traditional epics are usually written in an elevated writing style as a way of signifying the importance of the subject matter. An example of this style can be found in Homer's *The Odyssey* (c. 850 B.C.). The epic tells the story of a heroic character named Odysseus:

> Many were the men whose cities he saw and whose mind he learned, aye, and many the woes he suffered in his heart upon the sea, seeking to win his own life and the return of his comrades.

As you can see from this brief excerpt, this hero suffered many difficult tribulations and fought to win something important for his people. As you read about Moses, you will learn about the difficulties he encounters in following God's word while leading the people of Israel.

Homer's The Odyssey *tells the story of an epic hero named Odysseus. The Pentateuch tells the story of another epic hero, Moses. This painting, "Return of Ulysses to Penelope" from "The Odyssey," is by Bernardino Pintoricchio (c. 1454–1513).*

"The Israelites went into the sea on dry ground, the waters forming a wall for them on their right and on their left" (Exodus 14:22). This painting of "The Waters Are Divided" is by James J. Tissot.

Moses as Epic Hero

The last four books in the Pentateuch are an epic that includes the story of Moses' life. The story of his birth is told in Exodus 2 and his death is announced in Deuteronomy 34. His story is written as an inspiration for God's people—thus the epic style. Moses is considered to be the hero of a *traditional* epic because the legendary stories told of Moses were part of an oral tradition prior to being written, and the stories fulfill the qualifications of epic narrative.

Many elements of the story of Moses help us to determine that he is an epic hero. His humble beginnings make him an example of the common man, but his direct contact with God sets him apart as being exceptional. Moses then becomes the vehicle through which God performs miracles, such as parting the waters of the Red or Reed Sea. Throughout the stories, Moses demonstrates the qualities of bravery and wisdom. Moses also gives powerful speeches in his pursuit of God's calling, which is another qualification for determining whether a character is an epic hero. ■

ActiviTy

Look through the Pentateuch and find three separate examples of God speaking directly to Moses. In small groups, share your examples and create a composite list. Give the Scripture reference for each example. Post all the lists on a bulletin board.

SYMBOLISM

Read Exodus 4–7.

OPENING THE WORD

Reread Genesis 3. How is God's power over the serpent shown? How does this compare with the example in Exodus 7:8–12?

Many images in the Old Testament are symbolic. In Western traditions, the snake is often a symbol for evil or trickery. In the temptation story in Genesis 3, the serpent is described as being "more crafty than any other wild animal" (Genesis 3:1). When God confronts the woman with her sin, she excuses herself by saying that the serpent tricked her (Genesis 3:13). The symbolic nature of the serpent and its hostile relationship with humankind comes into play throughout classic literature. It is also important to note that in ancient times, some gods were represented as serpents. The Egyptians, for example, worshiped a serpentine god, Sito. Therefore, when Aaron's rod turns into a serpent and eats the Egyptian serpents, the situation represents the power of the God of the Hebrews over the Egyptian gods. ■

OPENING THE WORD

Working with a partner, read Exodus 16:1–17:7. Summarize the ways that God shows his power to sustain the Israelites in the wilderness.

Numbers can also be symbolic. For example, forty years was often used to represent the time span of one generation rather than an exact number of years. Numbers 32:13 states that God made the Israelites "wander in the wilderness for forty years, until all the generation that had done evil in the sight of the LORD had disappeared."

The term *wilderness* can symbolize any "bad place" that is dry, desolate, or frightening. But, because a person can find solitude in the wilderness, it can also symbolize a place for spiritual retreat. The blending of positive and negative connotations enriches this symbol. The same word that represents the dire need of the people also represents the place in which they meet God and are satisfied. ■

ARCHETYPE

archetype recurrent character type, image, or theme in literature

prophet a person who has a close relationship with God and communicates a divine message

An **archetype** is a complex form of symbolism. It is a character type, image, or theme that appears repeatedly in many different pieces of literature. For example, the flood appears in the literature of various world cultures and is therefore considered an archetype. The *savior* is another archetype, as is the **prophet.** A prophet is the vehicle of a divine message. This message is passed on through the prophet's words and actions. ■

ACTIVITY

After some research on archetypes, make a list of archetypal images that you have seen in modern movies, plays, or literary works. Focusing on one of those images, create a movie poster, playbill, or book cover for the work, focusing on the meaning of the archetype.

Moses as Archetype

In addition to being an epic hero, Moses also serves as an archetypal figure. Some archetypes that Moses fulfills are the good leader, the ideal judge, and the intercessor. He is also the archetypal threatened child who becomes a great figure—a recurring cross-cultural theme. Christians consider Moses, as an archetypal prophet and savior of his people, to be a precursor to Jesus. The author of the Gospel according to Matthew used many parallels to the Moses epic as he presented Jesus as the fulfillment of the Law.

For REVIEW

1. Why is Moses considered to be a *traditional* epic hero?

2. What are the archetypal roles fulfilled by Moses?

3. What does the word *wilderness* symbolize?

For DISCUSSION

Think of a modern-day setting that might be considered a wilderness. Imagine what it would be like to spend forty years in that type of environment.

JOURNAL

Who are your heroes? Why?

WHO WERE THE PEOPLE OF THE EXODUS?

Historical evidence shows that during his reign. Pharaoh Ramses II (c. 1290–1224 B.C.) undertook an ambitious construction program. A new palace and two new cities were constructed. Besides needing labor for construction, the building program required other workers to produce food for the laborers and to maintain the pharaoh's armies. Slaves made up this extensive workforce. In the Exodus story, Ramses II is believed to be the pharaoh who enslaved the Israelites, as well as the one on whom the ten plagues were inflicted.

These plagues, and how Moses led the enslaved Israelites out of Egypt, is in part a fulfillment of the promise that is made by God to Abraham, Isaac, and Jacob and recounted in Genesis. However, no mention of the **Exodus** or the enslavement of the Israelites exists in Egyptian historical records. The Book of Exodus is probably based on a real escape from slavery in Egypt, but it most likely involved a relatively small group of people unworthy of mention in the official records. The numbers in Exodus 12:37–38 are surely an exaggeration typical of the epic style. Nonetheless, archeological and textual evidence—from texts other than the Bible—convey a history of who the Israelites were.

Exodus the escape of the Hebrews from Egyptian slavery, under the leadership of Moses

The clay vessel in the form of a bull was found in a tomb in Israel.

This terracotta jug is typical of Canaanite pottery, with one handle and six holes at the spout.

WHO WERE THE ISRAELITES?

To understand who the Israelites were, it is important to look at the history of the ancient Near East as revealed through archeological and textual evidence. Scholars use textual and archeological evidence to construct a picture of the ancient Near East. Archeological evidence can provide a record of material culture. Material culture includes artifacts like pottery or tools, as well as food and refuse remains found in a collection of garbage or a fire pit. Textual evidence provides other sorts of information, such as dates, but the purpose for which a text was written should be kept in mind. Information could be presented in a particular way to portray a person or event in a particular light.

The people who eventually became the Israelite nation probably included more than the descendants of the slaves who left Egypt. Quite likely the **Israelites** who became a great nation included Canaanites, hapiru, shasu, and Sea Peoples, along with the original Hebrews.

Canaanites

Scholars agree that the land of Canaan was a place populated by many different peoples, including the group that would come to be known as the Israelites. Canaan, which later became part of Israel, was under Egyptian rule for many years (c. 1550–1200 B.C.). During this time, Canaanite kings were often at war with one another, and there were many rebellions against Egyptian authority. A war with the Hittites shortly after 1300 B.C. weakened the Egyptian empire, and a time of transition began in Canaan. During this transition, the many peoples who had settled in Canaan began to establish themselves as independent ethnic groups rather than remaining part of the composite ethnic group known as the Canaanites. The culture and religion of the Canaanites had a large influence on all of the cultures that developed from it.

Hapiru

Historians have noted a connection between the word **Hebrew** and a people called the **hapiru**—one of the peoples who inhabited Canaan. The hapiru are mentioned in the Amarna letters that were written in the fourteenth century B.C. and excavated in Egypt in the late 1800s. The letters, written by Canaanite kings under Egyptian rule, record the kings' complaints about the hapiru who raided their villages and fields. The Canaanite kings, who paid tribute to Egypt, asked for protection from these people. In the letters, the hapiru do not seem to be an ethnic group, but rather people living on the fringe of society. One letter refers to the hapiru as former slaves. Therefore, the hapiru may have been ancestors of the Hebrews.

A number of references to marginal or fringe groups appear in the Old Testament. In Genesis 23:4, Abraham says to the Hittites, "I am a stranger and an alien residing among you. . . ." Deuteronomy 26:5 presents Jacob as "a wandering Aramean" who "went down into Egypt and lived there as an alien, few in number, and there he became a great nation, mighty and populous." Verses such as these provide support for the theory that the hapiru were ancestors of the Hebrews. The term *Hebrew* was used to distinguish the early Israelites from other peoples of the ancient Near East, particularly the Egyptians and the Philistines.

Shasu

Still other groups of people who dwelled in Canaan may have been related to the Israelites of Exodus. The nomadic shasu's flocks frequently disturbed Egyptian land. Egyptian records mention that the shasu were sometimes taxed, but more notably the military records indicate that they were enslaved—like the Israelites.

Israelites a people who unified around 1050–1000 B.C. and included Canaanites, the hapiru, the shasu, Sea Peoples, and the original Hebrews

Hebrews peoples enslaved in Egypt who eventually became the community known as Israel

hapiru a class of people living in the countryside of Canaan, some of whom were former slaves; they may have been ancestors of the Hebrews

Activity

In small groups, make a list of countries today where two or more groups of different religions or ethnic background are having difficulty working together as one nation. For each example, name the core of the problem and discuss possible solutions.

Sea Peoples

Historians also recognize that the different groups migrating from the Aegean Sea and collectively known as the *Sea Peoples* may also be part of the combination of peoples who came to be known as the Israelites. In a mortuary temple of Ramses III (who reigned c. 1187–1156 B.C.), there is a mural, or relief, of battles being fought with the Sea Peoples on sea and land. Accompanying these images are women, children, and oxcarts—an indication the Sea Peoples were not just an invading army, but people coming to settle in Canaan. The Israelite tribe of Dan may have come from the Denyen, one of the Sea Peoples' groups. On the other hand, another group, the Philistines, became a major enemy of Israel. ■

Israel: A People

Canaan was certainly a place of mixed peoples. It was also an area that included different ways of life—farming, herding, fishing, and trading—in rural areas and cities. Despite the different lifestyles in Canaan, a similar material culture is found there, indicating that different groups shared similar traits. At the end of the Iron Age, the stability of Egypt came to an end and, in the highlands above Canaan, a decentralized, tribal society came into existence—Israel. The first appearance of the word *Israel* occurs in writing on a stele (a stone with carved writing) telling of the military victories of Merneptah, king of Egypt. The stele reads, "Israel is laid waste, his seed is not." This is significant because the word *Israel* is written with the Egyptian symbol meaning people, not country or city—people who referred to themselves as Israel and who opposed Egyptian rule.

This Egyptian stele was discovered near the turquoise mines of the pharoahs (13th century B.C.) in the Sinai area. Note the ankh (☥), symbol of life.

JOURNaL

How does studying the Old Testament help you understand the Jewish culture, faith, and history?

Jews term originally used to describe the people who resettled in the area of Judah following the Babylonian Exile; most commonly used to refer to followers of Judaism

Passover refers to when the Israelites were "passed over" by the angel of death as dictated by the tenth plague; a holiday celebrated by Jews as a day of deliverance

OPeNING THe WoRD

Read the story of the first Passover in Exodus, Chapters 11 and 12. What is the image of God that comes through in these chapters? If you had been there, how do you think you would have reacted to the events? Why?

Jews

Hebrews, Israelites, and Jews share a common history. Hebrews are the ancestors of the Israelites. The term *Jew* comes from the word *Judah*—one of the twelve tribes of Israel. Judah was also the name of an independent kingdom that formed after the nation of Israel split in two (922 B.C.). Babylonians destroyed Judah around 587 B.C. and took its people as prisoners. After the Babylonian Exile, these former prisoners returned to what was the land of Judah and became known as **Jews** from that point in history. ■

NEAR EASTERN CUSTOMS AND CULTURE

The Books of Exodus, Leviticus, Numbers, and Deuteronomy exhibit evidence of how the Israelites and their way of living were both a part of the Near Eastern world and its people, but also unique to it and distinct from it.

Scholars believe that when the Israelites were "passed over" by the angel of death, this event actually coincided with a spring festival that had its roots in a shepherding culture. This celebration would have coincided with either the annual spring change of pasture or the sacrifice of the firstborn animal to ensure fertility. Other evidence is that the spring festival, like **Passover,** would occur in the evening at the time of the full moon. The Seder meal celebrated during Passover recalls the entire Exodus event. All the groups who became part of Israel adopted the Exodus group's story as their own. They may have all formerly been under Egyptian rule, so the story of escape from Egyptian oppression would have appealed to them. In a sense, it was also their story. ■

Another characteristic of ancient Near Eastern culture evident in the Old Testament is the existence of prophets. Prophets were not uncommon in the ancient Near East, and they were considered divine messengers who would either hear, see, or dream a message from God. In a shrine dating back to the eighth century B.C., there is a reference to the prophet Balaam. In Numbers 22–24, Balaam refused to curse the Israelites. Balaam may have been a famous folk figure who is then described in Numbers as a charismatic prophet who spoke oracles from the God of the Israelites.

A nineteenth century illustration of Balaam.

HOW WERE THE ISRAELITES UNIQUE?

If characteristics of the Israelites were common among other peoples of the Near East, what made them so unique? The answer is found in the Israelites' beliefs about themselves and their relationship with God. The Israelite idea that God was a personal God and an autonomous creator and not a part of a pantheon of gods was a radical belief that developed gradually. This was an expression of monotheism. Most ancient Near Eastern peoples believed in polytheism, with a few exceptions, such as the Egyptian pharaoh, Akhenaton, who insisted that Aton, the sun god, was the only god to be worshiped and who also outlawed **idolatry.** It's important to remember, however, that the story of the Exodus was finally written long after the event when the understanding of God as the only God was much further developed than it was at the time of the event. In other words, the God of the Israelites was eventually understood as the one and only God of all.

idolatry false worship; honoring and revering a creature in place of God

Also radical was the belief that, for the Israelites, God himself, rather than a leader guided by a divinity, issued justice in the form of covenants. In the ancient Near East, covenants were a common way for people to make agreements among themselves as well as between a powerful monarch, like Egypt, and a vassal, such as a city-state in Canaan. In contrast to the covenant with Abraham, which was an unconditional promise, the Israelites' deity now assured protection and favor, but their obedience was required in return. In the covenant through Moses, God dictated laws that covered all relationships. For instance, in the Ten Commandments, the first three commandments are laws concerning the Israelites' relationship with God, while the other commandments dictate people-to-people concerns—such as how family life should be structured and what property rights people have.

For Review

1. Who were some of the peoples who dwelled in Canaan, and how do we know of their existence?

2. What characteristics of these peoples lead scholars to believe they may have been related to the ancient Israelites?

3. What are some similarities between the customs and culture of the Israelites and that of other ancient Near Eastern peoples?

4. What made the Israelites unique?

For Discussion

Reflect on the different backgrounds of the people who make up your classroom, school, church, family, and regional communities. Do you see any similarities or differences in the people who are a part of your everyday life? How is your social environment different or similar to that of ancient Canaan?

Activity

Locate a copy of the Passover Seder. Read through it (alone or in groups) and find correlations with the story in Exodus and with the Catholic liturgy of the Mass.

The Books of Exodus, Leviticus, Numbers, and Deuteronomy contain critical events in the story of God's people. How the events are interpreted reflects the situation of the people at the time the books were compiled. The exile was seen as a punishment for the people's failure to keep the precepts of the covenant. This shows that the covenant at the time of Moses included obligations and threats of punishment that were not present in the covenant as it was made with Abraham. The obligations also helped the people in exile rebuild their community.

Exodus

OPENING THE WORD

Read Exodus 5–12. What were the ten plagues? What occurrences might be considered plagues today?

The epic in the Book of Exodus in part fulfills the promise made by God to Abraham, Isaac, and Jacob, and to their progeny. Exodus recounts the story about the enslaved Israelites, their deliverance, and their covenant with God. Their deliverance is led by Moses, who begins his extraordinary life growing up in the pharaoh's palace. Throughout all of the events, God speaks and works through Moses. In fact, Moses is a hero only through the works of God who empowers him.

The pharaoh and his people represent the glory and power of Egypt. Egyptians believed that their pharaoh had superhuman powers and great wisdom. He uses this power to rule over and oppress the Hebrews, who were slaves. God intercedes and instructs Moses to ask the pharaoh to set the Israelites free. ■

The Plagues

Moses warns the pharaoh, not once but ten times, to free the Israelites or God will subject Egypt to another plague. The pharaoh endures nine plagues without complying, but finally he is unable to endure the tenth—the death of any firstborn male, human or animal, including the pharaoh's firstborn son. The pharaoh pleads with Moses to leave Egypt, and he and the Israelites do so. However, the pharaoh changes his mind and follows them to the Red or Reed Sea, intending to stop the escape. But because of God's power as exhibited through Moses, the Israelites are able to cross the sea, whereas the Egyptians drown.

Which plague do you think the artist Tissot was portraying in this painting?

Signs and Wonders

A *wonder* is something that instills marvel in the people who witness it due to its astonishing nature. A *sign* points beyond itself to something or someone else, even to God. The events in Exodus represent a conflict between God and the pharaoh; God always prevails. The plagues and the crossing of the sea may represent natural events that are made extraordinary through God. The plagues were an ordinary phenomenon of the time, based on natural phenomena, such as the annual flooding of the Nile, which often brought disease to the region. However, the plagues in this story are extraordinary for three reasons: The number or the degree or the severity of the plagues made them unusual. These plagues affected only the Egyptians. Moses called on God to begin these plagues; they are extraordinary because they are an act of God by means of Moses. If Moses can control nature, he must be inspired and aided by God, since humans acting of their own accord cannot control nature in that way.

The same is true for the crossing of the sea. The natural phenomenon of the sea rising has been recorded. However, in the story the Israelites cross, but the Egyptians drown—thus this is an extraordinary act of God. By helping the Israelites escape from Egypt, God is faithful to his promise to his people. ■

Opening the Word

Read Exodus 13:17–14:31. Now read Exodus 15:1–18. What differences do you note in the two accounts? Why might this be?

Read Exodus 16:11–12

Wanderings

During their wanderings in the desert, the Israelites complain of food and hunger, stating that things were better in Egypt. The people rebel against Moses and lack faith: "Is the LORD among us or not?" (Exodus 17:7). God, hearing them time and time again, provides food, water, and protection, again fulfilling his promise to be their God. The people at first did not recognize the *manna* from heaven as food. They asked, "What is it?" (In Hebrew this question is *man hu.*) Moses answers that it is "the bread which God has given to you to eat." The "bread" is a symbol of God providing for his people. Christians see the manna as a prefiguring of the Eucharist, the "Bread of Life."

The manna that God provided for the Israelites may have been similar to a substance that is considered a delicacy today by the Bedouin people, a nomadic group that roams the wilderness and desert areas of the Middle East. This delicacy is a sweet-tasting insect secretion that drops to the ground from the leaves of tamarisk thickets. The manna becomes firm in the cool night air and must be gathered early in the morning, or it will melt in the sun.

Uncertainty regarding the true nature of manna has led to a multitude of artistic representations. "The Gathering of Manna" is by James Tissot.

At Sinai

The covenant made at Mount Sinai is not the first expression of the covenant that God made with his chosen people. Recall God's covenant with Abraham in Genesis. God promises a great nation and people to Abraham, but he does not place any requirements or obligations on his people. God also does not include punishment as a consequence for failing to meet the covenant. At Mount Sinai, God fulfills the promise of a nation to the entire people—not just one individual. The covenant at Mount Sinai is the same covenant made with Abraham, but it establishes obligations and unifies the Israelites.

After three months of wandering, the people arrive at the foot of Mount Sinai where God calls Moses to him. Amid flames and thunder, God delivers to Moses the Law, the requirements of the covenant, including the Ten Commandments. The Israelites become afraid to approach, so Moses assures them that it is their God who has come to them, instructing them how to be free of sin; yet the people stay away. In Exodus 24, we read about the ratification of the covenant, which symbolized the union of God and his people. ■

Moses returns to the mountain and stays for forty days (a long time). During this time, the Israelites demand that Aaron make a god for them because Moses has not yet returned. Aaron has an idol made, and the people worship it. Once again, like Cain, the son of the first humans, the chosen people rapidly turn away from God and choose to sin. Coming on this scene, Moses is furious and throws the tablets with the commandments to the ground, breaking them. Moses asks those who are true followers of God to separate themselves from the idolaters. God threatens to destroy the Israelites, but Moses intercedes, and the Ten Commandments are written again by God. Interspersed into the end of Exodus, God explains further how he should be worshiped and who will be in charge of the worship.

Aaron melted down the jewelry of the Israelites to make the golden calf. This early twentieth century painting is by Vladimir Mazuranic.

OPENING THE WORD

Read the ceremony ratifying God's covenant with Abraham (Abram) in Genesis 15 and then compare it to the ceremony ratifying God's covenant with Moses in Exodus 24.

Political Event

According to the epic, the Israelites become a people at Mount Sinai. This is the most significant event for the Israelites. Through Moses, God gives the Law and ratifies the covenant with sacrifice and a meal. This expression of the covenant made with the nation rather than an individual (Abraham), has requirements, and the Israelites must keep the moral and ceremonial laws as a condition or demand of the covenant. God, of course, will always be faithful; he will always be their God, always calling them back to the covenant when they fail.

LEVITICUS

As a people, the Israelites represent a social unit or community. The priestly writers believed the Israelites as a community needed laws to live together and in relationship with God. This book contains cultic laws written by the Levites—the priests—during and after the return from exile. After Moses, the priests were all from the family of Levi (son of Jacob). The priests served as mediators between God and his people, performing sacrifices to make the people's gifts holy for God. The priests also served as teachers, oracles, and judges to settle disputes.

While the Book of Leviticus is a continuation of the listing of God's laws and commandments for the Israelites, it is basically a handbook for worship. The book portrays the priests as being instructed by God through Moses to tell the people of Israel all of God's statutes. For instance, explanations are given for how relationships between people should be conducted and what to do when a sacrificial animal is slaughtered. The final section adds additional instruction about offerings and religious vows. Leviticus as a whole stresses the centrality of formal worship to the Israelites' spiritual and moral lives.

NUMBERS

The Book of Numbers deals with the social organization of Israel based on the twelve tribes. In Chapter 3, you learned that the descendants of Abraham come to be organized into the twelve tribes. This is the book that sets up that definition of the people and contains "numbers" listing the numbers of Israelites. (These numbers are exaggerated.)

The Book of Numbers also explores the journey of the Israelites from Mount Sinai to the promised land and explains how God sustains them on their journey. God gives instructions to Moses regarding what is expected of the people when they reach the promised land. When the Israelites continue to act rebelliously, God still continues to protect them in the wilderness. While wandering, they encounter enemies whom God helps them conquer. Numbers concludes with a summary of the laws. ■

OPENING THE WORD

Read the story of Balaam in Numbers 22:1–35. Then create a story panel illustrating the events of the story.

DEUTERONOMY

Deuteronomy means "second law." The theme or main message of the Book of Deuteronomy is that the people will succeed or fail depending on how they follow the Law. This book contains material repeated from other books, and Moses, called a prophet in this book, tells his story before he dies. He gives insight into the events of Exodus and explains why the Israelites did what they did. Moses is told that God will send another leader to the people to lead the people into Canaan; this man is Joshua.

In this book, those who compiled the Law present Moses as telling the people of Israel all of God's statutes, ordinances, and codes, and then writing them down. Presented in this way, the Law gains great authority among the people. Moses, the prophet, is greater than any king. The Israelites would certainly become corrupt without these statutes. So, on the authority of Moses, God tells the people why he chose the Israelites—not because they were fewest in number, but because he loves them. The people are called to follow the laws not just out of duty but out of love for God.

This painting shows Moses parting from his friends before they entered the promised land without him.

For Review

1. What two extraordinary events in Exodus were based on natural phenomena?

2. What is important for the Israelites about the events at Sinai?

3. How does Moses recall to mind Abraham and Noah?

4. What is the purpose of the Book of Leviticus?

5. Why do you think the Book of Numbers was given this name?

6. What is the main theme or message of the Book of Deuteronomy?

For Discussion

Discuss the most significant events in the Pentateuch. How are the other four books different from Genesis? How do the last four books establish the foundations for the Israelites as a people?

Activity

Visit a synagogue and ask someone to explain the scrolls to you.

Stephen Bantu Biko

Seeker of Justice

Stephen Bantu Biko (1946–1977) was a charismatic black leader in the struggle for racial justice in the Republic of South Africa. Biko was a small child when the Nationalist party took control of the South African government and made racial discrimination the law of the land. The Nationalist party named its system of racial laws *apartheid*, meaning "apartness."

One action under the apartheid laws was to assign people to one of four racial groups on the basis of skin color. The groups were white (people of European descent), Bantu (black Africans), colored (people with mixed racial ancestry), and Asian (mostly people from India). Apartheid laws kept the four racial groups separate. Biko and his family were labeled Bantu. That designation circumscribed every aspect of his existence, as did the Hebrews' slavery in Egypt at the time of Moses. The laws ensured white people a high standard of living and the Bantu a life of poverty and degradation.

Biko graduated from St. Francis College and went on to the University of Natal's medical school. There he joined an interracial group, the National Union of South African Students (NUSAS), which advocated black civil rights. It was in meetings of this group that Biko observed an important dynamic. In meetings, white students talked and black students listened. This experience taught Biko that black South Africans were psychologically dependent on white people. He dropped out of NUSAS and the university and helped found the Black Consciousness Movement. Biko believed that once the minds of black people were free, liberation from oppressive apartheid laws would follow. By 1972 the Black Consciousness Movement had led to the formation of over seventy black organizations.

South Africa had laws to suppress voices of dissent. Anyone even suspected of criticizing the government or advocating change could be banned. Typically, banning meant a person could not leave home, speak publicly, receive more than one visitor

Stephen Biko fought against oppression and racism in the Republic of South Africa. He became a martyr in the struggle for racial justice.

at a time, or publish any written work. A banned person could not be quoted in the press or in any publication. In February of 1973 the minister of the interior banned Biko.

Despite being banned, Biko engaged in covert activity that promoted civil rights for black people. During the next two years he was arrested four times and was detained by the police for months at a time. The last arrest was August 18, 1977. While in custody he suffered massive head injuries at the hands of his jailers, and he died on September 12, 1977.

Biko's death led to the repressive South African government's worst nightmare: Biko became a martyr. Nations such as the United States, which previously had only criticized South Africa's apartheid policies, invoked punishing economic sanctions that would be lifted only when apartheid ended. Less than two decades after his death, justice rolled down on South Africa. By 1991 most of the laws of apartheid had been abolished. In 1993 a new South African constitution guaranteed all people equality before the law.

Isolation and Oppression

Do you have responsibilities? Have you ever been in a position of leadership? As part of a family, school, and community, you have obligations to others. How do you answer to these responsibilities? If you feel secure and safe in an environment, you may be comfortable enough to meet your responsibilities in your home or school.

Sometimes you may feel insecure or unsure about your surroundings. Perhaps, like Moses, you feel as if you are wandering in a wilderness. If you move to a new school or join a new team or club, you are beginning something entirely new. You are becoming acquainted with something that was previously unfamiliar. You may feel out of place and very much alone.

Immigrants to the United States often feel as if they are in a wilderness. The culture, language, and laws are all new. In the nineteenth and twentieth centuries, many immigrant groups coming to the United States established organizations to make their new home more like home. They set up their own banks and formed social clubs where they could meet and speak their primary language. Their churches were frequently their neighborhood centers for worship, social services, and social life. They found ways to assimilate, or become part of their new home, but they held onto the ideals from their country of origin that they felt were important to maintain.

The need to belong brings with it pressure to conform. Teenagers sometimes feel as if they must choose between isolation and oppression.

Moses was an Israelite but was raised as an Egyptian. He was different from the people around him. He faced many trials as he tried to follow God's commands. Often his people complained and rebelled against him, not trusting him to be their leader. He found strength in God to carry out his mission.

Unfortunately, many people today experience isolation or oppression. Exodus represents the ultimate liberation from oppression. We have had many other examples of liberation from oppression in modern times. Martin Luther King Jr. was a model of liberation for African Americans in the United States. (You will learn more about Dr. King in Chapter 8.) Nelson Mandela and Stephen Biko were leaders in South Africa. Daw Aung San Suu Kyi, a nurse whose efforts for political reform in Myanmar (formerly Burma) resulted in her being awarded the Nobel Peace Prize in 1991.

The Catholic Church also has a continuing commitment to achieve racial justice worldwide. In July 1999, the National Catholic Gathering for Jubilee Justice met with 3,300 participants from around the world. In one workshop, groups met to address racism and its harmful effects. On a local level, the gathering called for the Church to address racism within Catholic institutions—including schools. In all schools (Catholic and non-Catholic), students face the challenges of treating one another with respect and dignity. The ideas are simple: respect and treat others as you would like to be treated. However, putting these ideas into action takes genuine courage. Think about these ideas and the opening story of this chapter. How do you share respect for people who are different from you?

For Review

1. How did immigrants to the United States find their "way in the wilderness"?

2. Name some modern heroes who faced oppression and worked against it.

For Discussion

How does one live as a Catholic in a society that is not religious? In a society that discriminates against one or more groups?

Journal

When do you feel isolated? Who are the people who have led you out of isolation? Whom have you led out of isolation? Why did you do that?

The last four books of the Pentateuch continue the proclamation that God had entered into the history of the Israelites and, in his divine providence, formed them into his own people. These four books contain genealogies, laws, and richly detailed narratives that witness to God's awesome work. They also provide us with the story of Moses, the epic hero and leader of the Israelites. In reading these books, we come to understand the importance of the Exodus from Egypt and the years the Israelites spent in the wilderness. The Pentateuch paints a picture of the people chosen by God to be his people and his repeated efforts to care for them and teach them his ways. We gain an understanding of the covenant God made with his people through Moses and the obligations that the covenant placed on the people. By reading these books, we see that God is a caring provider. We see a God who is powerful, just, and forgiving.

Studying the archaeological and historical evidence relating to the Pentateuch gives us a sense of how the Israelites gradually departed from polytheism to practice monotheism. We see that this monotheism was revolutionary in its time. We also gain an understanding of who the Israelites were and how they came to be the foundation of our faith.

Who are they that fear the LORD?
   He will teach them the way that they should choose.
They will abide in prosperity,
   and their children shall possess the land.
The friendship of the LORD is for those who fear him,
   and he makes his covenant known to them.

                       Psalm 25:12–14

Now I know that the LORD will help his anointed;
he will answer him from his holy heaven
with mighty victories by his right hand.
Some take pride in chariots, and some in horses,
but our pride is in the name of the LORD our God.

Psalm 20:6–7

Events in Old Testament History

c. 1290 B.C.

Israelite exodus from
Egypt begins

c. 1400–1250 B.C.

Jericho destroyed

c. 1240 B.C.

Israelites enter Canaan

CHAPTER 5

Claiming the Promised Land

CHAPTER GOALS

Increase knowledge of the meaning of the Old Testament and deepen understanding of its value by studying the following:

- literary aspects of Joshua, Judges, and Ruth
- Israelite conquest and settlement of Canaan
- concepts of holy war and just war
- the value of conflict resolution

CHAPTER OUTLINE

Literary Interpretation: From Military History to Folklore

Historical Interpretation: Settling the Promised Land

Theological Interpretation: Holy War

Witness: Joan of Arc

Personal Challenge: Integrity and Tolerance

Summary

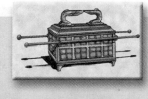

AFTER **1180** B.C.

Philistines settle in Canaan

C. **1220** B.C.

Judges begin to rule

C. **1020–1000** B.C.

Reign of Saul,
first king of Israel

For a long time, you and your friends have been playing basketball each Saturday afternoon on a neighborhood court. It's fun and you all look forward to the game each week.

One Saturday you arrive to find the court has been taken over by some other kids. One of your friends, the most quick-tempered of the group, immediately gets angry and wants to force the intruders off the court. Another more timid friend seems impressed by the size of some of the newcomers and starts edging away, observing, "Come on, let's look for another court. It's not worth getting into a fight over."

You're not sure what to do. You don't want to just walk away; that feels cowardly, and, besides, it doesn't seem fair that these outsiders have just taken over without asking. On the other hand, you don't want to get into a fight, particularly when you're not sure if you're right. After all, it is a *public* park; the court doesn't really *belong* to you. Should you stand up for yourself . . . or walk away?

After weighing the options, your group decides to resolve the conflict by talking about it calmly with the other group. Your group walks over to the court, and you present your case to the others in a calm, but frank manner. You are assertive, but careful not to be stubborn, giving the other group an equal opportunity to present its case. You listen carefully to what the group members have to say, trying to see things from their point of view.

As a group, you decide that if both groups compromise, neither group will end up feeling defeated. You all agree to set a time limit of one hour for each game. You walk away feeling that you have really struck a balance that unites integrity and tolerance. Who knows, maybe with your skillful way of planning and negotiating, you'll end up starting a neighbohood basketball tournament.

Keep this story in mind as you explore this chapter about the Israelites' conquest of Canaan. How is God present in your struggles?

Literary Interpretation

The Old Testament Books of Joshua, Judges, and Ruth follow immediately after the five books of the Law, or Pentateuch. Joshua is sometimes grouped with the Pentateuch, and this grouping is called the Hexateuch. The Book of Joshua is part of the ongoing story of God's chosen people—and the covenant that they have with God. The promise of land made to Abraham is fulfilled in Joshua. ■

Many of the stories in Joshua and Judges were told over and over again. The stories in Joshua were popular war stories that the Deuteronomistic writers wrote down from the oral tradition to emphasize the conquest of Israel and how God fights for Israel. The God of Israel entered into the history of the poeple to once again fulfill his promise to be their God and to make them his people. The inspired accounts proclaim God's constant providence.

Some Bibles list these books with the Penteteuch, but Joshua, Judges, and Ruth are usually listed as the first three Historical Books (see Chapter 1 chart). Joshua and Judges are works of military history, dealing with the conquest and settlement of Canaan, the land promised to the Israelites by God. Thus, Joshua and Judges continue the story begun in the first five books of the Old Testament. The Book of Ruth turns away from accounts of warfare to tell a story of family affection and ethnic tolerance.

Keep the opening story of this chapter in mind as you consider the victories and defeats of the Israelites and the presence of God in their lives.

MILITARY HISTORY

Military history is a type of literature that includes biographies and autobiographies of soldiers, and accounts of battles, campaigns, and wars. The Books of Joshua and Judges are both examples of a particular kind of military history that portrays God as actively involved in the battles and rewarding the people with victory when they have been faithful to the covenant. However, the two books deal with very different types of warriors.

Joshua as Hero

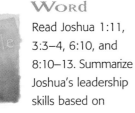
Recall that after the death of Moses, Joshua takes over in order to lead the Israelites into Canaan, the promised land. Joshua's extraordinary heroism has two dimensions—moral and military. Joshua always seeks to follow God's lead; he is a man fully acceptable to God. Joshua is also a brilliant and ruthless soldier who conquers Canaan in a swift and brutal campaign. As with the story of Moses, Joshua's story is exaggerated in the style of an epic, and the actual events of the conquest were far less swift and probably far less brutal. ■

One tribute to Joshua's reputation as a soldier is this statue at the U.S. Military Academy at West Point.

OPENING THE WORD

Other episodes in the story of Joshua parallel the career of Moses. Read the account of the Israelites crossing the Jordan River (Joshua 3:14–17; 4:4–7, 14–18) and compare it to Moses leading the Israelites across the Red or Reed Sea (Exodus 14:21–22, 26–31).

OPENING THE WORD

Read the story of Jephthah's vow (Judges 11:29–40). How does his vow reflect both a lack of faith in God and a failure of common sense? What story from the tradition should have prevented the vow and the sacrifice?

judge one of twelve charismatic military leaders of the Israelites during the period between the conquest of Canaan and the establishment of the monarchy

Parallel Writing

According to the story, Joshua himself is a heroic military leader of nearly the same stature as Moses, and his career often parallels the career of Moses. For example, before the siege of the city of Jericho, Joshua encounters a heavenly being who has come to aid the Israelites. Just as Moses was told by God in Exodus 3:5–10, Joshua is told, "Remove the sandals from your feet, for the place where you stand is holy" (see Joshua 5:13–15). ■

The writers of Joshua present the stories in terms of previous events. Still other depictions of Joshua are similar to those of Moses. As Moses parts the Red or Reed Sea (Exodus 14:21–22), Joshua parts the Jordan River (Joshua 4:7). God appears to Moses on Mount Sinai amid trumpet blasts (Exodus 19:16–19), and a series of trumpet blasts combined with the shouts of the people under Joshua's leadership cause the walls of Jericho to fall (Joshua 6:20). Both Moses and Joshua meet God and both send scouts ahead of them.

Judges

The Book of Judges collects the stories of men and women who deliver Israel from oppression. In ancient Israel, the title *judge* did not mean someone who presides over a trial; a **judge** was a brave, charismatic, resourceful military leader who was animated by the spirit of God. Although the judges are heroic, they are definitely on a smaller scale than Joshua is. Joshua is the successor of Moses as the leader of all those who entered the promised land; by contrast, the judges are associated with particular tribes of Israel. Unlike Joshua, who is both obedient to God and a brilliant soldier, some of the judges are morally flawed and even foolish. In general, the judges function as transitional figures between the heroic leaders of the past, Moses and Joshua, and the heroic leader to come, King David. ■

THE MORAL PATTERN OF JUDGES

OPENING THE WORD

Read Judges 3:7–11 and examine how it displays the moral pattern. How does Israel do evil? What happens as a result? How does God rescue Israel?

Read Judges 13–16.

The principal episodes in the Book of Judges reflect a repeating moral pattern: (1) The Israelites fall away from God—break the covenant, (2) God allows their enemies to oppress them, (3) the Israelites repent, (4) God raises up a savior to rescue them, (5) the savior overcomes the oppressors, (6) the Israelites have peace for a time—until they again fall away from God and the cycle repeats itself. For example, the story of Ehud (Judges 3:12–30) begins when the Israelites did "what was evil in the sight of the LORD"—worshiping the gods of the Canaanites. God allows Israel to be defeated by King Eglon of Moab, a country east of Canaan beyond the Dead Sea. When the Israelites repent and cry "out to the LORD, the LORD raised up for them a deliverer, Ehud son of Gera, the Benjamite, a left-handed-man." Ehud's left-handedness enables him to use a concealed sword against Eglon. Ehud then leads the Israelites against the Moabites, whom they defeat, killing all 10,000 soldiers. (The numbers 10 and 1000 both represent fullness—in this case, all the enemy's soldiers.) "And the land had rest eighty years." ■

Despite the repetition of this moral pattern, the Israelites do not seem to get the message. The Book of Judges implies that there is something inadequate about how they are organized as a people at this time. Near the end of the book, especially with regard to negative events, the statement is made: "In those days there was no king in Israel; all the people did what was right in their own eyes" (Judges 17:6; 21:25), suggesting that if they had a king, things would be better. This sets the stage for the monarchy in 1 Samuel. On the other hand, the three times an individual becomes powerful and almost becomes a king all lead to disaster—Gideon and idolatry in 6:1–8:28, Abimelech and family battles in chapter 9, and Jephthah and human sacrifice in chapter 11. This uncertainty on whether kingship is good or bad continues in the rest of the Deuteronomic History.

FOLKLORE AND MYTH IN SAMSON

OPENING THE WORD

Reread Judges 16:1–3, in which Samson carries off the city gates of Gaza, and compare it to the account of his death in Judges 16:23–30. How has Samson changed in the time between these two episodes?

ActiviTy

Use the Internet or your library to find pictures of sculptures or other fine art about Samson. Also find "strong" figures from other cultures, such as Hercules (Greek). How are the figures alike? How are they different?

Samson, the strong man, is a famous figure in the Old Testament. However, his story often seems less like military history or moral fable than it does like a heroic myth or legend or even a tall tale. For example, the episode of Samson killing a lion with his bare hands is similar to stories told about the Mesopotamian hero Gilgamesh and the Greek hero Hercules. The fact that Samson is vulnerable only if his hair is cut is reminiscent of the Greek hero Achilles, who could be wounded only in his heel. Samson does not seem inspired by religious or patriotic motives, but largely by a desire for revenge. ■ ■

This painting by the French artist James Tissot is titled "Samson Kills a Young Lion."

THE NARRATIVE OF RUTH

Read the Book of Ruth.

ACTIVITY

Select one of the three main characters in the Book of Ruth, and create an imaginary portrait of this individual. You may use any artistic medium you like. Before you begin, write down three or four personality traits that you think this character reflects, and then try to make your drawing, painting, sculpture, or other artwork embody these traits.

Although the Book of Ruth is set in "the days when the judges ruled," it does not deal with military history. Rather, it deals with family affection and ethnic tolerance. It is a tender, engrossing short story with a skillfully structured narrative and vivid characters. The German poet Goethe praised it as the most beautiful "little whole" of the Old Testament. Each of its four chapters presents a single episode and concludes with verses that summarize the preceding action and forecast what is to come. Although the tale is very brief, each of its three main characters, Naomi, Ruth, and Boaz, emerges as a well-developed individual. The fact that Ruth, a Moabite, is presented as a virtuous woman and an ancestor of one of Israel's greatest heroes, David, helps establish one of the story's chief themes, the value of tolerance.

About two-thirds of the Book of Ruth is presented in the form of conversation. The dialogue ranges from sharply humorous wordplay to moving eloquence. For example, in a famous passage marked by beautiful parallelism, Ruth refuses to abandon her mother-in-law Naomi:

> "Where you go, I will go;
> Where you lodge, I will lodge;
> your people shall be my people,
> and your God, my God."
> Ruth 1:16 ■

For Review

1. What factors contribute to Joshua's heroic stature?

2. Who were the judges?

3. What thematic pattern unifies the stories of the various judges?

4. How is the Book of Ruth structured?

5. How does the Book of Ruth show the value of tolerance?

For Discussion

Because of the strong links between the Book of Joshua and the first five books of the Old Testament, or Pentateuch, some biblical scholars have argued that Genesis through Joshua really forms a Hexateuch ("six books"). Discuss whether the Book of Joshua seems closer in character to the preceding texts in the Old Testament or to the Books of Judges and Ruth.

Activity

Read Joshua 6:1–20 together as a class. Then enact the dramatic scene of the fall of Jericho. One student should be the voice of God, and another student should play the role of Joshua. Seven students should represent the seven priests, while the rest of the class participates as members of the general army.

The Books of Joshua, Judges, and Ruth are set in the period of Israelite history between the death of Moses and the establishment of the Israelite monarchy. Joshua and Judges both deal with the conquest and settlement of Canaan. The Book of Joshua describes a swift, successful military campaign in the central hill country of Canaan and the distributions of conquered territory among the tribes of Israel. Another view is presented in the Book of Judges—that the Israelite conquest and settlement of Canaan was less epic and only partially successful; Judges presents a long series of conflicts between the Israelites and the Canaanites. The Book of Ruth ignores the larger history of the settlement to concentrate on the story of one family.

THE ISRAELITE STRUGGLE

OPENING THE WORD

Read Genesis 10:6, 15–20. These passages indicate how the Old Testament writers viewed the ethnic background of the Canaanites. From which of the sons of Noah were they descended?

In Chapter 4, you learned that the Israelite nation probably included many different peoples: the Canaanites, hapiru, shasu, and some of the Sea Peoples, along with the original Hebrews.

Who were the people against whom the Israelites struggled? The conflict between the Israelites and the Canaanites was, in a sense, "in the family," since these peoples were closely related. Both were part of peoples who had come from the desert regions east of Canaan; both spoke Semitic languages. Sometimes all the Israelites' enemies are grouped as "Canaanites"; sometimes they are referred to by specific names, such as the Amorites or Jebusites. At times the name *Canaanites* is reserved for the peoples dwelling on the coast of the Mediterranean Sea. (The word *Canaan* may refer to a red or purple dye from shellfish, a product for which the coastal Canaanites were well known.) ■

This Egyptian relief shows Philistine prisoners who were captured while raiding Egypt in 1180 B.C.

The Philistines and other Sea Peoples settled along the eastern coast of the Mediterranean Sea, known as the Great Sea.

ActiviTy

As a class, research the culture of the Canaanites or the Philistines. What is known about their religion, social and economic life, arts and crafts? How does this information enrich your study of the Old Testament?

Not all the Israelites' enemies were former desert nomads, however. A notable exception were the Philistines. The Philistines had not reached Canaan from the desert but from the Mediterranean Sea. The Philistines were one of the Sea Peoples, raiders originally from the region of the Aegean Sea who ravaged the eastern Mediterranean world around 1200 B.C. After an unsuccessful attack on Egypt, the Philistines moved north and settled the coastal plain of Canaan. The Philistines brought with them the technology for smelting iron, which made their armor and weapons superior to the bronze ones of the Israelites. The Philistines eventually disappeared from history, but they are remembered in the name the Romans gave to this whole region, *Palestine.* ■

CONQUEST AND SETTLEMENT IN JOSHUA

In the Book of Joshua, the Israelites conquer the Canaanite cities in a rapid series of assaults, while in Judges the conquest is a gradual process lasting many years. The Israelite occupation probably occurred in phases. Most of the infiltration was likely a relatively peaceful settlement of the sparsely populated hill regions, with occasional conflicts with the cities in the lowlands. Over time many of the earlier groups most likely joined the ever stronger Israelites.

The Canaanite world pictured in the Book of Joshua is a fragmented society of small city-states. The Canaanites had no central government. This would explain the recorded swift success of Joshua's initial campaign of conquest, which occupies only five years. After crossing the Jordan River and entering Canaan, the Israelites first attacked and destroyed the city of Jericho, a trading center located a few miles north of the Dead Sea near the western wall of the Jordan Valley. Jericho, whose name probably means "Moon City," is both the lowest (840 feet below sea level) and the oldest known (8000 B.C.) city in the world. Archaeological evidence indicates that Jericho was destroyed sometime in the middle of the late Bronze Age, which

OPENING THE WORD

Read in Joshua 8:1–29 the account of the capture of the city of Ai. What strategy did Joshua use to defeat the inhabitants of Ai? In this story, how is God portrayed? What does God do?

ACTIVITY

Listen to a recording of the African American spiritual "Joshua Fit the Battle of Jericho." Why do you think this story from the Old Testament would have inspired an enslaved people?

ACTIVITY

"Do the math" for the Book of Judges, adding up the periods during which the Israelites were oppressed by various enemies and the periods during which the land was at peace under the leadership of the different judges. What total do you get?

lasted from around 1500 to 1200 B.C., but this is too early to represent the Israelite attack described in Joshua. Perhaps the Israelites, in their success, appropriated the earlier destruction of Jericho into their glorified history.

Another important distinction is that the Canaanites worshiped fertility gods—named *Baal* and *Anath*. This difference is important because it is set in direct opposition to the God of the Israelites. The polytheistic religion of the Canaanites threatened Israel and God's plan for his people. ▨ ■

ISRAEL UNDER THE JUDGES

The Book of Judges follows the Book of Joshua and covers the history of Israel from the time of settlement until just before the establishment of the kingship under Saul, a period of roughly 200 years. The Book of Judges narrates the careers of twelve charismatic leaders who fought various enemies of Israel during this time, in most cases indicating for how long a period each "judged Israel." Adding up these periods—as well as the periods during which Israelites were oppressed by various enemies—produces a far larger total than 200 years. Allowing for some exaggeration and some overlap of judges in different tribes may bring us to a more realistic time span.

The Book of Judges should not be viewed as chronological history of the era from the settlement to the kingship, but as a collection of tales of the ancient heroes of the various tribes of Israel. Although Judges presents each of these individuals as having led all of Israel, the individuals are also closely identified with specific tribes. For example, Ehud is of the tribe of Benjamin, Gideon of Manasseh, Tola of Issachar, Elon of Zebulon, and Samson of Dan. ■

Judges of Israel

Name	Enemy	Term	Book of Judges
Othniel	Aram	40 years	3:7–11
Ehud	Moabites	80 years	3:12–30
Shamgar	Philistines	Not given	3:31
Deborah/Barak	Canaanites	40 years	4–5
Gideon	Midianites	40 years	6–8
Tola	Not given	23 years	10:1–2
Jair	Not given	22 years	10:3
Jephthah	Ammonites	6 years	10:6–12:7
Ibzan	Not given	7 years	12:8–10
Elon	Not given	10 years	12:11–12
Abdon	Not given	8 years	12:13–15
Samson	Philistines	20 years	13–16

Produced around A.D. 1250, this French manuscript illustration depicts two scenes from the Book of Ruth.

OPENING THE WORD

Read Judges 4 and 5. Did all the tribes of Israel participate in the battle? Who is given the glory for the Israelite victory over Sisera? Pay special attention to Judges 5:2–5.

The Role of Women in Judges

Two women play major roles in the Book of Judges. The first is the judge, Deborah, who is described as a "prophetess" rather than a warrior. Deborah and her general, Barak, organize Israelite resistance against a Canaanite army led by a general named Sisera. Although Sisera has "nine hundred chariots of iron," the Israelites, as is usual in these tales, utterly destroy the Canaanites: "All the army of Sisera fell by the sword; no one was left" (Judges 4:16). Sisera flees following the battle, taking refuge in the tent of a non-Israelite woman named Jael. While Sisera sleeps, Jael takes his life. Deborah celebrates the Israelite victory and Jael's participation in a song that may be among the most ancient passages in the Old Testament. ■

ISRAELITE CUSTOMS IN RUTH

The Book of Ruth was probably written after the exile, when many Jewish leaders were trying to restrict marriage and other interaction with outsiders. They were concerned that Judaism would not survive as a scattered people small in numbers. The Book of Ruth argues against these restrictions. It is also a valuable source of information about Israelite customs. For example, Ruth goes to glean in the fields of Naomi's wealthy kinsman, Boaz. *Gleaning* means gathering up the grain in the fields left behind by the reapers. According to Israelite law, people who were poor had the right to glean the fields, and farmers were required to leave part of the harvest for gleaning.

OPENING THE WORD

Reread Ruth 3. What roles do Naomi, Ruth, and Boaz each play in this episode?

Another Israelite custom in Ruth is *Levirate marriage.* If a married man died without a son, the Levirate law required his nearest male relative to marry his widow and provide him with a male heir. Ruth's kinsman by marriage, Boaz, fulfills the requirement after first arranging for a nearer male relative to renounce his claim. The arrangement between this man and Boaz is sealed by the Israelite custom of handing over a sandal. Boaz's acceptance of the sandal is accepted by witnesses as binding the agreement. ■

In the end, Ruth, a Moabite woman, becomes an ancestor of the great King David, so the restrictions on intermarriage are made to appear pointless. ■

ActiviTy

Retell the story of Ruth in the form of entries in a journal kept by Boaz. Be sure to include references to such matters as the barley harvest, arrangements for the reapers and the gleaners, and the Levirate law.

For Review

1. Who were the Canaanites and the Philistines?

2. How do the versions of the occupation of Canaan in the Books of Joshua and Judges differ?

3. In what two phases do historians believe that the Israelite occupation took place?

4. How did the makeup of Canaanite society contribute to the success of the Israelite conquest?

5. In the Book of Ruth, what was the Levirate law that Boaz followed?

For Discussion

Women from other countries and city-states play important roles in Joshua, Judges, and Ruth. In Joshua, Rahab, a woman of Jericho, helps the Israelites conquer the city (and according to Matthew 1:5, becomes the mother of Boaz); in Judges, Jael, a Kenite woman, kills Sisera, an enemy general; and Ruth herself is a Moabite. Why do you think the writers of the Old Testament gave these pivotal roles to non-Israelites and women?

ActiviTy

Research archaeological findings regarding the ancient city of Jericho. Focus on what is most interesting to you and create a graphic display of your findings. Present your display to the class.

The Book of Joshua is divided into three parts. Chapters 1–12 narrate the conquest of Canaan; Chapters 13–22 detail the distribution of the land among the different tribes; Chapters 23–24 bring the book to a conclusion, reporting Joshua's last words, his death, and his burial.

War is a religious activity for the Israelites. A pattern or code of war is evident in these stories. A standard of God always precedes them in the Ark of the Covenant (Joshua 6:2–4, 6–7). The Ark was a box that contained the tablets of the commandments and perhaps some other items. It was highly decorated and topped with carvings of two cherubim. The box symbolizes God's presence. The Israelites may have picked up the idea of a box from the Egyptians who put their gods in a box.

Another part of this pattern is the sacrifice before war (1 Samuel 7:8–10) and the importance of ritual purity. The war camp was to be a holy place, free of anything that was designated unclean (Deuteronomy 23:14). For instance, before the siege of Jericho, all of the soldiers were circumcised according to God's command. God explained to Joshua that circumcision removed the "disgrace of Egypt" from the men (Joshua 5:9). They were then purified and able to celebrate the Passover. Warriors were also forbidden to have intercourse with their wives during war so as to retain a pure focus (1 Samuel 21:4–5). Those who did not remain fully devoted to the conflict were discharged from war duty (Deuteronomy 20:5–8). ■

Opening the Word

Read Joshua 2:1, 8:4–8, and 10:9–10. Name four tactics of warfare that Joshua uses or displays.

The Ark of the Covenant was a symbol of the presence of God. When carried into battle, it symbolized the kingship and leadership of the God of Israel. The Ark was eventually placed in the temple of Solomon.

HOLY WAR

Before the capture of the city of Jericho, Joshua tells the Israelites, "Shout! For the LORD has given you the city. The city and all that is in it shall be devoted to the LORD for destruction" (Joshua 6:16–17). Following this command, the Israelites killed every living thing in the city—"both men and women, young and old, oxen, sheep, and donkeys"—sparing only the family of Rahab, a woman of Jericho who had hidden Joshua's spies (Joshua 6:21–23).

The character of the warfare described in Joshua and Judges is extremely brutal. For example, the destruction of Jericho reflects the ancient Israelite custom known as the **ban**, in which everything in a captured city—including the people, their livestock, and their possessions—is "devoted" to God, by being destroyed. Total destruction of the enemy would certainly ensure that there would be no intermarriage or weakening of the faith of the Israelites. Some of the livestock was unsuitable for consumption according to laws outlined in Leviticus, so the destruction of the livestock removed the problem.

ban ancient custom of completely destroying everything in a defeated city

To help understand this dreadful custom, it is important to remember that war for the Israelites was a religious act; it was "holy war." The background of holy war was the experience of the Israelites as desert nomads facing kings with trained, well-equipped armies including cavalry, such as Sisera's "nine hundred chariots of iron" (Judges 4:3). The Israelites believed that they literally had "God on their side" to offset their significant military disadvantage. God was the "LORD of hosts" and was personally engaged when Israel fought. When Israel won, the victory was God's. Holy war was sometimes fought only by volunteers. The number of the Israelite warriors was considered less important than the spirit of the Lord that animated them. At the same time, we must recognize that the concept of God presented is less developed than later concepts about God. ∎

OPENING THE WORD

Read Judges 7:2–3. Why does the Lord tell Gideon he has too many troops?

According to the rules for waging holy war set down in the Book of Deuteronomy, when the Israelites attacked a town, they were first to offer terms of peace. If the town surrendered peacefully, the inhabitants were to be spared (though they could be put to forced labor). However, if the town resisted, "then you shall besiege it; and when the LORD your God gives it into your hand, you shall put all its males to the sword" (Deuteronomy 20:12–13).

GOD AS WARRIOR

Some people find it difficult to accept the way God is presented as a warrior in these stories. However, it is important to remember that God is the Lord of history. Israel's life is based on this idea—and so is our faith. Our particular circumstances influence how we understand God to be Lord of history. Remember that the Exodus is interpreted as God's defeat of the pharaoh. God is present in this event to bring Israel to freedom. As part of the covenant, God governs all parts of Israel's life—even war. God's love and concern is always present.

ACTIVITY

The belief in "holy war" is still acted upon in the Islamic practice of *jihad*. Research jihad and explore how it is like and unlike "holy war" in the Old Testament.

The land of Canaan represents the fulfillment of God's promise of a land. God's promise to Abraham is fulfilled in Joshua. The land is God's "gift."

The presence of God is very clearly reflected in the repeated moral pattern of the Book of Judges: The Israelites sin by worshiping other gods or marrying other groups' women; their enemies oppress them; the Israelites repent; God raises up a leader who delivers Israel; the land is at peace until the people again "do what is evil." ■

JUST WAR

Throughout its history, one of the major efforts of the Christian Church has been to control warfare. The Christian theologian Saint Augustine of Hippo (A.D. 354–430) saw war as the result of sin, but believed that warfare could be valid if the violence were used to restrain evil and protect the innocent. Augustine tried to define what constituted "just war," proposing that violence is acceptable if certain conditions are met—just cause, right intention, last resort, and legitimate authority—all concepts that can be found to some degree in Israel's understanding of a holy war.

In their 1983 statement *The Challenge of Peace*, the U.S. bishops enumerated the conditions of a modern "just war" doctrine.

Conditions of Just War

Condition	Guidelines
just cause	War may be waged only to confront "a real and certain danger"—to protect innocent life, to preserve conditions necessary for decent human existence, and to secure basic human rights.
competent authority	War may be declared only by those with responsibility for public order, not by private groups or individuals.
comparative justice	No state has "absolute justice" on its side. Even a "just cause" has limits: Do the rights and values involved justify killing?
right intention	War can be legitimately intended only for the reasons set forth as a just cause. During the conflict, right intention means pursuit of peace and reconciliation, and the avoidance of unnecessarily destructive acts or unreasonable conditions (such as unconditional surrender).
last resort	For a resort to war to be justified, all peaceful alternatives must have been exhausted.
probability of success	If the outcome of force or resistance will clearly be disproportionate or futile, they are not justified.
proportionality	The damage inflicted and the costs incurred by war must be proportionate to the good expected for a nation and the world community.

Nonviolent conflict resolution applies to people and to nations.

OPENING THE WORD

Reread Judges 16:23–31. Does Samson's destruction of the Philistines seem to be an act of "just war"? Why or why not?

ACTIVITY

In the Middle Ages the Church attempted to control warfare through measures such as the Peace of God and the Truce of God, which sought to limit the periods during which hostilities could be conducted. Research the history of the Peace of God or the Truce of God to discover its specific provisions and how effective they were.

Conflict resolution and peacemaking are not tasks for nations only. Individuals and groups of every kind are constantly faced with situations of conflict that require the values and skills of nonviolent resolution. The story at the beginning of this chapter gives such an example of conflict resolution that does not resort to force or violence. When the art of peacemaking is studied and practiced more than the science of war, the world will be renewed. ■ ■

For REVIEW

1. What was the ban?
2. What was the background of the Israelite practice of "holy war"?
3. What were Saint Augustine's conditions for "just war"?
4. What is a "just cause" for war?
5. Who has "legitimate authority" to make war?

For DISCUSSION

In their famous "March to the Sea" during the Civil War, the army of Union General William T. Sherman destroyed everything in its path. Discuss whether Sherman violated the "right intention" condition of "just war." Has any war fought by the U.S. government met all the conditions of a just war?

ACTIVITY

Make a list of wars or armed conflicts today that are being fought on religious grounds. Which conditions of a just war apply to each? Which do not?

Joan of Arc

Warfare in the Middle Ages was often motivated by religious faith. One of the most famous warriors inspired by faith was Joan of Arc (1412?–1431). Joan was a pious, illiterate peasant girl born in the village of Domremy in the French province of Lorraine. Three years after she was born, the French were defeated by the English at the battle of Agincourt. This was the last in a series of disastrous defeats for France in the long conflict with England known as the Hundred Years' War. Much of France was occupied by the English, and in 1420, the French were forced to sign a treaty agreeing to surrender the crown of France to the English king when the reigning French king died.

Then in 1428, when the French had all but lost hope, Joan appeared, claiming that heavenly voices had given her a mission to rescue France from the English invaders and restore to the throne the French heir, Charles the Dauphin. She claimed that Saint Michael the Archangel, Saint Catherine of Alexandria, and Saint Margaret of Antioch spoke to her, telling her she must rescue the French city of Orléans (which had been besieged by the English for many months), and that she must see Charles crowned king of France at Reims.

Visionary experiences such as Joan's were not uncommon in the Middle Ages; but they were often associated with individuals who were physically weak or mentally unbalanced. Joan was neither; she was, in fact, very healthy in both body and mind, working in the fields and doing women's tasks at home. The Middle Ages were also a period of widespread superstition. Many people believed in witchcraft, and a tree and fountain near Joan's village of Domremy were believed to be enchanted. Both Joan's claim to hear voices and the folklore of her village would later be used against her by her enemies.

Traveling across enemy territory to see Charles, Joan cut her hair short and wore men's clothes for security. Her courage and conviction impressed the Dauphin, who permitted her to lead troops against the English at Orléans. Inspired by her fearlessness, the French soldiers defeated their enemies and

This medieval miniature pictures Joan of Arc in armor and carrying her banner. Joan was motivated by her faith and thus is a model for us.

liberated the city. After this victory, Joan accompanied Charles to Reims, where he was crowned king of France on July 17, 1429. The following year, she was captured in battle by the Burgundians, who sold her to their English allies. The English turned her over to the Church for trial. Before and at her trial, she was questioned closely and for long periods of time about her voices, Domremy's enchanted tree and fountain, and her habit of wearing men's clothing. Even today her answers are impressive. Condemned as a heretic and witch, Joan was burned at the stake at Rouen on May 30, 1431.

In 1455, at the request of her mother and two brothers, Joan's trial was reopened and she was declared innocent of all the charges against her. In 1920 the Church canonized her as a saint.

Strengthened by her faith, Joan fought for France at a time when war was the only option. We can live by our faith today through employing the methods of peacemaking and conflict resolution rather than warfare. After all, it takes as much courage to be a peacemaker as it does to be a warrior.

Integrity and Tolerance

We began this chapter by talking about uniting integrity and tolerance, of standing up for what you believe, and by also showing a willingness to consider other people's points of view.

The Books of Joshua and Judges offer many examples of standing up for one's beliefs. Joshua never loses his faith in God throughout the time he leads the Israelites, and at his death God renews the covenant between himself and his people. Deborah knew what God wanted for his people and did what was necessary to defeat the Canaanite army under Sisera. Samson, though a flawed leader, put his faith in God one last time and died a heroic death.

Some striking biblical examples of faith in God involve non-Israelites, such as Jael, the Kenite woman who killed the enemy general Sisera, and Rahab, the woman of Jericho who took the risk of hiding Joshua's spies.

An example of *not* standing up for one's beliefs can be found in the story of Achan in the Book of Joshua, which shows the consequences of an individual's lack of integrity, both to himself and his community. After the capture of Jericho, Achan violates both God's command and Joshua's by stealing some of the city's treasure, all of which was to be destroyed. As a result of God's displeasure over this violation of the ban, the Israelites are defeated in their first battle with the men of Ai. When Achan's crime is revealed, he and his whole family are stoned to death. ■

The concept of God in Joshua and Judges is less developed; it is a concept of a rather merciless tribal deity, for whom any kind of accommodation with the Canaanites is a sin. The Book of Ruth reflects a very different idea—a God of compassion and caring who sees both Israelites and non-Israelites equally as his people. The theme of tolerance and understanding is most clearly expressed in the character of Ruth herself, a virtuous Moabite who becomes an ancestor of both David and Jesus.

OPENING THE WORD

Read the story of Achan in Joshua, chapter 7. How is his guilt revealed? How does he explain his conduct to Joshua?

CONFLICT RESOLUTION

The Second Vatican Council called for a new attitude toward war, which had become so terrible in the twentieth century. The council pointed out the reckoning we will face as a result of our deeds of war. We are called instead to be peacemakers. We, as a Church, are to rid ourselves of "enemy" thinking, and instead to view others as brothers and sisters in Christ. The bishops in Vatican II ask us to strive to be "great-souled" people. We need to enlarge our compassion and to see the horrible reality of war, its destruction and death.

We are asked to examine our heroes. Are they peacemakers? Do they exhibit compassion as well as commitment? Do we view peacemakers as highly as warriors? And how can we educate ourselves in the art of conflict resolution? The story of conflict resolution at the beginning of this chapter gives one example of how we can turn away from violence and work to resolve our differences by peaceful means. ■

OPENING THE WORD

Read Ruth 2:8–13. In this passage, how does Boaz exhibit the instincts of a peacemaker?

The understanding of God that Jesus preached is similar to that found in the Book of Ruth—compassionate and caring toward all people. Jesus himself was nonviolent. He chastised Peter for cutting off the soldier's ear in the garden. He went to the crucifixion without violence. The Beatitudes (Matthew 5:3–12) are clearly a call for nonviolence. In recent times, we have had calls for nonviolent conflict resolution from Christian activists such as Dr. Martin Luther King Jr. (1929–1968) and Dorothy Day (1897–1980). They not only rejected violence, but they also worked to resolve conflicts peacefully. As followers of Jesus, we can do no less. ■

A tireless advocate of social justice and peace, Dorothy Day observed, "If I have achieved anything in my life, it is because I have not been embarrassed to talk about God."

ActiviTy

Research the career of a peacemaker of the twentieth century, such as Dr. Martin Luther King Jr. or Dorothy Day of the United States, Mohandas Gandhi of India, or Aung San Suu Kyi of Myanmar. Write a short essay about the courage of this individual.

For Review

1. Why was Achan punished?

2. How does the concept of God in Joshua and Judges differ from that in Ruth?

3. To what did Vatican II contrast "enemy thinking"?

4. According to Vatican II, how are heroes to be evaluated?

For Discussion

Name some twentieth-century American heroes. What distinguishes them as heroes? Do we regard peacemakers as highly as warriors?

ActiviTy

Make a list of important dates in this chapter—from the stories of David to the example of Dorothy Day. Create a time line using these dates, and add pictures noting the history of conflict and conflict resolution.

JourNaL

Have you ever had to be a peacemaker? What measures did you take toward resolving the conflict? What did you learn from the situation?

Summary

The Books of Joshua and Judges deal with the conquest and settlement of Canaan—the land promised to the Israelites by God. The world these books describe is harsh and violent, one that is animated by fierce loyalties to the Israelite community and equally fierce hatred for outsiders; it is a world scarred by brutal conflicts in which there were no noncombatants. The positive models these books offer are examples of moral integrity, of holding fast to one's faith in God despite the cost. The inspired writers proclaimed the greatness of the God of Israel who, in his providence, brought the people through the many trials of settling the promised land.

The Book of Ruth turns from the history of warfare to tell a story of family loyalty and ethnic tolerance. The lessons of Ruth go beyond simple loyalty to one's own community to a larger understanding of the needs of other people. It is a tale about peacemakers. In our personal lives and as members of communities and nations, we need to abandon "enemy thinking" in viewing others and educate ourselves in the art of conflict resolution. We too need to become peacemakers.

He reached down from on high, he took me;
*   he drew me out of mighty waters.*
He delivered me from my strong enemy,
*   and from those who hated me;*
*   for they were too mighty for me.*
They confronted me in the day of my calamity;
*   but the LORD was my support.*

                    Psalm 18:16—18

He chose his servant David,
    and took him from the sheepfolds;
from tending the nursing ewes he brought him
    to be the shepherd of his people Jacob,
    of Israel, his inheritance.
With upright heart he tended them,
    and guided them with skillful hand.

Psalm 78:71–72

Davidic Monarchy Period in Israel

1100 B.C.
Assyrian ruler Tiglath-pileser I
holds Northern Syria

1000–994 B.C.
David is king of Judah

961–922 B.C.
Solomon is king of Israel

1020–1000 B.C.
Saul rules the people of
Israel

994–962 B.C.
David is king of all Israel

c. 960 B.C.
Solomon builds temple at
Jerusalem

CHAPTER 6

Building a Kingdom

CHAPTER GOALS

Increase the student's understanding of the temple period and the monarchy by studying the following:

- some literary forms and examples
- the succession of kings and development of a unified kingdom
- an understanding of king and messiah as God's anointed
- the qualities of good leadership
- personal applications of the concept of idolatry

CHAPTER OUTLINE

Literary Interpretation: Oracles, Poetry, and the Formula of Kingship

Historical Interpretation: Monarchy and Dynasty

Theological Interpretation: Theocracy and Messianism

Witness: Thomas More

Personal Challenge: Recognizing Idolatries and Setting Priorities

Summary

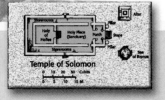

Temple of Solomon

776 B.C.
First recorded Olympic
Games held in Greece

587 B.C.
Temple at Jerusalem
destroyed by Babylonians

922–587 B.C.
Divided Monarchy

753 B.C.
Rome founded on
Tiber River

Your school is holding student government elections. You want to be thoughtful and fair and not regard the election as a popularity contest. The president of the student council is an important office. That person must be responsive to her or his peers, yet be able to think independently when the occasion demands.

There are four individuals running for council president. You have eliminated two of them because one is too popular and one is not well-known. In your estimation, the contest is between the remaining two.

One nominee is a boy who is on the cheering squad. He possesses a lot of energy and enthusiasm as well as the ability to convince others to participate in causes he feels are important. If he makes a mistake, he is able to acknowledge it and continue on a better path. However, if someone challenges his opinion, he finds that difficult to accept. This boy studies hard to get high grades, yet seems to know when it's time to take a break and have a good time. At home, he has a lot of responsibility for his younger siblings because his mother is a single parent. He never complains about having to do this.

The other nominee is a girl who is captain of the debate team. She has done a good job coaching others and encouraging them to do their best. She has a way of examining both sides of an issue and making clear, impartial decisions. She has grades that are good but not outstanding. Extracurricular activities play a big part in her schedule, and she volunteers at the local hospital, waiting on tables in the snack bar. This girl is a favorite of some teachers, perhaps for good reason. She is very interested in religion and isn't shy about that.

You have only one vote. For whom will you cast your ballot for student council president? What further information do you wish you had about the candidates? How would you go about finding out more?

In this chapter you will learn about biblical examples of the leadership qualities of wisdom, prudence (good judgment), and strength. As you study the Scriptures, think about how those qualities apply to modern situations.

Scrolls of the Torah are hand-written in Hebrew, which reads from right to left. This scribe is repairing a Torah scroll.

FAitH SHARiNg

Two times this week, think about times when you have had to vote for something or someone. This could include a class or club election, an opinion poll, an evaluation sheet for an activity or event, or a consumer survey for a product appealing to teens.

- How carefully would you vote in each case? How much thought would you put into each decision?
- Do religious values affect the way you vote? What values would you be unwilling to compromise?

In this chapter you will read parts of four historical books: 1 and 2 Samuel and 1 and 2 Kings. After the Book of Judges, the religious history of Israel continues to unfold to show the rise of a monarchy in Israel. ■

As with many other books in the Old Testament, the writers, inspired by God, present religious truth within a historical framework. This history of the monarchy, in which God did wondrous deeds for his people, shows the blessings (given through obedience to the covenant) and the suffering (results of disobedience) of God's people. The main literary style is the narrative, which was discussed in a previous chapter.

Many of the accounts are vivid and are presented as eyewitness testimonies of certain historical events. Of course, the writers wrote and rewrote these stories many times—ending with a version written after 586 B.C. It was written for those Jews who remembered the destruction of the temple and had gone into exile. These documents were intended to encourage repentance and give hope by reminding the Jews that God had remained faithful to his promise throughout a succession of disobedient kings. The readings of 1 and 2 Kings, when combined with the Books of Samuel, paint a portrait for us of admirable leadership. Studying these portraits can help us evaluate potential leaders in modern times, even the president of the student council.

STYLE OF AN ORACLE

An **oracle** consists of words of wisdom or advice given by God through a spokesperson. (Note that the terms *oracle, oral history, oral surgery,* and *oration* all share the root word *oral,* which is related to the mouth.) In 2 Samuel 7, Nathan gives us textual clues that what he is to convey is the word of God. Examples of such clues are: "Go and tell my servant David: Thus says the LORD" (2 Samuel 7:5) and "Thus says the LORD of hosts" (2 Samuel 7:8). Some biblical oracles are judgment speeches ("bad news") and some are oracles of salvation ("good news"). Both types of oracles are conditional. They depend on the action or inaction of the people in response to the oracle.

POETRY

Opening the Word

Read Psalms 30 and 139. Point out parallel lines that use contrast. Read Psalms 103 and 144, noticing the strength of rhythm in the English translation. Say one of the two psalms aloud while beating the rhythm with a pencil or light percussive instrument.

"Sing to the LORD a new song, his praise in the assembly of the faithful."

Psalm 149:1

Many of the psalms have been attributed to King David, who was a musician and poet as well as a political leader. His name is attached to more than 70 psalms; that is, the psalm was *to, for, by,* or *in the style or spirit of* David. Many of the psalm poems have a parallel structure and rhythm. In parallel structure, a numbered verse has several parts that continue, contrast, or overlap each other. An example of contrast is: "If I ascend to heaven, you are there; if I make my bed in Sheol, you are there" (Psalm 139:8). The rhythm of the poetry was enhanced with musical instruments that accompanied psalm-singing.

In poems and songs, the rhythm is based—in part—on the number of syllables in a line and the stresses on the words. In the poetry of the psalms, important words were stressed and unimportant words were unstressed. Psalm 150 uses rhythm and repetition, and names some of the instruments played in worship: "Praise him with trumpet sound; praise him with lute and harp!" (Psalm 150:3).

There is much we don't know about Hebrew poetic techniques, since the original pronunciation has been lost and poetry depends so much on the sound of the words. There are also musical instructions at the beginning of many psalms, and their meanings have been lost.

Activity

Look in a hymnal for songs that are based on psalm texts. Identify any selections that you like and note the Scripture, the writer of the text, and the date of two or three of the selections. **Optional:** Organize a small choral group to sing the songs, play a recording of them for the class, or use the songs in a class prayer.

Hannah's Song

Read 1 Samuel 1:9–2:10.

vow a solemn promise

Songs, which are another form of poetry, appear throughout the Scriptures. An example of this literary technique is found in 1 Samuel. Hannah, the wife of Elkanah the Ephraimite, was a devout woman. When she went to the shrine at Shiloh, she prayed, wept, and poured out her soul. Hannah prayed fervently for a son and made a **vow** to God. She promised to offer her son to the Lord as a consecrated person. Her son Samuel became the one who recognized and anointed Saul, the first king of Israel. After her son was born, Hannah thanked God in song for answering her prayer. ■

OPENING THE WORD

After reading Hannah's song, turn to the Magnificent (Luke 1:46–55), Mary's response to Elizabeth following the annunciation, when Mary learned that she would bear a child who was divine. Here are two women with remarkable pregnancies, for different reasons. Compare their thoughts and words in graphic or written form.

THE FORMULA OF KINGSHIP

Read 1 Kings 14:21–31, 15:25–31.

In the two Books of Kings, the reign of each king after Solomon is given by means of a formula. First there is an introduction which has a time frame, forebearers, and accomplishments. That is followed by details of the king's death, descendants, and sometimes references to annals or other books, some since lost. The report formula and a rough chronological order throughout 1 and 2 Kings makes it easy for readers to recognize the cycle of faithfulness and unfaithfulness to the covenant.

For REVIEW

1. What is an oracle? What part do oracles play in the history of Israel?

2. Give examples of several poetic elements found in psalms associated with David.

3. What is the effect of the formula report about the rulers in 1 and 2 Kings?

For DISCUSSION

Consider people who seem to speak with authority, such as a parent, teacher, priest, or politician. Do they claim to be speaking for God, explaining his will for your life? Who is entitled to make such a claim? How can you decide whether it is God's guidance you are hearing?

ACTIVITY

Write a brief biography of a deceased U.S. president that follows the form given for the kings of Israel and Judah. As a class, collect the biographies and put them in a chronological bulletin board display.

Read 1 Samuel 13:19–22.

AcTiviTy

Research to find out what products the Philistines made from iron and why this new material was such an improvement over what they had used previously.

monarchy rule by a single head of state, often a hereditary office

dynasty a succession of rulers in the same family line, frequently father to son

OpeNiNG the WorD

Read 1 Samuel 8:10–22 to understand why Samuel opposed the idea of appointing a king. Why do the people insist upon having a king despite Samuel's cautions?

JourNaL

Think of a time when you asked your parents for permission to do something and they told you why it would not be a good idea. What did you do? What were the consequences? If you didn't follow your parents' advice, did you later regret it?

THE IRON AGE

From about 1400 to 1200 B.C. the Hittites kept a great secret. They had extracted iron from ore and had made tools and weapons from this "new" metal. These iron instruments were superior to those made from bronze and copper. Around 1200 B.C. this new technological secret spread to other peoples, and the Philistines mastered the technology. ■

The Philistines' control of this metal gave them an economic advantage over the Israelites, but the Israelites persisted in their struggle to build a strong nation. For the Israelites, creating a **monarchy** meant establishing a political and religious unit. To create this unit, they sought a king.

MONARCHY AND DYNASTY

During the monarchy in Israel's history, many of the kings were wise, prudent, and strong, but they also had character flaws. They brought about a centralization of leadership to unite the people, strengthen their faith, and build a holy city. They worked to meet the expectations of God and of the people. The prophets spoke of a king, a messiah, who would be a descendant of King David. A king's descendants who continue to rule in succession may be called a **dynasty.** Tracing the Davidic line (descendants of David) became an important factor in establishing a messiah's authenticity and authority.

Look back to the story that opened this chapter. Choosing a leader, following a leader, being a leader, and building up loyalty and team spirit are probably things to which you can relate. The children of Israel had been a wandering people, a loose confederation of tribes, and it was natural that they would desire a king to pull things together.

The Israelites' desire for a monarchy developed gradually as they observed the nations around them. Some of Israel's judges were almost powerful enough to be considered kings. As the tribes became more prosperous, they wanted the trade and stability a central authority would provide. The threat from the Philistines convinced them that they needed a united defense. In one story, the prophet-judge Samuel opposes the idea of an Israelite king. The Israelites reject Samuel's advice, and Saul becomes their first king. ■ ■

JoUrNaL

Recall times when you witnessed holy oil being used in a religious ritual such as Baptism, Holy Orders, or Anointing of the Sick. Describe the ritual, noting sensory details. Imagine how the recipient might feel.

Read 1 Samuel 9:27–10:8, 1 Samuel 12.

Anointing with Oil

Saul was marked for leadership by being anointed with oil. In the ancient world, perfumed or scented olive oil or ointment was a cosmetic often worn on festive occasions by women and men. Healing herbs and other ingredients were added to the oil and ointment to form a salve or medicine. In Israel and other Middle Eastern countries, special people and objects were set apart for political or religious service by a ritual of consecration during which oil was poured over their heads.

KING SAUL (C. 1020–1000 B.C.)

Saul, during his short unsuccessful reign, had trouble forming a centralized nation. Saul died by his own sword after being wounded in a disastrous battle with the Philistines. He is a tragic figure in the history of Israel. ▪

The land of King David's people still provides shepherds' fields today.

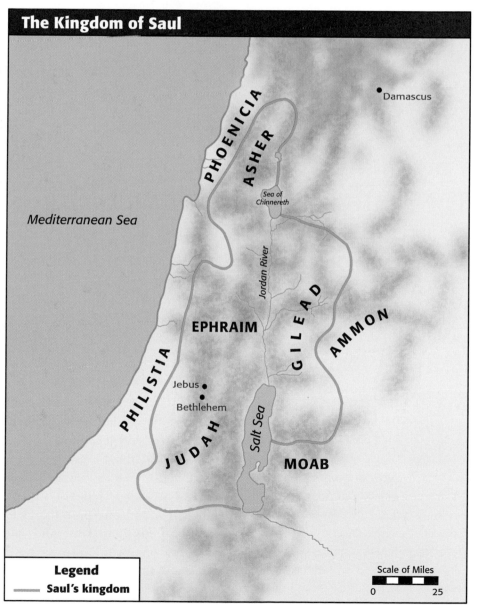

The Kingdom of Saul

PHOENICIA
ASHER
Damascus
Sea of Chinnereth
Mediterranean Sea
Jordan River
EPHRAIM
GILEAD
AMMON
PHILISTIA
Jebus •
Bethlehem •
JUDAH
Salt Sea
MOAB

Legend
—— Saul's kingdom

Scale of Miles
0   25

King David made great strides in uniting the people and expanding the territory of the kingdom. This painting is by James Tissot.

OPENING THE WORD

King Saul's torment is described in 1 Samuel 16:14–23. What were his symptoms and therapy? Do you think his problem was evil spirits, mental illness, or both?

JOURNAL

The story of David and Goliath is a favorite of many. Recall an example in your own experience in which someone "weaker" overcame someone "stronger." Write a reflection about this struggle in which the apparently weaker or smaller person wins. How is your example inspirational?

KING DAVID (c. 1000–961 B.C.)

Many times during his reign, King Saul was troubled and restless. Some said God's spirit left him and an evil spirit came to dwell in him. According to one tradition, a servant sent for a shepherd boy named David who was known for his courage, strength, and ability to play the harp. The boy soothed Saul with music and was liked so well that he became the king's armor-bearer. The judge Samuel found David and anointed him as the Lord's chosen. Saul and David had an on-again, off-again relationship, punctuated by jealousy and rivalry as indicated by the taunt in Scripture: "Saul has killed his thousands, and David his ten thousands" (1 Samuel 18:7 and elsewhere). The two of them quarreled and threatened each other, but they also admired one another greatly. David was close friends with Saul's son, Jonathan, and he married Saul's daughter, Michal. ▨ ▨

The City of David

At the age of thirty-seven, David was anointed king, and he ruled and united Israel for forty years. He brought the Ark of the Covenant in from the outlying territory, and Jerusalem came to be called the City of David. His armies conquered the Philistines, the Moabites, and the Syrians. David recognized God's favor to him and his people: "Is there another nation on earth whose God went to redeem it as a people, and to make a name for himself, doing great and awesome things for them, by driving out before his people nations and their gods? And you established your people Israel for yourself to be your people forever . . ." (2 Samuel 7:23–24). David was a courageous and faithful leader. Some have compared the developments in Israel at the time to the U.S. establishment of a federal republic with a stronger central government under its constitution.

KING SOLOMON (c. 961–922 B.C.)

Read 1 King 3:1–15.

Solomon was a son of David and Bathsheba. Solomon consolidated his forces, drove out dissidents, and ordered the execution of Adonijah, his step-brother, a competitor to the throne. Early in his career Solomon prayed for understanding and the ability to discern between good and evil. He did not ask for long life or for victory in battle. This pleased God, who granted him wisdom exceeding that of any other leader, with riches and honor to follow. Solomon married a daughter of the Egyptian pharaoh and kept many women of other nations in his household. The Song of Solomon (Song of Songs), the Book of Wisdom (Wisdom of Solomon), Ecclesiastes (Qoheleth), and Proverbs are attributed to this wise leader, although he probably was not the actual author.

Building and Breaking

Read 1 Kings 10–11.

ACTIVITY

Among the riches in King Solomon's court was an ivory throne. Using the Internet or another resource, find information about the status of ivory today and the countries of origin.

Solomon's reign brought many improvements and great splendor to Israel. Solomon appointed officers, established administrative districts with a prefect (chief officer) in each, and modernized the military by giving soldiers horses and chariots. He also established a prosperous import-export business and collected taxes to finance an extensive building campaign—a palace, fortification walls, and a central temple. He was a man of many dreams and visions. The Queen of Sheba in Arabia brought trade goods to Solomon's court and challenged him with hard questions. She wanted to see for herself this king of wealth and wisdom, and she was properly impressed. When Solomon died—1 Kings 11:43 expresses this with the words that he "slept with his ancestors and was buried"—his son Rehoboam succeeded him. During Rehoboam's rule, the kingdom split into north and south. ■

For Review

1. What is the difference between a monarchy and a dynasty?

2. What were some uses of oil in biblical times?

3. Who were the main people with whom David interacted?

4. List some of Solomon's achievements.

For Discussion

Together as a class, read Exodus 28–29 and 1 Kings 8:3–11. Name the privileges and responsibilities of a priest in ancient Israel. Then compare those to the privileges and responsibilities of a priest in the Catholic Church today.

Activity

Role play an interview between King Solomon and an eyewitness of the time period. As a class, ask him or her questions that require wise answers.

Theological Interpretation

A variety of opinions and traditions influenced the material finally included in the Books of Samuel and Kings. Many unknown sources were used by those who wrote the Deuteronomic history after the exile in Babylon. As a result, the books have inconsistent views of kings. Kings, in the final analysis, sometimes led the people into living out their covenant responsibilities, and they sometimes led them into evil ways.

SAMUEL AS PROPHET AND JUDGE

The role of Samuel is explained by two traditions, both found within 1 Samuel 1–12. In one tradition, Samuel, the seer and prophet, gives advice to Saul. From his "high place," he has the authority to appoint a king in the name of God. He secretly anoints Saul as "prince" of the people.

In the other tradition, Samuel is a judge who finds the idea of a monarchy displeasing. He appoints his own sons as judges, but the people continue to demand a king. They tell Samuel, "You are old and your sons do not follow in your ways; appoint for us, then, a king to govern us, like other nations" (1 Samuel 8:5).

These two traditions represent the struggle to form a unified nation under God. Samuel's remarks (1 Samuel 7:3–17) are important because he believes that the people are to be ruled by a **theocracy.** He believes that the formation of a kingdom with an earthly king is a violation of the covenant. The Israelites had to redefine monarchy to keep the proper order of command. To keep with the covenant, they understood power in this order: God, Law, King, People. This is distinct from the traditional understanding of monarchy: King, Law, People.

theocracy a nation ruled by God

DISLOYALTY TO GOD

When the leaders lose favor with God, they fail and fall away from right relationship with God. When Saul believes he is above the law, he falls (1 Samuel 15). David commits adultery with Bathsheba and commits murder, and he too falls (2 Samuel 11:1–12:14). Solomon worshiped other gods and failed (1 Kings 11). Israel was a covenanted people. This required observance of the law and worship in the temple.

AN ORACLE FROM GOD

In 2 Samuel 7, the prophet Nathan receives a word from God for King David about building a house—a house for his name and for the ark—a house where God's magnificent deeds can be remembered. The people have been on the move, and it is time for them to be planted and to put down roots. God's house, too, has been a portable tent and tabernacle. As the leader of Israel, David feels a responsibility to begin construction of this temple.

A TEMPLE FOR WORSHIP

Read 1 Kings 6–8.

worship to honor or revere a divine being, usually within a religious ritual

JOURNAL

List some of the temple furnishings mentioned in 1 Kings 7. Write about the function of each and the sense or senses to which they would appeal.

OPEN THE WORD

Psalms were used in temple worship, just as we use them in our liturgy today. Many of them were attributed to King David. In pairs, read two of the following psalms and find references to the temple and what took place there.

Psalm 11 (Song of Trust in God)

Psalm 24 (Entrance into the Temple)

Psalm 26 (Plea for Justice)

Psalm 122 (Song of Prayer and Praise for Jerusalem)

Psalm 134 (Praise in the Night)

God promised to build a house for David—a dynasty lasting forever. David wanted to build a house for the Lord, even though the prophet Nathan spoke against the plan. The temple, built by David's son, Solomon, took seven years to build and required the work of thousands of laborers (1 Kings 9:20–23). The first commandment states that people are to **worship** God alone and not turn to idolatry. Religious practice could be more easily regulated in a central place. Priests brought the Ark of the Covenant and installed it in the innermost room. The ark contained the stone tablets on which the commandments were written. As a dark cloud filled the temple, Solomon blessed the assembly and presented lavish burnt offerings and grain offerings. The dedication ceremony and accompanying festivities lasted seven days. ■ ■

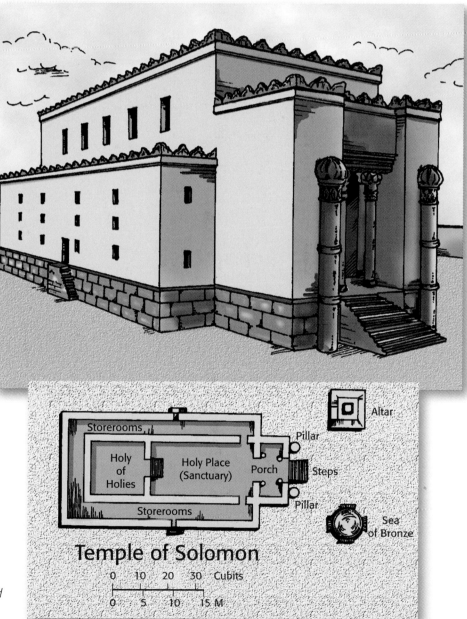

Temple of Solomon

0 10 20 30 Cubits

0 5 10 15 M

The temple built in Solomon's time may have been modeled after a Canaanite temple. Solomon's temple was decorated with ivory, bronze, and gold.

messiah king or deliverer expected by the Jews; the "anointed one"

messianism belief in a messiah as the savior of the people

Each king of Israel was a *mashiah* or "anointed one" singled out by God for leadership. You have read about oil being poured as part of a consecration ceremony. From the Hebrew word *mashiah* we get **messiah**. **Messianism** was a movement that developed centuries after King David. Believers expected a deliverer in the here-and-now, although no one knew exactly when. King David was perceived as fulfilling the role of messiah-king in an earthly practical sense, and David was an anointed one. He met the kingly specifications by providing law and justice, securing God's blessing for his people, defeating enemies, and ruling on a large scale. The followers of Messianism hoped that one of David's descendants would establish his kingdom again.

Activity

Listen to a recording of G. F. Handel's oratorio *Messiah*. What Scripture passages do you recognize? How does the musical score help you appreciate the majesty of the words?

Christ as the Anointed One

Christos is the Greek word for "anointed one." Of course, "Christ," as applied to Jesus, means the same thing; it is not his surname. For Christians, the deliverer has come and will come again at the end of time. Christians consider Jesus the Messiah, the Christ. The prophet Isaiah spoke of the coming deliverer with a sequence of honorific titles:" Wonderful Counselor, Mighty God, Everlasting Father, Prince of Peace" (Isaiah 9:6). ■

Jesus the Christ has been portrayed in differing cultures around the world. This "Lakota Victory Christ" is by Rev. John Giuliani.

For REVIEW

1. What two views of the monarchy are found in the historical books?

2. How does building the temple relate to the first commandment?

3. What are two words meaning "anointed"?

For DISCUSSION

From what you have read, what would be your reaction to a temple service in Jerusalem in Solomon's time?

Thomas More

Man of Conviction

Thomas More was an English statesman and scholar (1477?–1535). He studied the classics and new humanistic learning at Oxford, then attended law school. His associates were philosopher Desiderius Erasmus and painter Hans Holbein, and he was a contemporary of the Protestant reformer Martin Luther. More was aware of the threat of material success to spiritual life. After four years in seclusion, he discerned his vocation as a layperson and a married man. In 1520 he was made a knight, so his name is often written with "Sir" before it.

As Plato's *Republic* and St. Augustine's *City of God* did, More's writing envisioned an ideal state, an island *utopia* with a just and equal society. More's book *Utopia*, published in 1516, is a social satire with a proposal for a commonwealth. In this work, More spoke against war, religious intolerance, and misuse of property. He advocated a kind of communalism in which "the father of every family or every householder fetcheth whatsoever he and his have need of, and carrieth it away with him without money, without exchange, without any gage, pawn, or pledge. For why should anything be denied unto him, seeing there is an abundance of all things . . . ?"

Eventually More enjoyed the company of the king and queen of England and, though you would not have guessed it from his picture, he enjoyed a good party. He served as lord high chancellor during the era when King Henry VIII sought an annulment of his marriage to Catherine of Aragon in order to marry Anne Boleyn. King Henry took matters into his own hands and created a schism in the Catholic Church. To which side would More give his oath of loyalty? He secluded himself once again as his strength of character and his moral conviction were tested. In the end, More refused to

Thomas More dreamed of a just and equal society free of material concerns and in harmony with God's law. He made a decision to live according to his beliefs and refused to compromise them.

go along with the king in his revolt against the pope. The king first deprived More of his books and writing materials, and then set up a rigged trial in which More was convicted of treason. He was executed for treason, in effect, for rejecting the English king as head of the Church in that country, superior to all outside rulers, including the pope. More was canonized a saint in 1935.

Recognizing Idolatries and Setting Priorities

A continual challenge to the leaders of Israel was the tendency of people to become impatient and anxious, to return to religious practices dating from before they believed in one God, or to borrow practices of their neighbors.

RECOGNIZING IDOLATRIES

JOURNAL

Write about how you feel when you are in your own or another church in your community. How does the arrangement of the building, seating, and decor assist you in your worship of God?

According to the Exodus epic, when Moses came down from Mount Sinai with the tablets on which the commandments were written, he found that the people had produced a golden calf as an idol to worship. The golden calf has been an example of false worship and idolatry for all time. The oracle of Nathan instructed the leaders of Israel to give the people a place to worship properly to prevent them from turning to idolatry. ■

Representations of the Divine

When you read the first commandment in Exodus 20:2–5 or Deuteronomy 5:6–9, you may be surprised at how much is implied. The people are directed not to make images of heavenly things—such as God, angels, the pearly gates, or perhaps also saints or common people who have died. They are also directed not to make images of earthly things—plants, animals, and humans—or of things such as rock, water, or sea life. The monotheistic religions of Judaism and Islam observe similar prohibitions to some degree. In Islam, artists do not make images of animals or humans. Important public places, especially mosques, are decorated with geometric or floral patterns and Arabic lettering.

The Dome of the Rock in Jerusalem was built over a place sacred to Jews and Muslims. Use the Internet or an encyclopedia to research the events believed to have happened here.

A variety of art forms are visible in this photo of the interior of San Marco in Venice, Italy. An iconostasis separates the sanctuary from the nave of the church.

ActiviTy

Bring to class a religious image that helps you pray or reflect. In small groups, discuss how religious images help you pray or make good decisions.

Religious Art

What might we as Christians consider idolatry? Two interpretations will be mentioned here. Some religious groups have a conservative understanding of imagery in places of worship. Traditional Quaker and Amish meeting houses, Reformed and Evangelical communities, and some others place less emphasis on sculptures, paintings, or stained-glass windows. Eastern (Orthodox and Catholic) Christians treasure and honor their icons—stylized paintings of religious subjects, often saints. In the Church in the East, a historical challenge called the *iconoclastic controversy* was settled in A.D. 843 in favor of using icons. Catholics tend to favor colorful church buildings with two- and three-dimensional art, and some ■ Catholic places of worship are filled with beautiful detailed decoration. ■

These forms of religious art are not idolatry, however. Such art points to or symbolizes aspects of God or God's creation, starting with holy people; the art is not God. Representations of the Trinity, the Holy Family, and the saints remind us of God's love and faithfulness. Pictures and carvings show us scenes from the Old and New Testaments of the Bible. An outsider seeing someone praying in front of such representations might call this idolatry. These representations are not a replacement for God but, rather, reminders of God and our faith. The prayer before images of saints is a prayer of intercession, asking the saints to intercede with God the Father through Christ for the intentions of the one praying.

SETTING PRIORITIES

Revering God and keeping his name holy is at the top of the list of the Ten Commandments. Other objects or material things may become so important to us that God is shifted down from first place. Finer and larger homes, cars, clothing, and gourmet food may tempt some and claim their devotion. This was a major concern of Saint Thomas More and other religious leaders over the ages. Money, or misuse of money, can be a problem for Christians. Other entertainment, activities, or habits may become so important to us that we forget about God. Sports, hobbies, grades, games, and even health and physical fitness can claim too much of our attention. Some habits can resemble addictions. An insider seeing these behaviors might call them idolatry.

For high school students at the beginning of the twenty-first century, idolatry can have an extended meaning. It can be anything that gets in the way of their spiritual life. The possession of things and the need to participate in certain activities can cause students to get off track. Fads can become gods that are worshiped. Sports can claim their energy and devotion. Activities intended for relaxation can become unhealthy competition.

Our Church leaders provide teaching, guidance, and examples to help us live in relationship with God and according to God's commandments. As was true for the Israelites and the faithful Catholics of England at the time of Henry VIII, having good leaders to follow is crucial in our walk with God. ■

JOURNAL

Write a journal entry describing how you might change your life to become less driven by other things and people. Are you "addicted" to computer games? Are you unable to resist a trip to the mall? Is this a type of idolatry?

For REVIEW

1. How did Thomas More deal with the use and misuse of money?

2. What is an icon?

3. What is utopia?

For DISCUSSION

In the time of the first temple, worship was often accompanied by animal sacrifice and grain offerings. What do you understand sacrifice and offering to be today?

ACTIVITY

Prepare a graphic presentation about one of the early kings of Israel (Saul, David, or Solomon) showing their admirable qualities and deeds and their not-so-admirable qualities and deeds. Then prepare a graphic presentation on your own admirable qualities and deeds. (This latter need not be shared.)

The question of how political leadership links with spiritual leadership concerned God's people after they were settled in Israel. They tried to be faithful to the God of Abraham, Isaac, and Jacob, but continued to fall away. The people felt they needed a single leader with fortitude and vision instead of an assortment of itinerant preachers and judges at large in an agricultural world. Oracles guided the choice of a succession of kings who were anointed for their vocations. A central city and temple for worship enabled people to resist idolatry and remain faithful to God.

The Saul–David succession culminated in the riches of Solomon's kingdom. After that time there was a division between Judah and Israel. Throughout these transitions, God remained faithful to his people, even though they and their leaders at times turned away from the covenant. As always, God was at work in the history of his people. He promised them a messiah, the ultimate leader. Christians interpret Old Testament prophecies to refer to Jesus, whom they believe is the anointed one sent to save God's people and all people. This salvation is of a spiritual nature, not a military conquest.

For this I will extol you, O LORD, among the nations,
    and sing praises to your name.
Great triumphs he gives to his king,
    and shows steadfast love to his anointed,
    to David and his descendants forever.

                                        Psalm 18:49–50

Depart from evil, and do good;
    so you shall abide forever.
For the Lord loves justice;
    he will not forsake his faithful ones.
The righteous shall be kept safe forever,
    but the children of the wicked shall be cut off.
The righteous shall inherit the land,
    and live in it forever.

Psalm 37:27–29

The Time of the Divided Kingdom

1000–500 B.C.
Vedic Period in India

c. 900 B.C.
Chavín culture established
in Peru

800–700 B.C.
Rise of Greek city-states

1020–587 B.C.
Age of kings

c. 922 B.C.
Division of Hebrew Kingdom

869–849 B.C.
The prophecy of Elijah

The Kingdom Divided and the Prophetic Word

CHAPTER GOALS

Increase students' knowledge of the time of the Divided Kingdom and the role of the prophets by studying the following:

- literary impact of the Books of Amos and Hosea
- historical significance of the Assyrian Empire
- concepts of justice and accountability

CHAPTER OUTLINE

C. 760 B.C.
Prophecy of Amos

C. 755–732 B.C.
Prophecy of Hosea

C. 730s–722 B.C.
Assyrian invasion of northern Israel

C. 716 B.C.
Nubian kings added Egypt to their empire

663 B.C.
Assyrians pushed Nubians out of Egypt

While eating your breakfast before school, you take note of a feature article on the front page of the newspaper.

You sigh and shake your head, setting the newspaper aside. You are a student at Central High School, and you heard about Friday's fight. You are surprised, though, that the two students are being expelled. You expected them just to be suspended. There is a flyer on the kitchen table for a school board meeting. You figure it must have come in yesterday's mail. It is an invitation for Central High students, parents, and teachers to attend a special meeting on Wednesday. The board wants to establish rules for how to deal with situations such as the outbreak at the game. They want to clearly outline the determinations for the suspension or expulsion of a student in a given situation. You look over the flyer and resolve to go to the meeting. You decide that you want to take part in the decision-making process at your school. After all, the decisions made by the school board affect you too. That's a very good reason for you to get involved. You want the decisions that they make to be good ones.

Keep this story in mind as we study Amos, Hosea, and 1 and 2 Kings. How do you make decisions? Which of your beliefs and values are most important to you?

MORNING NEWS

Local teens expelled for outburst at game

Two sixteen-year-old students were expelled from Central High School Monday for having instigated a violent outburst. The teens were attending a football game last Friday, when they started a fist-fight with three students from the rival school, Lincoln High. The fight spread throughout the stands as other students joined in the scuffle. Fifteen students incurred minor injuries and were taken to Memorial Hospital for treatment. The two teens are being held accountable for inciting the violence that led to these injuries. School authorities stand by their decision to expel the students, stating that this was not the first offense for either teen.

The Old Testament prophets alerted the Israelites to the fact that they needed to make some important decisions about whether to follow the will of God or face the consequences. God would hold them accountable for their actions.

You face choices every day. For important decisions, you probably encounter a "gray area"—where is it difficult to figure out what is the right thing to do. What are your responsibilities? To whom are you accountable? As the opening story states, difficult decisions are part of everyone's life. ∎

PROPHETIC LITERATURE

Prophetic literature usually takes the form of anthologies of sayings and sermons delivered on different occasions and compiled later by followers of prophets. The inspired prophetic books of the Old Testament anticipate the fulfillment of God's purposes. Through them we see God at work in the lives and preaching of the prophets. Each book contains the story (sometimes) and speeches of the prophet for which it is named. Some prophets, such as Hosea and Amos, are considered minor prophets because of the brevity of the books named for them. These eighth-century B.C. prophets foretold the destruction of Israel at the hands of the Assyrian Empire and presented the people with some tough decisions.

"Assyria shall be [Israel's] king. . . ."
Hosea 11:15

This bas-relief is from a palace in Nineveh in Assyria.

The Old Testament prophets were not fortune-tellers. Predictions that the prophets made were conditional and were based on what God revealed to them.

Prophets

Prophets in the Old Testament were called by God and given a divine message to convey to God's people. Most were men, but some were women. They came from many backgrounds and were not always prophets permanently. Conscious of God's authority, the prophet confidently and courageously communicates God's message to the people. When reading prophetic literature in the Old Testament, remember that the prophets were not like modern-day fortune-tellers. Predictions that a prophet voiced were based on what God had revealed to the person through his religious and other life experiences. The prophets were authentic messengers of God. The prophets' predictions were conditional, however; they depended upon whether the people of Israel heeded God's warning. The nation was successful when it listened to the prophets.

prophecy the words of God, delivered through a spokesperson known as a prophet; generally calls for the Israelites to live justly and avoid idolatry

Prophecy

The means by which the divine message, or **prophecy,** is expressed varies greatly from prophet to prophet. Although the message itself comes from God, each prophet has an individual speaking style and uses different types of literary devices to convey that message.

LITERARY TECHNIQUES IN THE PROPHECIES OF HOSEA AND AMOS

Hosea delivered his prophecies to the northern kingdom of Israel as they were suffering through a war with Assyria. Hosea, as a member of the community to which he spoke, was able to identify with his listeners. He often used the word *we* when addressing the Israelites.

The prophet Amos was not from northern Israel and used the word *you* instead of *we* when speaking to the Israelites. He could not identify with them as Hosea was able to do. Amos was a shepherd before being called by God, and many of Amos's metaphors are drawn from that work.

PERSUASION

persuasion an appeal intended to convince a specific audience to share a particular belief or perform a certain action

The technique of **persuasion** requires that the writer or speaker begin with a position and then find evidence and arguments to convince the audience to share that belief. Effective persuasion appeals to both the logic and the emotions of a specific audience, intending to convince them to perform an action or adopt a certain belief. Persuasive articles appear in many publications, especially those that have a certain bias. For example, some magazines are politically conservative, while some others are liberal. The articles are often written to influence the reader toward one bias or the other. The prophet Hosea uses persuasion in calling the people to repent and in issuing his directives, or instructions. ■

OPENING THE WORD

Read Hosea 4:1–14 and 10:12. What do you think is the essence of Hosea's message?

IMAGERY

When speaking of God, Hosea employs images from the Israelites' daily lives. He uses images such as father, husband, bear, leopard, lion, evergreen cypress, dew, and rain. He depicts Israel as a woman in childbirth, a person who is sick, a wife, an olive tree, morning mist, and smoke. These images were familiar to the Israelites, and therefore the comparisons were more meaningful. Because of the imagery and figurative language used, it's easy to apply the prophet's message to other situations. This was frequently done by New Testament writers who applied many prophecies to Jesus. ■ ■ ■

OPENING THE WORD

Read Hosea 9:10. What does the imagery in this verse suggest about Israel?

Read Hosea 14.

ACTIVITY

Write a modern version of Hosea's prophecies, using metaphors of your own, drawn from present-day circumstances.

OPENING THE WORD

Read Hosea 11:1–3. How is God depicted in this passage? Why is this significant?

"They shall again live beneath my shadow, they shall flourish as a garden; they shall blossom like the vine, their fragrance shall be like the wine of Lebanon."

Hosea 14:7

Amos used many pastoral images in his prophecy because he was a shepherd and farmer.

Pastoral Imagery

The literary term **pastoral** is used in reference to things pertaining to a rural setting or a rustic way of life. The prophet Amos draws from his experience as a shepherd and farmer and uses pastoral imagery to convey God's warning to the people of Israel. One example of this is his reference to a loaded cart:

> "So, I will press you down in your place,
>   just as a cart presses down
>   when it is full of sheaves."
>
> Amos 2:13 ■

pastoral drawn from a rural setting or rustic way of life

Opening the Word

Read Amos 4 and 5. Identify the pastoral imagery in these two chapters.

ALLEGORY

The Book of Hosea may be read as an allegory, a type of extended metaphor. An **allegory** is a symbolic story with two levels of meaning. On one level is the *literal* meaning of the story: The turtle and the rabbit had a race, and the turtle won. The *allegorical* meaning addresses something about human nature or relationships: It is more important to be wise and determined than it is to be quick. In the Old Testament, allegories present a deeper religious lesson or meaning.

allegory a story with symbolic characters that presents religious truths or generalizations about human nature

Hosea as Allegory

Hosea compares the Israelites' betrayal of God, through their idolatry and oppression of the poor, to the unfaithfulness of his wife, Gomer. This allegory is designed by God, as we can see in the following verse:

> The LORD said to me again, "Go, love a woman who has a lover and is an adulteress, just as the LORD loves the people of Israel, though they turn to other gods. . . ."
>
> Hosea 3:1

Chapter 7

Read Amos 1 and 2.

OPENING THE WORD

Read Amos 7:1–3 and 7:4–6 and note the parallelism in the two visions. Write the verses down and, using colored pens or pencils, highlight the parallels you find.

Hosea's personal life becomes an allegory of divine compassion and unconditional love. Gomer, Hosea's unfaithful wife, is representative of the unfaithful Israelites. Hosea's love for his sinful wife is an allegory of God's love for his sinful people. ■

PARALLELISM

One of the literary techniques used in Amos is parallelism. We learned about parallelism in Chapters 1 and 2. In Amos, parallelism demonstrates that Israel and the surrounding nations are judged by the same standards:

> Thus says the LORD:
> For three transgressions of Edom,
>   and for four, I will not revoke the punishment. . . .
>
> Amos 1:11

> Thus says the LORD:
> For three transgressions of Israel,
>   and for four, I will not revoke the punishment. . . . ■ ■
>
> Amos 2:6

ACTIVITY

Create a research file of newspaper articles that discuss recent incidents of the kinds of crimes mentioned in Amos and Hosea. Based on your findings, write a brief argument for the relevance of these prophetic books to modern times.

For REVIEW

1. Name three images Hosea uses to describe God.

2. Why does Amos use pastoral imagery?

3. Hosea's marriage to Gomer is an allegory for what concept?

For DISCUSSION

Old Testament prophets used metaphors and other figurative language to warn the people of Israel. Has a parent or teacher ever used a metaphor or an allegory in order to convey the potential consequences of an action you had done or were contemplating? Was the metaphor or allegory effective?

ACTIVITY

Clip magazine photos (or create your own illustrations) of the images Amos and Hosea used to describe God. Make a collage of these images and include a Scripture citation for each picture.

JOURNAL

What quality of God is most important to you? Why?

THE DIVIDED KINGDOM

Divided Kingdom the result of the division of Israel into two separate nations: Israel and Judah

Israel was unified under the kings Saul, David, and Solomon. The kings ruled over the twelve tribes and their respective territories. When Solomon died, Israel split into two rival kingdoms—Judah to the south and Israel to the north. Israel and Judah existed side by side for several centuries. During the time of the **Divided Kingdom,** Israel and Judah were each ruled by a succession of kings. As well as fighting other invaders, such as the neighboring Arameans, there were many power struggles within the Divided Kingdom itself.

During the reigns of Uzziah of Judah and Jeroboam II of Israel, the prophet Amos's oracles focused on Israel's domestic wrongdoings and predicted doom; however, he called for the people to reform. He stressed that they were once a united family due to the Exodus from Egypt they shared through experience and story. Other prophets from those times, such as Elijah and Hosea, warned of both cultural and political dangers to the chosen people in the Divided Kingdom. The prophets called upon the people of the Kingdom of Israel to make a decision and to act on it. They warned the people that they would be held accountable to God for their actions.

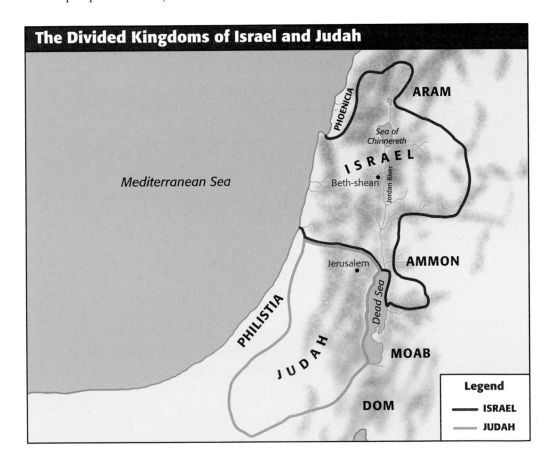

The Divided Kingdoms of Israel and Judah

PHOENICIA

ARAM

Sea of Chinnereth

I S R A E L

Beth-shean

Jordan River

Mediterranean Sea

AMMON

Jerusalem

Dead Sea

PHILISTIA

J U D A H

MOAB

DOM

Legend
—— ISRAEL
—— JUDAH

1. The god Baal was honored throughout the ancient Near East and Middle East. The prophets proclaimed the universal power of the God of Israel.

2. The prophet Hosea challenged both Israel and Judah to forsake the worship of Baal. Art by James J. Tissot.

THE PROPHETS

Elijah was a prophet in the northern kingdom of Israel during the reigns of Ahab and Ahaziah (869–849 B.C.). Ahab was a powerful king who expanded Samaria, Israel's capital city, and fought many wars against Syria. According to Assyrian records, he also participated in battles against Assyria in an attempt to help the neighboring regions of Syria and Palestine. Ahab looked to Baal, an ancient Canaanite storm god, to replenish the land with rain (1 Kings 16:30–33). Baal's followers believed that he provided rain and insured fertility.

The belief in Baal and its various forms had so permeated ancient Near Eastern life that the Semitic word for Baal was synonymous with lord, owner, and husband. Elijah stressed that the God of Israel was universal in power and therefore the sole provider of rain and fertility, as well as the God of history and politics.

Hosea, another eighth-century prophet also condemns Israel's worship of Baal. God, speaking through Hosea, states that, "I will remove the names of the Baals from her mouth, and they will be mentioned no more" (Hosea 2:17). In his prophecies, Hosea describes the political climate during the eighth century. Scholars believe that when Hosea mentions military activity in 5:8–12, he is either referring to an Assyrian invasion or a battle between Israel and Judah. Hosea accuses both kingdoms of looking toward the two superpowers of the time—Egypt to the west and Assyria to the east—for security. Hosea prophesies that because of such infidelity to God, "They shall not remain in the land of the Lord; but Ephraim shall return to Egypt, and in Assyria they shall eat unclean food" (Hosea 9:3). This prophecy was realized when the Assyrians captured Samaria in 722 B.C. and annexed the land, placing about 27,000 Israelites in captivity.

The walls of Samaria, capitol of the Northern Kingdom; Assyria conquered Samaria in 722 B.C.

WHAT MADE THE ASSYRIANS SO POWERFUL?

The Assyrians came from the hilly regions above the Tigris River and had already been established as a major power in the ancient Tigris-Euphrates area. By the eighth century they had subdued Babylon and had begun a push west toward the Mediterranean. Several factors contributed to the Assyrians' success. Besides having a large and effective army, they were ruthless conquerors. Many Assyrian royal inscriptions describe how they subdued captive cities with ruthless acts of terror. The Assyrians frequently used these methods as a way of exerting their power and destroying any existing sense of national unity. They also put their own governors into newly conquered lands and displaced the former inhabitants.

Judah succumbed to Assyria in the latter half of the eighth century B.C. and was required to pay tribute. Unlike Israel, however, its internal affairs were still governed by the House of David. Assyria had also conquered Egypt by 663 B.C. However, by about this time, the Assyrian empire was already in decline due to effective resistance by conquered peoples and its inability to rely on the troops it acquired in other lands.

For Review

1. When did Israel divide into two kingdoms? What were the kingdoms?

2. What were the two main concerns of the prophets Hosea and Elijah?

3. List three reasons why the Assyrians were effective conquerors.

For Discussion

Discuss how the Israelites might have struggled to maintain their beliefs under Assyrian dominance. What do you think would happen if an Israelite showed that he or she did not believe in Baal?

Activity

Research the Assyrian conquest of the Middle East. Create a map showing the areas the Assyrians controlled, along with the dates.

The story at the beginning of this chapter presents an unfortunate situation and also the events that follow. Actions have consequences. Our set of beliefs often informs our decisions about consequences.

The prophets Elijah, Elisha, Amos, and Hosea all preached God's call to justice. Each answered to God as the sole authority. Each lived out a single-minded commitment to challenge the Israelites to maintain right relationship with God. The Israelites had drifted from their loyalty to God. They had become less than enthusiastic in their commitment to God by worshiping Baal alongside him. Breaking the first commandment had become routine, and other sins—adultery, covetousness, and disregard for people who were poor—were widespread.

These four prophets all made it clear that they served a jealous God who called for justice. They sought to guide the Israelites back to God, who awaited their return with open arms. God's compassion is evident throughout the Scriptures. It was evident in the Israelites' history and in the life of each prophet. God's call to be faithful was the message the prophets modeled and publicly announced.

OPENING THE WORD

Read Amos 7:7–9. What is the meaning of the plumb line in this prophecy? What other images could be used to get this message across today?

Reread Amos 5:15–24.

AMOS

Amos reiterates God's jealous nature and delivers God's judgment on Israel. He reminds the people of Israel that it is not for their own merit that they were chosen as the people through whom all nations would come to know God. God's covenant with them brought responsibility, not merely privilege. Their pride and egotism had led to their repeated sin and departure from God's commandments.

The Lord judges the Israelites for their worship. Their worship of him contained the right elements, but they lacked the clean hearts necessary to truly honor God. Formal rituals were being substituted for social responsibility. Amos 5:24 states, "But let justice roll down like waters, and righteousness like an ever-flowing stream." This was God's assurance that in the end **divine justice** and righteousness would prevail. ▪ ▪

divine justice the moral standard by which God judges human conduct; the realization of that standard by God; an expression of God's righteousness, pity, love, and grace

JOURNAL

Which aspects of your life would measure up if someone were to apply a "plumb line" to them? Reflect on whether an aspect of your life might not measure up to the commitments God requires. How might you remedy the situation?

"Thus says the LORD:
For three transgressions of Israel,
and for four I will not revoke
the punishment;
because they sell the righteous
for silver,
and the needy for a pair of
sandals—
they who trample the head of the
poor into the dust of the
earth,
and push the afficted out
of the way. . . .
Amos 2:6–7a

Opening the Word

Read Amos 9:11–15. What hope for the future does Amos give the people of Israel? How is this passage an expression of royal messianism?

Journal

Write down whether the following statements are true or false: (1) I recycle; (2) I give my outgrown clothes to a local thrift shop or charity; (3) I gave extra change to someone who needs it; and (4) I regularly thank God for the many ways he has blessed me. How do these statements relate to the message in Amos?

Amos's Work History

Many of the common people identified with Amos's work with sheep and cattle and trusted his prophecy. The disparity between those who were rich and those who were poor was a focus of God's message through Amos. The rich were financially able to make extra sacrifice and to tithe, and seemed to do so as an atonement for their widespread abuse of the lower class. Amos recognized their complacency and in his prophecy pointed out that those who were rich were oblivious to the pain and strife they wrought on those who were poor. In Amos 6:7 we see God's warning: "Therefore they shall now be the first to go into exile, and the revelry of the loungers shall pass away." God holds the people accountable for their actions. ■ ■

HOSEA

Hosea is the allegory of God's love and faithfulness to a betraying and adulterous people. The marital allegory includes an allusion to the divorce procedure of Mosaic law. The wording in Hosea 2:2 (2:4 in NAB)—"she is not my wife, and I am not her husband"—closely resembles the declaration a husband was required to make upon putting his wife out of his house and thus divorcing her.

Gomer returns to the security of her husband after being unfaithful to him. The prophet calls the Israelites to return to God after being unfaithful to him (they had turned to idolatry and oppressed those who were poor). Gomer refused to see that all she owned was from Hosea, just as the Israelites refused to acknowledge that their very existence was due to God's goodness. The Israelites were instead giving credit to other gods for their vineyards and orchards. In the allegory, Hosea is told by God to restore his marriage (Hosea 3:1). This mirrors God's love for the people of Israel despite their infidelity. Hosea's message, given after the destruction began, was more gentle than that of Amos.

A Message for All

Hosea's message was directed to everyone in Israelite society—ordinary people and priests alike. The priests of the day profited from the people's sin because of the contributions they received when people made sin offerings. The offerings were so numerous that some items were sold or given to relatives, thus increasing the priests' power and prestige in the community.

Hosea also warned the southern kingdom, Judah, not to follow Israel's example. The sinfulness of the people of Judah was not as terrible as that of the Israelites, but they were equally chastised for their "adulterous" behavior. In Hosea 5:10, the princes of Judah are compared to people who move boundary markers, or landmarks. Moving territorial boundaries to increase one's property was obviously stealing, a serious crime in Mosaic law.

Tribute

Hosea also was consistently opposed to paying tribute, a monetary payment to a stronger nation for protection. At this point of history Israel was paying tribute to Assyria. However, God is a jealous God who insisted that tribute was owed to him alone—the monetary tribute being a symbol of the spiritual tribute due him. There was only one way for Israel to regain God's blessing—repentance. Hosea asked that Israel return to the wilderness to make a fresh start. Hosea spoke a message from the Lord, who did not give in to his wrath but subdued it by compassionately drawing his people to himself.

"Return, O Israel, to the LORD your God."

HOSEA 14:1

"As [Elijah and Elisha] continued walking and talking, a chariot of fire and horses of fire separated the two of them, and Elijah ascended in a whirlwind into heaven."

2 Kings 2:11

ELIJAH

Elijah is one of the most memorable prophets because of the dramatic miracles that occurred during his life and at his death. Ravens brought food to Elijah, and he multiplied a poor widow's pantry, raised a child from the dead, caused a king's soldiers to be consumed by fire, parted the Jordan river, and rode to heaven in a flaming chariot. The miracles of Elijah and Elisha focused on substances that Baal was credited for dominating: fire, rain, and farm crops. God worked through Elijah in such dramatic ways in order to catch the attention of a nation lulled into complacency with a false god of convenience, Baal. God is Lord of nature, as well as of history and politics.

Triumph Over the Priests of Baal

The people of Israel were torn between worshiping Baal and worshiping the God of Israel. They could not make up their minds and decide upon their loyalty. To influence their decision, Elijah orchestrated a very public showdown against Baal. The focus on fire at the showdown made a point of Baal's supposed strength. That Elijah chose a bull for the sacrifice on his altar to God is particularly telling of his personal devotion. When a priest chose a bull, it signified that the sacrifice was offered in atonement for his personal sins. This underlined the fact that the power witnessed in this demonstration was the power of a pure and holy God, not that of the man offering the sacrifice. The twelve stones Elijah chose symbolized the twelve tribes of Israel prior to the division of the kingdom.

Three times Elijah doused the altar with water to show his strong confidence and faith in God. Imagine the saturation and its dampening effect on a potential blaze! Because of the location of the showdown, the water used would have to have been salt water. Salt was an important element in Hebrew life. It preserved food, sustained livestock, was a universal medication, and was seen as a symbol of fidelity. To offer a sacrifice without salt was unsatisfactory. The salt symbolized the priest's own self being surrendered. It also made the smoke that was produced smell sweeter to those present as it rose to God. ■

Read 1 Kings 18:17–46.

JOURNAL

When receiving an apology, what impresses you the most? How can you tell if it is sincere? Describe an offense you have committed and the apology you gave. Did you end your apology by asking for forgiveness? Explain how doing so provides completion for you and prompts the recipient to take your apology more seriously.

Ahab and Elijah

Read 1 Kings 19:3–18.

JourNaL

Describe an incident wherein you had just accomplished something that was spectacular, beyond your average effort. Perhaps it was a phenomenal victory in sports or the completion of an assignment in record time. How did you feel afterward? How long did that feeling last?

It was the dramatic nature of this showdown that convinced King Ahab of Elijah's credibility. Elijah experienced a holy fear of God's power. In telling his wife Jezebel about the events of the day, Ahab unleashed on Elijah a formidable enemy. Jezebel became furious when she learned that Elijah had killed the prophets of her god, Baal. Being quite human, Elijah ran away upon the threat of Jezebel even though he had just proven God's great power and invincibility. Ahab, however, saw how clearly Elijah spoke for God. ■

When Elijah was fearful, he was drawn to Mount Sinai, the place of Moses' meeting with God. God started tending to Elijah's needs immediately—first by angels and then through the word of God himself. Never did God condemn Elijah for his fear. Twice Elijah repeated a litany of his deeds and the Israelites' ignorant response. God spoke to Elijah in the sheer silence. Elijah's stay at Mount Sinai was brief, but it was sufficient time for him to shed his doubt and fear, reconnect with God, and grow in his understanding of God. ■

ELISHA

JourNaL

Where do you go when you are overwhelmed with fear and doubt? What makes this feel like a safe place?

Elisha was the perfect replacement for Elijah. His youthful enthusiasm and dedication to learning is unmatched in the Old Testament. He walked as the apprentice to a great prophet, yet Elisha never changed his own character in the style of hero-worship. Elijah fought the powers of evil; Elisha kindled the powers of good. His last moments with Elijah were particularly telling of his character. When asked what he would like Elijah to do for him before he left, Elisha's response was one of pure wisdom coupled with respect for his teacher. He requested of Elijah, ". . . let me inherit a double share of your spirit" (2 Kings 2:9).

For REViEW

1. What class issue is presented in Amos? Give two examples of exploitation.

2. What worship practices did God condemn through Amos?

3. What allegory does Hosea use to describe Israel's relationship with God?

4. To what place does Elijah retreat when he is overcome by fear? What is significant about this location?

For DiscussioN

Discuss the concept of a just and jealous God. Can you see evidence today of a just and jealous God? Provide examples.

AcTiviTy

Apply the concept of justice to a trial being publicized today. Write an argument as to whether justice is being served in the case. Present your argument to the class.

Pope John XXIII

The Pope Who Embraced the World

Angelo Giuseppe Roncalli (1881–1963) was born into a peasant family in a small village near the town of Bergamo, Italy. When he left his family at age eleven to prepare for the priesthood, no one knew that he was destined to become a pope and peacemaker whose words would move the world's two superpowers back from the brink of nuclear war.

Roncalli's 1958 election to pope came as a surprise; at the age of seventy-six he became Pope John XXIII. Though he was a cardinal, he was relatively unknown outside Vatican circles. Due to his advanced age, observers thought Roncalli was meant to be a transitional pope. He was not likely to live long, so little was expected to happen during his reign. Under the reign of Pope John XXIII, however, many things did change.

Pope John XXIII's casual openness charmed visitors. When he met U.S. President John F. Kennedy and the first lady, he called Mrs. Kennedy simply *Jacqueline*. When he met with the daughter and son-in-law of Soviet premier Nikita Krushchev (who were avowed atheists), he gave them a blessing to take back to all their relatives as a gesture of reconciliation. The rapport established as a result of these meetings was to prove valuable.

The pope also extended himself to ordinary people. During his first year as pope, Pope John XXIII received more than 240,000 visitors in audiences—far more than any of his predecessors had in one year.

In January 1959, Pope John XXIII announced plans for an ecumenical council that would change the Church. It would bring together all the Catholic archbishops, bishops, and heads of religious orders in the world, as well as observers from other Christian denominations and other faiths. This event would be known as the Second Vatican Council. The hope was to establish ways for the Church to relate meaningfully to people in a rapidly changing world and move the whole world toward reconciliation. The decisions of the council are evident today in

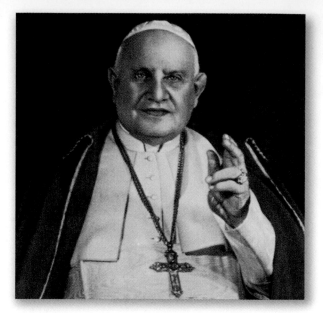

Pope John XXIII believed in resolving conflict peacefully and treating all people with respect. He demonstrated the positive impact the Church can have on world events.

Catholic liturgy and practice and in the way the Catholic Church relates to other faiths and the cultures in which it exists.

In October 1962, in the midst of the council, a crisis was brewing. The Soviet Union was building missile sites in Cuba that threatened U.S. security, and Soviet ships carrying missiles with nuclear warheads were steaming toward the island. The two superpowers—the United States and the Soviet Union—were careening toward war. On October 22, President Kennedy announced a naval blockade of Cuba. As Kennedy spoke, behind-the-scenes diplomatic negotiations were in progress.

The result of the negotiations was that both Kennedy and Krushchev agreed that words from the pope might defuse the situation. On October 26, Pope John XXIII delivered a public appeal by radio to the two heads of state. He pleaded, "Hear the anguished cry which rises to heaven from every corner of the earth, from innocent children to old men, from the people in the cities and villages: Peace! Peace!" The leaders listened. Krushchev withdrew the missiles. Kennedy saluted his statesmanship. Words from the pope who hoped to reconcile the whole world did, in fact, help bring the Cuban missile crisis to an end.

In his encyclical Peace on Earth *(Pacem in Terris), 1963, Pope John XXIII listed many of the rights people ought to experience. Find the encyclical on the Internet (www.vatican.va) and list the rights detailed there. How do you experience each right? What duty comes with each right?*

Accountability

Pope John XXIII treated all people with the utmost respect and, as a result, had a positive impact on the world. He never lost sight of the fact that he was accountable to God for his actions, nor did he get caught up in personal motivations or personal weaknesses. He had a positive influence on world leaders at a time of very important decisions.

Sometimes our personal insecurities can be detrimental to our walk with God; recall the problems the prophets faced. We become judgmental of others in order to feel better about ourselves. We are disrespectful of other people and don't treat them as well as we should. This negative attitude may be communicated in subtle ways, such as through body language and private thoughts, or through blatant actions and speech. Do you look down on people because of their age? Their faith or lack of it? Their religious affiliation? Their culture or race? ■

God knows everything about you. God is omniscient and therefore is not ignorant of your thoughts or deeds. Our shortcomings can be turned around as long as we recognize them and ask God to help us change. Then we must take determined steps to do so. The Bible reminds us in Romans 8:28 that "all things work together for good for those who love God." That's a promise you can cling to through all your doubts and insecurities.

Under the direction of Pope John XXIII, the Catholic bishops of the world gathered in St. Peter's Basilica for the Second Vatican Council.

Personal doubts and insecurities can also be a stumbling block as we try to make decisions. Sometimes we decide to do something based on what other people will think about us. For this reason, we need to base our decision making on our relationships with God and others, the commandments God has given us, and his call for justice and compassion. We must not forget that it is God to whom we are ultimately accountable.

The teen in the opening story recognized the importance of using good judgment when making decisions. The teen also recognized that we need to get involved in the decision-making process of our school or community because the outcome of those decisions affects our lives as well as the lives of those around us.

For Review

1. How can our personal insecurities be detrimental to other people?

2. What do we have to do in order to turn our shortcomings into assets?

For Discussion

We are ultimately accountable to God. How does your accountability to God inform how you are accountable to other people in your life—parents and other family members, authority figures, or people in your community?

Activity

Interview a Catholic relative or community member who was born before 1950. Ask him or her to recall the Church prior to the Second Vatican Council. What were his or her impressions of Pope John XXIII? What positive changes did he or she experience as a result of changes initiated by the council?

Important decisions are often made in a period of upheaval and uncertainty. The story at the beginning of this chapter is an example of an upsetting situation that stirs people's beliefs. This situation also calls for answers and actions.

The time of the Divided Kingdom was a time of great upheaval. The people of Israel had many conflicts with the people of Judah and with surrounding kingdoms. Assyrian armies posed a strong threat to the political independence of the Israelites. The people turned from God and began to disregard his commandments. Something had to be done. The Old Testament prophets reminded the people of Israel that they would be held accountable by God for their actions. The decisions they were making in their lives had repercussions. God worked through the prophets to bring the people back into right relationship with him.

Amos, Hosea, Elijah, and Elisha went to great lengths to explain to the Israelites the concept of a just and jealous God. Hosea depicted God as a jealous husband who demanded fidelity from his wife, Israel. God also called for justice and mercy. Fortunately for the Israelites, and also for us, God is compassionate and forgiving. He is always ready to reconcile with those who repent and return to him.

For the LORD will not forsake his people;
he will not abandon his heritage;
for justice will return to the righteous,
and all the upright in heart will follow it.

Psalm 94:14–15

By the rivers of Babylon—
    there we sat down and there we wept
    when we remembered Zion.
Of the willows there
    we hung up our harps.
For there our captors
    asked us for songs,
and our tormentors asked for mirth, saying,
    "Sing us one of the songs of Zion!"

Psalm 137:1–3

The Time of the Babylonian Exile

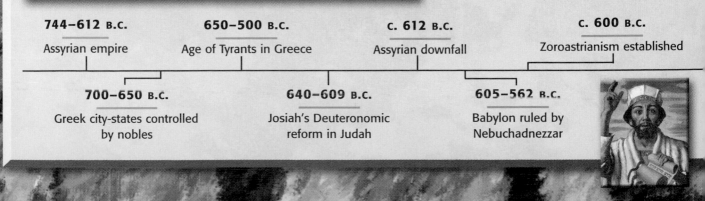

744–612 B.C.

Assyrian empire

650–500 B.C.

Age of Tyrants in Greece

C. 612 B.C.

Assyrian downfall

C. 600 B.C.

Zoroastrianism established

700–650 B.C.

Greek city-states controlled
by nobles

640–609 B.C.

Josiah's Deuteronomic
reform in Judah

605–562 B.C.

Babylon ruled by
Nebuchadnezzar

The Fall of Judah and the Babylonian Exile

CHAPTER GOALS

Increase knowledge of the meaning of the Old Testament and deepen understanding of its value by studying the following:

- characteristics of prophetic literature
- historical background of the Babylonian Exile
- theological commentary on the message of the prophets
- explanation of the call to social justice

CHAPTER OUTLINE

Literary Interpretation: Prophecy and Wisdom

Historical Interpretation: Prophets Before and After the Exile

Theological Interpretation: Major and Minor Prophets

Witness: Martin Luther King Jr.

Personal Challenge: Social Justice

Summary

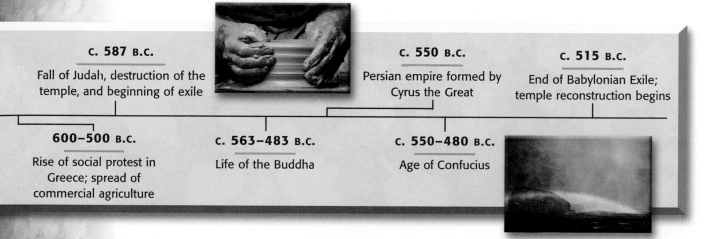

C. 587 B.C.
Fall of Judah, destruction of the temple, and beginning of exile

C. 550 B.C.
Persian empire formed by Cyrus the Great

C. 515 B.C.
End of Babylonian Exile; temple reconstruction begins

600–500 B.C.
Rise of social protest in Greece; spread of commercial agriculture

C. 563–483 B.C.
Life of the Buddha

C. 550–480 B.C.
Age of Confucius

Imagine that your parents have just informed you that in one month you will be moving to another country to live for the next few years.

You begin to think about all of the challenges this move presents for you: How easy will it be to make new friends? How will I learn a new language? Will I take everything with me?

You decide to face this new challenge with a positive attitude. You log onto the Internet and pull up information on the country. You want to have a better understanding of where you are going and what it will be like when you get there. You research the culture of the country so that you will be able to relate to the people who live there. You want to understand their beliefs and cultural practices to be sure that you will be respectful of them.

Your parents remind you that the three of you will have each other for encouragement too.

Keep this story in mind as we study the Babylonian Exile, a time when the Israelites had to leave their homeland.

The twentieth-century painting of Isaiah by Eugene Spiro captures the prophet's stern warning of judgment.

The teen in the opening story is concerned about what life will be like in a new place, away from all that is familiar. Such a challenge can make it difficult for one to remain focused on his or her faith in God. The Israelites faced the same challenge during the Babylonian Exile. Many of them were forced to leave their homeland and had to rely on the prophets to guide them during this time of uncertainty. ■

PROPHECY AS COMMENTARY ON HISTORICAL EVENTS

We learned about Old Testament prophets in Chapter 7 and focused on the literary styles of Hosea and Amos. In this chapter we will study a larger group of prophets: Isaiah, Second Isaiah, Jeremiah, Ezekiel, Micah, Nahum, Habakkuk, and Zephaniah. In these prophetic books, we see patterns and literary styles repeated throughout. The general sequencing in prophetic literature—warnings of doom followed, after the destruction, by the promise of eventual restoration—helps the books to end on a positive note.

Mode of Pronouncing Judgment

The prophets of the Old Testament pronounced God's judgment upon Jerusalem, confronted leaders and false prophets, reproached the people of Israel, and gave oracles against other nations as well. You will see examples of this mode (pattern of expression) of pronouncing judgment throughout the prophetic books. For instance, in Isaiah 1:14–15 the prophet delivers an oracle of judgment regarding Judah's religious superficiality:

> Your new moons and your appointed festivals
> my soul hates;
> they have become a burden to me,
> I am weary of bearing them.
> When you stretch out your hands,
> I will hide my eyes from you;
> even though you make many prayers,
> I will not listen;
> your hands are full of blood.

FAITH SHARING

Over the next week, develop responses to the following questions: In what ways does God show his love for his people? How can his people show their love for him?

Read Jeremiah 2:6–11, 3:12–15, 5:18–24.

Mode of Offering Encouragement

After warning people of impending doom, the prophets offered encouragement and consolation. They explained that if the people returned to God and persevered through the hard times ahead, they would see the eventual restoration of God's people. You will see examples of the mode of prophetic encouragement throughout the prophetic books. For example, the prophecy of Micah 7:8–9 focuses on the future victory of God's people: ■

> Do not rejoice over me, O my enemy;
>> when I fall, I shall rise;
> when I sit in darkness,
>> the LORD will be a light to me.
> I must bear the indignation of the LORD,
>> because I have sinned against him,
> until he takes my side
>> and executes judgment for me.
> He will bring me out to the light;
>> I shall see his vindication.

ACROSTIC

acrostic an ordered poem in which the first letters of individual lines or verses, when combined in order, form their own pattern, phrase, or word

The Book of Lamentations is attributed to the prophet Jeremiah. It was written using a literary device called an **acrostic.** In the acrostics of the Old Testament, each line begins with a letter of the Hebrew alphabet. This method was probably used as a mnemonic device, or memory tool, to help people remember the verses. Very few English translations of the Old Testament have attempted to maintain this device, however, so the pattern is lost in translation. Lamentations 3 was originally an acrostic in which each letter of the twenty-two-character Hebrew alphabet was represented by a set of three verses. The other chapters of the book each have twenty-two verses.

Nahum 1:2–8 and several psalms (9, 10, 25, 34, 37, 111, 112, 145) were also written in the form of an acrostic. This very structured form of poetry works well in Lamentations because it provides a ritualized way of expressing grief, much like a funeral liturgy. Because the form is so commonly used, it provides familiarity at a time of great upheaval.

ALLEGORY

allegory a story with symbolic characters that presents religious truths or generalizations about human nature

The prophets often used allegories to explain God's covenant with Israel. The most common **allegory** used was one in which the covenant was compared to a marital commitment. As we learned in Chapter 7, the Book of Hosea is an example of this type of allegory. Another example of a marital allegory can be found in Ezekiel 16. God chastises Israel, calling her, "Adulterous wife, who receives strangers instead of her husband!" (Ezekiel 16:32). Other allegories found in the Book of Ezekiel include the allegory of the vine (15), the allegory of the eagles (17:1–21), the allegory of the cedar (17:22–24 and 31:1–18), and the allegory of the pot (24:1–14). Isaiah's vineyard song (Isaiah 5:1–10) illustrates a **social justice** theme: people who are rich, who build up large estates by taking land from those who are poor, are condemned.

social justice practice by which social rules and government procedures follow a standard of righteousness and fair treatment

REFRAIN

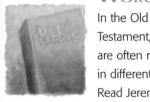

OPENING THE WORD

In the Old Testament, verses are often repeated in different contexts. Read Jeremiah 49:19 and compare it to Jeremiah 50:44. Why do you think the verse is repeated?

The prophets of the Old Testament often used repetition to reinforce elements of their message. Scholars have pointed out that Ezekiel uses the word *mortal* in reference to himself as the prophet about a hundred times, and uses the phrase "and they/you will know that I am the LORD" about fifty times. Similarly, a line that recurs throughout a poem or song in such a way is called a *refrain*. Throughout the Book of Isaiah, key phrases and lines are often repeated, or used as a refrain. Verses might begin with similar lines, such as Isaiah 51:9a ("Awake, awake, put on strength, O arm of the LORD!") and Isaiah 52:1a ("Awake, awake, put on your strength, O Zion!"). ▪

For REVIEW

1. The prophets commented on historical events using which two modes?

2. What is the literary device that was used by the writer of the Book of Lamentations?

For DISCUSSION

Old Testament prophets lived unusual lives, often standing apart from the community as being "different." Do you think this helped or hindered their message? How would a modern prophet go about voicing his or her message? What effect would the person's way of life have on the public reception of his or her message?

ACTIVITY

Create an acrostic using the word prophet. Each line of your acrostic should describe the role of Old Testament prophets in commenting on historical events.

THE ANCIENT WORLD FROM THE EIGHTH TO SIXTH CENTURY B.C.

Many prophets bore witness to and gave commentary on the political upheavals in the ancient world from the eighth to the sixth century B.C. During this time, the superpowers of the ancient world—Egypt, and the great civilizations of the Tigris-Euphrates river valley, Assyria and Babylonia—struggled for control. The **Kingdom of Judea** was located geographically in the middle of these struggles and was directly impacted by them.

Kingdom of Judea the kingdom south of Israel that existed from the time following Solomon's death in 925 B.C. until the destruction of the temple in 586 B.C.

PROPHETS BEFORE THE EXILES

Isaiah prophesied during the reigns of four kings of Judah from 783–687 B.C. He forewarned Judeans of Assyria's looming presence: "it will sweep on into Judah as a flood" (Isaiah 8:8). In response to this presence, Judah was pressured to rebel against Assyria, first by Israel and later by Egypt and Philistine. Isaiah warns of the folly of this later alliance. He tells the Judeans that they will be "dismayed and confounded" (Isaiah 37:27), because Egypt will be led away by the Assyrians. The Assyrians eventually did take control of the capitals of Israel and Samaria, and later of Judah.

The politics of Judah's powerful neighbors and its effect on Judah were not the only considerations of prophets at this time. While Micah was a contemporary of Isaiah, his prophecies addressed mainly the internal social evils present in Judah. Micah was originally a rural farmer, unlike the city-dweller Isaiah, and was a champion of those who were underprivileged. Micah, an advocate for social justice, preached against the evil policies of Jerusalem: "Its rulers give judgment for a bribe, its priests teach for a price, its prophets give oracles for money" (Micah 3:11). Micah's prophecies influenced King Hezekiah who established social reforms. ■

ACTIVITY

The United States is often referred to as a superpower. Work with a small group to discuss what it means to be a superpower. Make a list of the characteristics of a superpower and then assess whether these characteristics apply to Assyria (scan Isaiah 5:26–30 and the Book of Nahum).

Assyria, the superpower that Isaiah had feared, lost influence and control as Babylon's power began to strengthen. The prophet Nahum speaks directly of the events surrounding the fall of Assyria's most important city, Nineveh. In 612 B.C. Babylon captured and destroyed Nineveh. Nahum sees the fate of the Judeans at the hands of the Assyrians and the subsequent "Devastation, desolation, and destruction!" of Nineveh as an act of God's intent for his people (Nahum 2:10). He also reassures them: "Though I have afflicted you, I will afflict you no more. And now I will break off his yoke from you and snap the bonds that bind you" (Nahum 1:12–13). He encourages the Judeans to celebrate their festivals, for "never again shall the wicked invade you" (Nahum 1:15).

During the reign of Josiah in Judah (640–609 B.C.), a reform of Judaism took place. The reform was based on a book of the covenant found in the temple and included the requirement of the elimination of the worship of other gods, centralization of worship in Jerusalem, and a public

*"All the trees of the field shall know
that I am the LORD.
I bring low the high tree,
I make high the low tree;
I dry up the green tree
and make the dry tree flourish.
I the LORD have spoken;
I will accomplish it."*

Ezekiel 17:24

OPENING THE WORD

Read 2 Kings 22, the story of the finding of the book of the covenant during the reign of Josiah. Who is Huldah, and what is her role in the reform?

Babylonian Exile period of history when the Babylonians forced most of the inhabitants of Judah to migrate to Babylon

exile an individual banished from his or her home; banishment from one's land

JOURNAL

When have you felt like an exile? Describe the circumstances. How did you cope? What were your feelings during and after your time in "exile"?

recommitment of the nation to the covenant. Josiah is one of the few kings praised in the Deuteronomic History because he consulted a prophet before his reform. The "found" book may have been an early version of Deuteronomy. ■

PROPHETS DURING AND AFTER THE EXILES

Babylonia did turn out to be as wicked as Assyria. While Nahum did not prophesy this, Jeremiah did. Jeremiah states, "Even if you defeated the whole army of Chaldeans [Babylonians] who are fighting against you, and there remained of them only wounded men in their tents, they would rise up and burn this city with fire" (Jeremiah 37:10). The Babylonians forced many of the Jews from the southern kingdom into exile in 597 B.C. Ten years later the Babylonians forced another deportation of the Jews and destroyed the temple in Jerusalem.

Ezekiel is the only prophet who came to his calling during the **Babylonian Exile.** As God speaks through him, he tells the **exiles** that they are being punished for their infidelities and idolatry but will eventually be restored. He assures them that the national powers that have forced them into exile are under his control. In Ezekiel 29:20 he tells them, "I have given him [the Babylonian king Nebuchadnezzar] the land of Egypt as his payment for which he labored, because they worked for me, says the Lord GOD." ■

After the Babylonians had deported Jews a third time, in 582 B.C., their strength began to wane. Cyrus of Persia came into power. He was religiously tolerant and, beginning in 535 B.C. or maybe as early as 538 B.C., he allowed the Jews to return home and restore the temple in Jerusalem. Chapters 40–55, called Second Isaiah, respectfully acknowledge Cyrus as an agent of God's plan for Israel. Second Isaiah refers to Cyrus as being "anointed" by God.

The Prophets in the Eighth to the Sixth Century B.C.

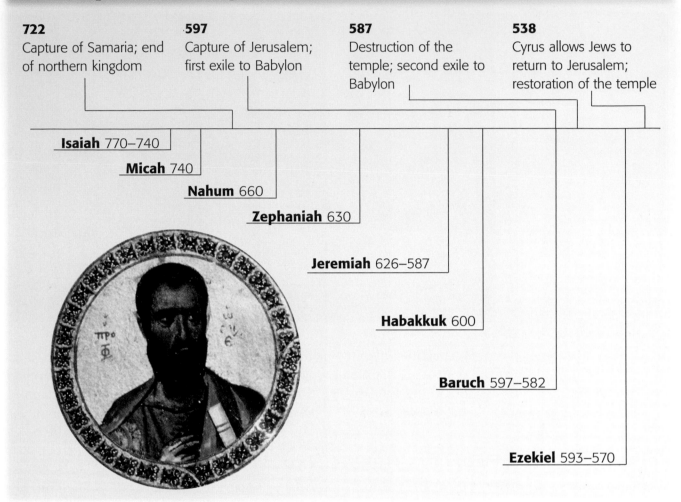

722
Capture of Samaria; end of northern kingdom

597
Capture of Jerusalem; first exile to Babylon

587
Destruction of the temple; second exile to Babylon

538
Cyrus allows Jews to return to Jerusalem; restoration of the temple

Isaiah 770–740

Micah 740

Nahum 660

Zephaniah 630

Jeremiah 626–587

Habakkuk 600

Baruch 597–582

Ezekiel 593–570

For Review

1. Who were some of the superpowers in the eighth to the sixth century B.C.?

2. Which prophet warned the kingdom of Judah not to ally itself with Egypt?

3. In what way was Micah a social reformer?

4. Which Persian leader allowed the Jews to return to their homeland?

For Discussion

If prophets who resembled those in the ancient world existed today, what do you think their message would be? How do you think the prophets and their message would be received?

Activity

Choose a current event about which you are concerned. It could be something of relevance to your community, your country, or the world. Write a few paragraphs about your concern. Suggest a plan for changing the situation and for attracting public support for your cause.

Theological Interpretation

THE MAJOR AND MINOR PROPHETS

The prophetic books of Isaiah, Jeremiah, and Ezekiel comprise what are referred to as the major prophets. This title is indicative not of quality but of length. Minor is the term used for the shorter books of prophecy, which include Nahum, Micah, Habakkuk, and Zephaniah. Each prophet's message foretells Israel's doom, as well as a final salvation or restoration through repentance. Yet each prophet's background and setting lends unique features to each one's delivery.

Read Isaiah 6:1-8.

JOURNAL

What are some of the calls one experiences in life? How do you know if you have been called by God to perform a specific action?

OPENING THE WORD

Read Isaiah 3:12–26 and note the prophet's reaction to the king and other people who were rich. Then read Isaiah 16:5.

Read Isaiah 10:20–22.

JOURNAL

How often do you exhibit a penitent heart? Reflect on the peace and trust that you have with God.

Read Isaiah 26:7–11, 30:15.

ISAIAH

Isaiah is considered the greatest prophet of the Old Testament. He is quoted more than fifty times in the New Testament. His prophecy spanned the reign of five kings of Judah, and his ministry was strong despite his listeners' disregard for his message. Clearly seeing the great gulf between sinful people and God, Isaiah proclaimed his own uncleanness in a vision prompting the angels to touch his mouth with a live coal. Only then did he accept his call. ■

It is in Isaiah's prophecy that we first are given the bridge to fill the gap between the sins of humans and the call of God. In Isaiah 6:5 the prophet cries out, "yet my eyes have seen the King, the LORD of hosts!" This is the first instance of a prophet referring to a king other than the rulers of the day. Isaiah and the other prophets firmly establish in their message that Israel will be punished, but that God will provide salvation through a Davidic king. ■

Another message that Isaiah delivered is found in his frequent reference to a "remnant." This refers to a portion of people that would be spared God's punishment, because they alone had remained faithful to the covenant. Jeremiah and Ezekiel and some of the minor prophets include this concept, but it is Isaiah who communicates the sense of salvation for a remnant rather than for the whole nation or people.

Clearly, national pride or solidarity will not guarantee being spared God's wrath. This leads Isaiah's listening audience, past and present, to the realization that personal faith and commitment are far more reliable as the means to salvation. In Isaiah's time, that was quite a novel idea. He develops this message further, giving guidance on how to develop that personal faith. A personal faith calls the individual to yearn for a relationship with his or her Creator and to live in obedience to God's will—to live justly. ■

JEREMIAH

Read Jeremiah 24.

OPENING THE WORD

Read Jeremiah 31:31–34. These verses have been called the "gospel before the gospel." Why do you think these verses are referred to in such a way?

Read Jeremiah 7:1–15.

JOURNAL

When do you feel you have a heart to know God? When do you think of yourself as a "child of God"? What would be signs that you have given your heart to him fully?

Read Jeremiah 1.

Jeremiah does not preach of the renewal of the covenant made on Mount Sinai but of its replacement. As a priest, Jeremiah intercedes repeatedly for the people, but he also admonishes the Israelites for their reliance on formal religion as their only expression of faith. In fact, his vision of the baskets of figs in Jeremiah 24 clearly sets the Israelites in exile as the remnant God will redeem. Jeremiah 24:7 states: "I will give them a heart to know that I am the LORD; and they shall be my people and I will be their God, for they shall return to me with their whole heart." ■ ■

The theme of justice appears in Jeremiah's prophecy, as it does with most prophets. In the temple sermon (7:1–15), Jeremiah condemns those who oppress refugees, orphans, and widows, and who think God will overlook their sins because they come to the temple.

Jeremiah's prophecy is full of lessons he teaches by the use of objects. Probably the most recognized is that of the potter and the clay (see Jeremiah 18). Through this analogy and others, Jeremiah communicates God's plans for Israel. God could destroy Israel as easily as a potter can crumple a pot on the wheel. The people of Israel had become useless and ruined like a spoiled linen belt. In Jeremiah 27:2–11 the prophet predicted destruction to any nation not submitting to Babylon's yoke of control. Even so, in Jeremiah 51:59–64 Babylon itself would sink and rise no more, like a sunken scroll.

Jeremiah was initially reluctant when called to be a prophet. He said, "Truly I do not know how to speak, for I am only a boy" (Jeremiah 1:6). However, God reassured him with the promise of his presence and his rescue of Jeremiah. Jeremiah spent much time in exile, both physically and emotionally. Despite being criticized, rebuked, and exiled, Jeremiah remained faithful to God throughout his life.

God shapes the history of Israel just as a potter molds his or her clay. The destiny of the people of Israel is in his hands.

EZEKIEL

JOURNAL

Do you think that a teen whose father is in prison can be trustworthy? Do you think that a teen whose parents are atheists can be a devoted Christian? How do these questions relate to the concept of personal responsibility for sin and for goodness?

Read Ezekiel 37:1–14.

As a prophet, Ezekiel's interest in the temple and the liturgy is unequaled. Perhaps this is because he was both a priest and a prophet. His calling to the role of prophet was unique in that he was the first to be called to go outside of Palestine—to Babylon. This singular experience reiterated to Ezekiel the message that God reaches the individual despite his or her lineage or his or her geographical location.

Ezekiel exhorted the individual to be alert for God and ready to repent (see Ezekiel 3:16–21). His commitment to priestly legislation has earned him the title of "The Father of Judaism." The absolute majesty of God is a strong undercurrent throughout Ezekiel's message. Historians believe that Ezekiel influenced the Law of Holiness, which is found in Leviticus 17–26. Portions of Ezekiel's prophecy were considered dangerous because of its strong images, prompting some groups to require that a reader be at least thirty years of age. Ezekiel makes a strong case for personal responsibility for sin and for goodness. ■

Ezekiel's view of salvation is one that begins with total obliteration. The temple that was used in idolatry will be destroyed, as will the worshipers. Then a new temple and restoration would occur. Ezekiel's prophecy comes to fruition with the new temple that was built right after the exile (520–515 B.C.).

SECOND ISAIAH

Read Isaiah 42:1–9, 49:1–7, 52:13–53:12.

Second Isaiah or Deutero-Isaiah is the title given to chapters 40–55 of the Book of Isaiah. The distinction is based on anonymous authorship of these chapters, which likely were composed and written down by disciples of the prophet Isaiah about 150 years after the first chapters. These chapters are characterized by consolation and peace. The "anointed one" to which the text refers is believed to have been Cyrus of Persia, consistent with the political times.

The author of Second Isaiah wrote that redemption was clearly coming and promises a deliverance based on the end of time (end of the world). He distinguishes between the ages, then and now, "things of old" and "new things." The exile is God's judgment and will be followed by a time of eternal salvation. This clear time delineation furthered the Israelites' understanding of God as the only god to be worshiped and served to an understanding of God as the *only* god. God was not only a practical choice for Israel, he was the only choice.

NAHUM

Read Nahum 1:2–13.

The prophecy of Nahum is full of nationalism. His message is that God would act exclusively on behalf of Judah in order to realize the hope of Israel. He had witnessed cruelties in Assyria and so was overjoyed at the city's destruction. He portrayed God as the avenger, but with mercy.

Read Micah 6 and 7.

Activity

With a small group, create a plan of social action about something that interests you. You might clean up a wilderness area or a neighborhood park. Or write a letter of protest to a U.S. corporation that employs child labor in another country.

Read 2 Chronicles 36:9–23 and Ezra 1:2.

Activity

Read Micah 6:8. Then write the verse on a flash card with the Scripture reference on the back of the card. Work with a partner to memorize the verse.

Read Habakkuk 1:1–4, 2:12–20.

Journal

Have you ever questioned God in prayer? If so, how did you feel? Was your prayer answered? (Remember silence is an answer too.)

Though the fig tree does not blossom . . .
yet I will rejoice in the LORD. . . .
Habakkuk 3:17, 18

MICAH

A contemporary of Isaiah, Micah, had firsthand experience with the evils he attacked. A laborer from an obscure village in the foothills of Judea, he characteristically focused much attention on the capital cities—pinpointing them as centers for moral corruption. Micah vividly portrays the decay of the Israelite society and proclaims that God will use Assyria to punish the sins of Jerusalem. Although a native of the southern kingdom, Micah favored the Moses-Sinai tradition of Israel. But his prophecy of God's punishment is not limited to either the northern or southern kingdom. Micah was particularly attuned to the socioeconomic injustices that abounded (see Micah 2:1–2). He itemizes Israel's sins—from idolatry and covetousness to hate, dishonesty, and family discord. ■

Micah laid out his argument like a lawyer, with God as the plaintiff. The three sections (Micah 1–2: Trial of the Capitals, Micah 3–5: Trial of the Leaders, and Micah 6–7: Trial of the People) begin with the clear message of punishment and doom, and conclude with a message of hope and salvation. The fulfillment of Micah's prophecies can be found in 2 Chronicles and Ezra. ■

HABAKKUK

Habakkuk is distinctive as a prophet because he is the first one to question God's ways of governing the world. The best part is that God answers willingly. He says that Babylon was the correcting rod, the Lord's avenging instrument. ■

ZEPHANIAH

Read Zephaniah 1:4–6, 2:8–11, 3:1–5.

Zephaniah was influenced by Isaiah, although he lived several decades after him. His message condemned practices common during the early part of Josiah's reign before the reforms, such as worshiping the sun, moon, and stars. His prophecy warned of judgment, but he allowed for the faithful remnant of Israel to be spared. He also protested against the sinful ways of the Assyrian court ministers.

THE GOSPEL WITHIN THE PROPHECIES

Old Testament prophecies are a graphic depiction of a main principle of the gospel. Sin divides people from God, and the divide gets bigger and bigger as the sin goes unconfessed and the sinner remains unrepentant. Both personal sins and social sins accumulate and make the chasm bigger. Only in seeking God can the gap be closed. The prophet's call to repentance is just as viable in the twenty-first century as it was in the seventh and eighth centuries B.C. Christians recognize in Christ the king promised in Isaiah and Micah; he bridges that gap.

Christians believe that Christ bridges the gap that separates us, as sinners, from the goodness of God.

For Review

1. According to Micah 6:8, what three things does God require of you?

2. What do the prophets say that God wants from the Israelites?

For Discussion

What social sins of Israel prevail in our society today? What efforts are being taken to correct these problems? How can the Church be a part of the solution?

Activity

Research a social justice issue and find out how Jews and Christians are involved in solving the problem. Present your findings to the class.

Martin Luther King Jr.

Messenger of Social Justice

Growing up in the South in the 1930s and 1940s, Martin Luther King Jr. knew the pain and humiliation of being kept out of places where only white people could go. White restaurant and hotel owners refused to serve African Americans. White officials devised ways to keep them from voting. Worse yet, an African American observed violating any of the complex codes regulating conduct between the races might find himself or herself in the hands of an angry, lawless mob.

At age fifteen "M.L.," as his parents called him, entered Morehouse College in his hometown, Atlanta, Georgia, as part of a program for gifted students. While at Morehouse, King decided to become a minister, as his father and grandfather had been before him. He was ordained and went on to earn two more degrees—a Bachelor of Divinity from Crozer Theological Seminary and a Ph.D. from Boston University. While in college, King discovered the teachings of Mohandas Gandhi, the Indian pacifist who led his country's struggle for independence from Great Britain. Gandhi's pacifism was to have a profound effect on the direction of King's ministry. King's thinking was also influenced by the Sermon on the Mount and by the author Thoreau.

In 1955 an African American woman named Rosa Parks was arrested in Montgomery, Alabama, for violating a city ordinance requiring that she give up her bus seat to a white passenger. Local ministers urged African Americans to protest the arrest by not using the bus system until the law giving white people preferential seating was changed. Boycott organizers asked a new, young preacher in town— Martin Luther King Jr.—to lead them. The boycott succeeded, and in 1956 the Supreme Court ordered Montgomery to end racial segregation on buses.

During the Montgomery Bus Boycott, threats made against King's family caused him to suffer a personal crisis. He wondered whether leading the struggle for African Americans' civil rights was worth

Martin Luther King Jr. fought against racism and other forms of oppression. He dedicated his life to promoting social justice.

the risk. While alone in prayer, he turned himself over to God and heard a voice telling him: "Martin Luther, stand up for righteousness. Stand up for justice. Stand up for truth. And lo, I will be with you, even until the end of the world." From that moment, he never again questioned his mission. Like the prophets of the Old Testament, King chose to stand up for social justice.

In August of 1963 over 200,000 people turned out for a peaceful march on Washington—a demonstration of support for the civil rights of African Americans. It was here that King made his stirring, prophetic "I Have a Dream" speech. In December 1964 King was awarded the Nobel Peace Prize in recognition of his leadership of a nonviolent quest for social justice.

King's concern for the plight of a group of underpaid sanitation workers on strike took him to Memphis, Tennessee, in April 1968. In a speech to encourage strike supporters, he acknowledged that he might not live a long life. But King said he was not afraid of dying. He had already "been to the mountain top." An assassin's bullet ended his life the next day.

Social Justice

The life of Martin Luther King Jr. provides us with a powerful example of a man who fought for social justice. How can we follow his example? ■

CARING FOR PEOPLE WHO ARE POOR

The prophets of the Old Testament also spoke of a need for social justice. They warned that God will deal harshly with those who turn the other way when faced with the challenge of helping people in need. For example, during their time in exile, there were members of the Israelite community who were better off than others. These people had a responsibility to care for the people in their community who were poor.

We too have a responsibility to care for people who are poor or oppressed in our community. We should stand up for social justice. One way that we can make a difference in our community is to volunteer with organizations that help people who are poor. We can also donate money to these organizations if we are not able to offer our time. Most of all, we must remember to treat people who are poor with respect. Their unfortunate situation does not make them any less important to God—quite the contrary.

Actively working to help those who are poor is one way to stand up for social justice. Whom do you know who does this?

FIGHTING OPPRESSION

Another way that we can demonstrate concern for social justice is to focus on groups within our society that are oppressed by others. Depending on the community in which you live, this might include people of a certain social class, ethnicity, or religious background.

The teen in the opening story would feel oppressed in the new country to which he or she is moving if the people there did not make him or her feel welcome. Immigrants to this country often need additional support in adjusting to their new surroundings. You can help make that transition easier for immigrants with whom you come into contact.

Welcoming newcomers into our communities takes a conscious decision on our part. Who are the recent immigrants in the area? What are their stories?

For Review

1. What great leaders influenced Reverend Martin Luther King Jr. in his ministry?

2. How did a courageous act by Rosa Parks affect Martin Luther King Jr.'s ministry?

3. Name two ways that Christians today can pursue social justice.

For Discussion

Listen to a recording of Martin Luther King Jr.'s "I Have a Dream" speech. Then discuss the importance of this speech and the emotions it continues to inspire in those who hear it.

Activity

Working with a small group, compile a list of the social service organizations active in your community and what is required of their volunteers. Your local phone directory would be a good first resource for this activity.

The Old Testament prophets were called by God to communicate his message to the people of Israel. They warned the people of the consequences that would befall them if they did not repent from their sinful conduct. God was angered by the constant wavering of the Israelites between loyalty to him and to neighboring empires. They confronted false leaders and gave oracles against other nations as well. The prophets also encouraged the people with the promise that if they persevered and remained focused on God, he would restore them to their homeland.

During this period in Israelite history, the cause of social justice was of great importance. The prophets pointed out that the people were angering God through their neglect of those who were poor. The people were called to demonstrate their obedience to God through their care for one another.

Many times he delivered them,
    but they were rebellious in their purposes,
    and were brought low through their iniquity.
Nevertheless he regarded their distress
    when he heard their cry.
For their sake he remembered his covenant,
    and showed compassion according to the abundance
        of his steadfast love.

Psalm 106:43–45

Create in me a clean heart, O God,
  and put a new and right spirit within me.
Do not cast me away from your presence,
  and do not take your holy spirit from me.
Restore to me the joy of your salvation,
  and sustain in me a willing spirit.

Psalm 51:10–12

The Time of the Restoration

C. 525 B.C.

Height of Etruscan
expansion in Italy

515 B.C.

Reconstruction of temple
complete

C. 500 B.C.

Nok Iron-Age culture
beginning in Central Africa

522–486 B.C.

Persian king Darius I extends empire
from the Nile to the Indus River

509 B.C.

Overthrow of the last king of Rome;
Roman republic established

C. 500 B.C.

Desert dwellers of New Mexico/Arizona
grow first drought-resistant type of maize

CHAPTER 9

The Restoration and New Beginnings

CHAPTER GOALS

Increase knowledge of the meaning of the Old Testament and deepen understanding of its value by studying the following:

- literary characteristics of apocalyptic literature, satirical humor, the novella, and fairy tales
- historical context for the restoration of Jerusalem
- explanation of visions of the apocalypse and a future messiah
- role of the Church in the modern world

CHAPTER OUTLINE

c. 500 B.C.	447–432 B.C.	359–336 B.C.
Beginnings of the Monte Albán culture in Oaxaca, Mexico	Parthenon built in Greece entirely of marble	Philip II of Macedonia unifies Greece

c. 450 B.C.	390 B.C.
Zenith of Greek drama	Gaul invasion of Rome; Gauls withdraw after being paid ransom in gold

Although you're busy with school, sports, and spending time with your friends, you feel that you can squeeze in time for a little bit of volunteer work. (Besides, your mom keeps asking you to do it.) You want to do something for people in your community who are in need. You decide to volunteer some of your time at a local soup kitchen and sign up to spend a Saturday serving lunch to the homeless.

When you arrive, you're uncomfortable and nervous. You've never done anything like this before, and you don't really know what to do. As you walk through a hallway, you overhear some conversation about where some of the homeless people slept last night: under bridges, in vacant garages, in abandoned buildings. Off the hallway, you notice a storage room. The staff is organizing soap, toothbrushes, and some clothes to distribute to the men, women, and children.

A supervisor gives you the job of handing food trays to the people in line. You put on your apron and begin. At first you're just going through the motions, but as more and more people express their thanks to you, you start to feel really good. You start to hand out a few kind words along with the trays: "There you go, sir. You have a nice day now." You begin to feel comfortable and enjoy yourself. You eye the line of people and see that it's thinning out. You really don't want it to end.

After everyone is served, you join the rest of the volunteer staff in cleaning the premises. You do it willingly, realizing that it is another way to give of yourself and to help other people. On your walk home from the soup kitchen, you start thinking about how to arrange your schedule so that you can volunteer more regularly.

Keep this story in mind as we study a time of new beginnings in Israel's history.

THE CHRONICLES

chronicle a listing of historical events; an historical account or narrative with a purpose; a creative reinterpretation of historical events

The two books of the **Chronicles** are grouped with the historical books of the Old Testament. They are a creative reinterpretation of history that presents a review of Israel's history in terms of God's unfolding plan rather than in a pristine chronology. Stories are condensed or expanded to meet the needs of this theme. ■

A large emphasis is placed on the reigns of David and Solomon, but the personal shortcomings and difficulties these two men faced are omitted. For instance, none of the problems detailed in 2 Samuel 1–4 are mentioned by the authors of the Chronicles. David is placed on the throne quickly and easily: "So all the elders of Israel came to the king at Hebron, and David made a covenant with them at Hebron before the LORD. And they anointed David king over Israel, according to the word of the LORD by Samuel" (1 Chronicles 11:3). In addition, the Book of Chronicles uses a long genealogy from creation to King David (1 Chronicles 1–8) to give the impression that all the previous events were a preparation for David. ■

FAITH SHARING

Over the next week, think about the following questions. What is the challenge that God has placed before you? In what ways are you equipped to handle it? How will God compensate for your weaknesses?

ACTIVITY

In a small group, draft an outline for a skit based on a historical event in Israel's history, but one that is geared toward a particular theme. Perform your skit for the rest of the class.

Shakespeare's Henry IV is an example of a chronicle play.

The "Four Horsemen of the Apocalypse" by Edward Jakob von Steinle was inspired by the Book of Revelation 6:1–8.

VISIONS OF THE APOCALYPSE

apocalypse a revelation of future events

An **apocalypse** is the presumed unveiling of future events, particularly the final struggle between the powers of evil and God, with God victorious and his kingdom established forever. When we hear the word *apocalypse* in the context of the Bible, we generally think of the New Testament Book of Revelation. What you may not know, however, is that the Book of Revelation draws upon apocalyptic literature found in the Old Testament.

Read Zechariah 14.

Isaiah 24–27 and many of the visions of Zechariah and Joel represent early apocalyptic development. The Book of Daniel, chapters 7 through 12, is the clearest apocalyptic in the Old Testament. This apocalyptic literature differs from prophecy in that it describes a divine intervention and the beginning of a new age, whereas prophecy interprets more ordinary historical events as actions of God. Moreover, apocalyptic is usually written in response to real or perceived persecution.

OPENING THE WORD

Work with a partner to analyze the influence of the Book of Zechariah on the Book of Revelation. Base your analysis on the following pairings:

Zechariah 4:10 and
  Revelation 5:6
Zechariah 6:1–7 and
  Revelation 6:2–8
Zechariah 13:1 and
  Revelation 21:6, 22:1–2
Zechariah 14:6–7 and
  Revelation 22:5
Zechariah 14:9 and
  Revelation 11:15, 15:3–4

ZECHARIAH'S VISIONS

The prophetic Book of Zechariah is an extremely visionary text, providing admonitions to repent, hope for a messiah, and revelations about a messianic community of the future that would be centered in Jerusalem. This book presents visions in the style of dialogues between God, the prophet Zechariah, and an angel who interprets the visions for Zechariah. Zechariah experiences a vision of the end times, but after witnessing destruction, warfare, and suffering, he sees victory: "And the LORD will become king over all the earth . . . for never again shall [Israel] be doomed to destruction; Jerusalem shall abide in security" (Zechariah 14:9, 11). Zechariah's more hopeful visions and oracles speak of a time when enemies will become a thing of the past, there will be peace between all people, and the worship of God will be universal. ◼

JOEL'S VISIONS

Read Joel 2:28–3:21 or in NAB—Joel 3:1–4:21.

The prophet Joel calls the people to return to God. He uses the example of the plague of locusts that has devastated the land as a warning of things to come. He presents apocalyptic prophecies of the day of the Lord, complete with judgments and blessings. He speaks of an apocalypse that will be an earthly disaster of cosmic proportions: "I will show portents in the heavens and on the earth, blood and fire and columns of smoke. The sun shall be turned to darkness, and the moon to blood, before the great and terrible day of the LORD comes" (Joel 2:30–31 or in NAB—Joel 3:3–4). ■

JOURNAL

Have you ever begrudged someone their good fortune? Was it because you didn't think they deserved it? What does the lesson of Jonah teach us about this type of response?

ActiviTy

Draw or paint a vision of the apocalypse. You may focus on a single image or portray a larger scene. Use appropriate Scripture as the caption for your illustration.

Read the Book of Jonah.

antihero a character who is placed in the role of a traditional hero but is not idealized in any way

satirical humor humor that exposes human folly through a form of ridicule in order to achieve a moral purpose

JONAH AS ANTIHERO

The Book of Jonah is a prophetic book, but it is written in the form of a teaching story or parable. Jonah is an **antihero**—his portrait is contrary to what we designate as being heroic. An antihero is usually presented as more of an ordinary person, complete with character flaws and human weaknesses. In the Book of Jonah, **satirical humor** is used throughout to ridicule Jonah's weaknesses and expose his human frailties. This satire is really aimed at the people's expectations and demonstrates the futility of disobeying God; as Jonah learns from his mistakes, so must the chosen people and so must we. ■

The idea of the "great fish" that swallowed Jonah may have been based on what we know today to be a whale. Art by Sister Helena Steffensmeier SSSF.

"Then Jonah prayed to the LORD his God from the belly of the fish, saying: 'I called to the LORD out of my distress, and he answered me. . . .'"

Jonah 2:1–2

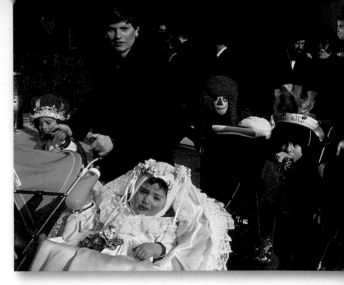

Jewish families in New York celebrating the festival of Purim.

NOVELLA

novella a suspenseful tale that revolves around a specific situation

In the twentieth century, usage of the term *novella* grew to encompass any piece of fictional prose that was longer than a short story but not as long as a novel. However, earlier usage of the term referred to any tale that revolved around a specific situation. The term *novella* derives from the Latin term *novella narratio,* which means a "new kind of story." Many novellas are full of suspense and drama—as the Book of Esther is. The hero or heroine of a novella must work out the resolution of a particular conflict. The Book of Esther models these characteristics, as Esther and Mordecai expose the evildoings of Haman. The suspense reaches its peak just before the people reveal Haman's sadistic plot to King Xerxes in time to save the Jews from persecution and death.

fairy tale a myth with an earthly setting, human characters, and a happy ending

The Book of Esther is similar to a classic **fairy tale.** Esther, like Cinderella, comes from humble beginnings to become the wife of royalty. Haman is a caricature of evil, and the powerful are not really in control (the king is easily manipulated). This story of Esther goes beyond that happy ending, however, to show how her position as the queen of Persia benefits all the Jews. In her position of power, she is able to expose the evil Haman, who has issued an order that every Jew be put to death. An event of coincidence resolves the plot (6:1–11). The book also uses irony. The events are set in motion when the first queen disobeys the king. But Esther, her supposedly obedient replacement, ends up controlling events.

Read Esther 7:2–8:16.

For Review

1. How do 1 and 2 Chronicles differ from other historical books?

2. What is the theme of an apocalyptic vision?

3. Describe an antihero. What type of humor is often used when telling the story of an antihero?

For Discussion

Many modern movies depict the destruction of the earth or the end of civilization as we know it. How do these portrayals relate to the apocalyptic literature found in the Old Testament?

Activity

The Jewish festival of Purim celebrates the story of Esther. Research this festival by using print materials or electronic resources or, if possible, by speaking with members of the Jewish community. Present your findings to the class.

THE PERSIAN EMPIRE AND ISRAEL'S HISTORY

The historical and postexilic prophetic books most likely were written between the sixth and fourth centuries B.C., when the ancient Middle East was part of the Persian empire. The Old Testament writers were active participants, but they also reinterpreted the events of previous times and their time to portray Israel as one single community—a people intent on one place of worship in Jerusalem. The Book of Chronicles, for example, emphasizes David's role in establishing the nation's worship.

The people of Israel had been split apart and faced the challenges of reconstructing the temple and restoring their way of life after returning from exile. At that time, worship became more important for defining Jewish identity, since the people no longer had an independent nation.

The Persian empire's breadth was as great as its duration; it extended from Egypt in the west to the Indus River in the east. The founder of the empire, Cyrus the Great, was responsible for laying the cornerstones on which the empire thrived: military capability and efficient administrative systems. A characteristic of Cyrus the Great that affected the restoration, but did not extend to all of his successors, was his politically smart tolerance of other people's religious customs and practices.

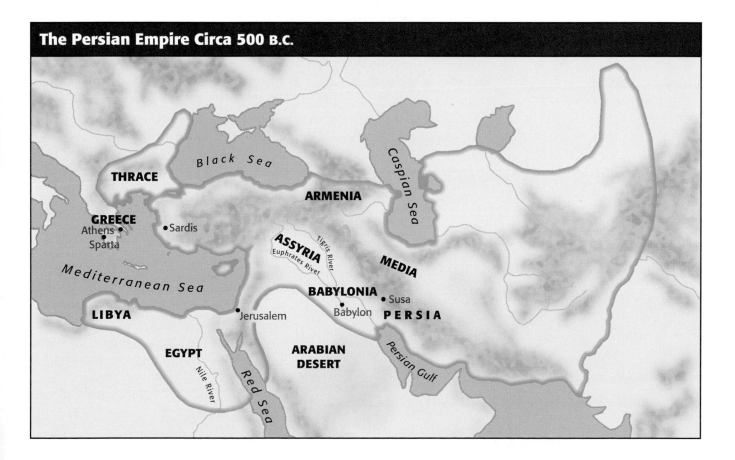

The Persian Empire Circa 500 B.C.

CYRUS THE GREAT

Cyrus was the son of the daughter of the king of Medes and of a vassal prince. The historian Herodotus recounts that the king of Medes had a dream in which his infant grandson, Cyrus, would someday overthrow him. In a story that resembles the upbringing of Moses, the king orders Cyrus slain, but the king's chief adviser gives the infant to a shepherd who raises Cyrus. He lives and, as a young man, revolts against his grandfather. The king's army surrenders to Cyrus. With the surrender of the army, Cyrus inherits the empire of the Medes.

CYRUS AND THE BEGINNING OF THE RECONSTRUCTION

Cyrus's empire-building was the result of his military prowess and diplomatic skill. In 539 B.C. Cyrus conquered Babylonia. The rule of Syria and Palestine came with his conquest of Babylonia. (Babylonia was the place where many Israelites of the former kingdom of Judah were prisoners—in exile—under Babylonian rule.) Cyrus showed compassion to these exiles—Jews of the **Diaspora.** In one edict, he freed the exiled Jews and allowed them to return to Jerusalem to reconstruct the temple after years of being scattered and being exposed to idolatrous religious practices in Babylonia. Because this was such a significant event in Israelite history, Cyrus is referred to in Isaiah as being part of God's plan for Israel.

Despite Cyrus's edict, the relationship the Jews had with the Samaritans adversely affected the reconstruction of the temple. The Samaritans wanted to help reconstruct the temple. The Jews, however, regarded the Samaritans as unholy, due to their intermarriage with peoples the Assyrian conquerors had placed in Judah. The Jews forbade the Samaritans to work on the temple. As a result, the Samaritans did their best to interfere with its reconstruction, and they succeeded. As Ezra 4:4–5 states, "Then the people of the land discouraged the people of Judah, and made them afraid to build, and they bribed officials to frustrate their plan throughout the reign of King Cyrus of Persia and until the reign of King Darius of Persia."

Diaspora the community of Jews in Babylonia after the Exile; **diaspora**—communities of Jews who have scattered all over the world, including places such as India, Africa, and Spain. *Diaspora* is derived from the Greek word meaning "scattered."

satrapy an administrative province ruled by a governor called a *satrap*

DARIUS

Darius, like Cyrus before him, was able to unify the diverse peoples of the Persian empires through administrative channels. The empire was divided into provinces called *satrapies.* Each **satrapy** was ruled by a governor, a satrap. The satrap was responsible for law and order, local military operations, and the collection of tribute. Zerubbabel, a descendant of David, became a governor of Judah under Darius. Zerubbabel and the high priest Joshua were responsible for the completion of the temple in 515 B.C.

Cylinders told the stories of such events as Cyrus's conquest of Babylon and the return of exiles to their homelands.

This bas-relief, found in Iran, probably includes Darius, either as the king or as the crown prince behind the king.

Some historians attribute Darius's tolerance of the religious beliefs of others to the fact that he was a follower of a religion founded by Zoroaster. The religion, known as Zoroastrianism, centered around one god, known as the father of justice, but emphasized a dualism between good and evil. A follower of Zoroastrianism must think and say good thoughts and perform good deeds to reach paradise. Another example of Darius's religion affecting his politics is his order that the satrap in Egypt consult with the local priests when codifying laws.

ARTAXERXES I

Continuous rebellions threatened the stability of the empire after Darius's reign. Xerxes I succeeded Darius, followed by Artaxeres I, another Persian emperor who directly affected the history of Israel.

Nehemiah, a treasured member of the royal court and a Jew, had been dismayed at reports of Jerusalem being in ruins. Artaxerxes I (possibly Artaxerxes II) sent Nehemiah to Jerusalem to help Jerusalem fortify its walls. Artaxerxes, however, may have had a political motive for sending Nehemiah. Artaxerxes's military had been fighting rebellions in Egypt. Perhaps it was in order to keep Egypt's nearest neighbor, Judah, pacified or under control that he sent Nehemiah to Jerusalem as governor. Artaxerxes also sent back to Jerusalem Ezra, a scribe, and others who were part of the **remnant**.

remnant exiles and former exiles who remained faithful to God

The Persian Emperors

Cyrus	Darius	Xerxes	Artaxerxes I	Artaxerxes II	Artaxerxes III
590–529 B.C.	522–486 B.C.	486–465 B.C.	465–425 B.C.	404–359 B.C.	359–338 B.C.

Whether Artaxerxes had political motives or compassion for the Jews who were facing hostility from their neighbors in Jerusalem, the fact that Ezra and Nehemiah were allowed to return to Jerusalem greatly affected the history of Israel. Nehemiah's reforms as governor helped the Jews define who they were as a community; a member of the community needed to be of Jewish descent, and no intermarrying was allowed. Ezra reaffirmed that the Jewish community must live by the law of God. Indeed, this was decreed by Artaxerxes. Artaxerxes tells Ezra, "All who will not obey the law of your God and the law of the king, let judgment be strictly executed on them" (Ezra 7:26). Both Ezra and Nehemiah worked to end mixed marriages and the influence of other cultures and languages, believing that was necessary in order for the scattered people to survive.

Keeping the Persian empire together proved to be hard and constant work for the remaining Persian emperors. Artaxerxes II was able to keep the empire together through treacherous means. Sparta and Egypt were openly rebellious, and the emperor failed to keep Egypt as part of the empire. Later, many satraps, including those of Greece, Sparta, and Athens, rose in revolt, but they were defeated. Artaxerxes III was a cruel ruler who put most of his relatives to death to assure his throne. His initial failure to regain control of Egypt encouraged Phoenicia and the island of Cyprus to revolt. After quelling that revolt, Artaxerxes III again turned his sights toward Egypt, and he finally succeeded in defeating that nation. Egypt again became a Persian satrapy. Artaxerxes III and his elder sons were then killed by an influential eunuch in the court of Artaxerxes III.

For Review

1. How was Cyrus the Great able to build the Persian empire?

2. How did Cyrus the Great affect the history of Israel?

3. Describe the political motive Artaxerxes II may have had in sending Nehemiah back to Jerusalem.

For Discussion

Discuss what it takes to be a great leader. Is it administrative, diplomatic, or military skill? If it is a combination of these attributes, which is the most important? Support your ideas with examples from the Persian emperors as well as from other political and spiritual leaders.

Journal

When have you felt like a member of a remnant? Did the situation ever change? If so, why? If not, was that for the best? Explain.

Theological Interpretation

The promised land of postexilic Israel splintered into many small enclaves. Jerusalem was in ruins, and the Jews were driven into poverty. The prophets in these books focused on restoring a way of life and a religious community. With these challenges, the people of Israel struggled with a sense of the "absence" of God. It was difficult to remain focused on God's promise when it did not appear that he was watching over them any longer.

Another theme that appears in the Books of Jonah, Chronicles, Ezra, and Nehemiah is the relationship between religion, culture, and nationalism. Jonah, for example, criticizes the people for wanting their prophets to be concerned only with their own nation. The other books try to define Jewish identity in a way that would survive the loss of the nation. The issue of tolerance (or intolerance) follows from this discussion.

HAGGAI

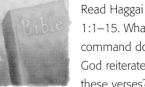

OPENING THE WORD

Read Haggai 1:1–15. What command does God reiterate in these verses? How could these words apply to you in your own life today?

Haggai was the driving force behind the rebuilding of the temple in Jerusalem. His call to finish the rebuilding overruled all the excuses made by the people. Fifteen years had passed since their return from exile, and yet the people had done very little to reconstruct their house of worship. Preoccupied with the harassment by neighboring nations, they had instead become consumed with providing and protecting their own housing and material possessions.

Haggai was keenly aware of the importance for strengthening the Israelites' faith of the re-establishment of religious symbols and rituals. He also knew the value of the community effort involved in the temple reconstruction. Haggai's emphasis on rebuilding what the Babylonians had torn down was a rallying cry. The effectiveness of his prophecy was tremendous; the people began rebuilding just twenty-three days after Haggai's first message. ■

Haggai's focus was on the need to rebuild the temple.

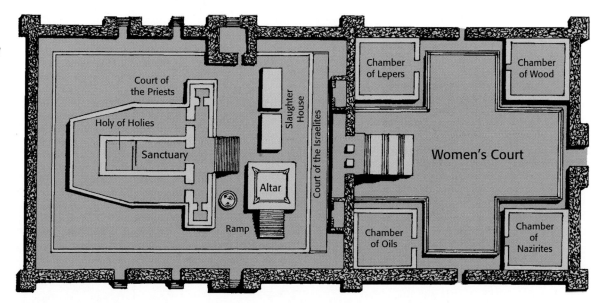

Read Haggai 2:3–9.

JouRNaL

List the five things that take top priority in your life. Where does God fit on the list? Brainstorm two ways to improve his standing in your daily life.

AcTiviTy

Research the celebration of the Feast of Tabernacles in the Jewish tradition. Does your parish celebrate this feast in any way? If so, describe when and how.

JouRNaL

Reflect on an instance when you consciously placed your relationship with God above a personal goal or desire. What were the results? How did you feel?

The Israelites had begun the temple with zeal, but discouragement had stopped their enthusiasm. Their new focus became self-centered; God's house was left unfinished, abandoned while they toiled at other work. Once again God was directing the Israelites back onto his course. Haggai openly addressed the rumblings of the Israelites as they began the temple reconstruction. In Haggai 2, Haggai delivers his message during the Feast of Tabernacles, targeting the older Israelites who remembered the glory of the temple built by Solomon and who were discouraged by the limits of the new temple.

Haggai delivers the Lord's clear message that this temple would see greater glory than Solomon's. In Haggai 2:4, Haggai asks all the people to be courageous and to work. He emphasizes that they have been delivered from exile and that they are God's covenant people. They need to work— not just be children of God but *working* children of God. Haggai delivers God's call to make his house, his work, a priority. Haggai declares God's willingness to bless us from our initial steps in obedience. The foundation alone is all that the Israelites have accomplished, yet the Lord declares it to be the beginning of his blessing. When God is given first place, he blesses his people richly. ■ ■ ■

ZECHARIAH

Like Haggai, Zechariah's message is one of encouragement of the temple reconstruction project. In an apocalyptic style, Zechariah delivers encouragement to the Israelites as they rebuild and as they renew hope in a messianic kingdom to come. Zechariah directs the people to look ahead to the day of the Lord.

Zechariah, a priest as well as a prophet, delivers his first message from God two months after that of Haggai. In the first six chapters of Zechariah, Zechariah recounts eight visions he has experienced. The first vision is of "riders," messengers from other nations (see Zechariah 1:7–17). This vision is in response to the lament by the Israelites that sinful nations were prospering. The "riders" promise God's judgment on even the apparently prosperous nations.

The second vision is of horns (see Zechariah 1:18–21). The four horns symbolize the nations that had overpowered Israel. In the vision, the horns are cast down, indicating that the oppressor nations would pay for their sinfulness as Israel had. The third vision is of a measuring line (see Zechariah 2:1–13). As the Israelites continue to rebuild Jerusalem, God would remain as their protective wall; they would need no others.

Zechariah's fourth vision is of a heavenly court (see Zechariah 3:1–10). In this vision the high priest Joshua, who now leads the community, has his filthy clothes removed and clean garments placed on him. According to the vision, the accusations of Satan (Hebrew word meaning "adversary" or "accuser") hold no sway over the people God chooses to restore. This is one of the earliest appearances in the Bible of the adversary Satan.

The fifth vision is of a lampstand (see Zechariah 4:1–14). The lamp holds an infinite reservoir of oil symbolizing the infinite care God will show his people. The sixth vision, one of a "flying scroll," represents God's curse (see Zechariah 5:1–4) for those who go against God's Law. No one is exempt from God's punishment for sin. This reiterates that the individual—not just the nation—must live righteously. The seventh vision is of a woman in a basket (see Zechariah 5:5–11), who represents the wickedness in all the land. In the vision, an angel packs the woman back into the basket and returns her to Babylon. This signifies God's removal of sin from society, both from the nation and from the individual.

The final vision is of four horses and chariots (see Zechariah 6:1–8). In this vision, the horses patrol the world in search of evil, especially in the north—the route from Babylon. This reassured the Israelites that all the world was now at rest and Judah could rise again in freedom.

These visions of Zechariah held an expansive message for the Israelites, proclaiming that they will not be his chosen people exclusively. Enemies will become a thing of the past.

Zechariah emphasized the importance of religious ritual just as Haggai did. In Zechariah 7, Zechariah answers a question as to the number of days for fasting. He responds by telling what is most important: "Render true judgments, show kindness and mercy to one another" (Zechariah 7:9).

The second part of the Book of Zechariah (chapters 9–14) was added to the original book and is more messianic. A messianic oracle in Zechariah 9 refers to the entry of Zion's king on the foal of a donkey. The symbolic significance of the donkey was in defiance of the then-current practice of a monarch arrogantly riding in horse and chariot. The donkey was a vehicle of nobility in the days of Genesis and Judges. Zechariah's message communicated that the king to come would be a humble and noble king. His vision of this messiah king is further elaborated in Zechariah 10:4–5. This king would be strong, trustworthy, stable, and victorious. In Zechariah 11, Zechariah explores the roles of an evil shepherd. His message is that the messiah will be a good shepherd.

The Book of Zechariah gives us an image of the messiah as a good shepherd. This painting of "The Good Herdsman" is by the Danish artist Christian Dalsgaard (1824–1907).

". . . all nations will count you happy, for you are a land of delight, says the LORD of hosts."
Malachi 3:12
Painting by William Manners (1885-1904).

JOURNAL

Have you ever offered God less than your best? What step can you take today to improve your walk with God?

Read Malachi 3:6–12.

JOURNAL

Is there anyone in your class who seems to be particularly strong in his or her faith? Would you call him or her one of the "faithful few" to whom Malachi referred? What can you do in your own life to be more faithful to God?

MALACHI

Malachi's message is delivered more than eighty years after the completion of the temple. The actual name of this prophet is unclear because the Hebrew meaning of *malachi* is "my messenger." So the name "Malachi" was possibly a "pen name." Even though the temple had been completed, Malachi's message remains one of confrontation. The Israelites had once again placed their priorities on things other than God. They were neglecting the temple and being willfully disobedient. But prior to his argument, Malachi delivers God's message, "I have loved you, says the LORD" (Malachi 1:2). A good and wise father, God precedes his correction with an assurance of his love for his children. His instruction begins with the priests, saying that the sacrifices they offered were not satisfactory. They were presenting crippled and blind animals, which was dishonoring to God. ■

In Malachi 2, Malachi addresses the ignorance of the priests about God's word, since they had caused many people to stumble. Next Malachi directed his message to the people. They, too, were dishonoring God by divorcing their Jewish wives and marrying non-Jewish women. The Israelites were justifying their defiance of God's law by twisting God's word.

Finally, Malachi's message called for the people to reform their offerings. If they were to give the entire tithe (ten percent) of their harvest to God, he would open the floodgates of blessing. The current bad harvest from drought and pestilence was a result of the Israelites' withholding of tithes. Malachi concludes his prophecy with reference to the "remnant"; the faithful few will be spared God's final judgment. ■

THIRD ISAIAH

Read Isaiah 56–66.

OPENING THE WORD

Reread Isaiah 66:7–13. Who is being described as a mother in this passage? In what ways do God and the Church serve as maternal figures?

Isaiah, as a book of the Old Testament, has three divisions, with each division being based on authorship. It is believed that Second and Third Isaiah were compilations of multiple authors, all disciples, or members of the school, of the prophet Isaiah. Third Isaiah comprises chapters 56–66 and spans the time period 540 to 510 B.C. As with the message of his fellow prophets, the message of Third Isaiah is a lament for the falling away of the Israelites from God's plan and a call for renewal.

In particular, the message includes a radical concept for that time period: God's blessing of both people of other nations and of eunuchs (Isaiah 56), and so to all who honor God. Justice is the theme of Third Isaiah. In the past neither people of other nations nor eunuchs were allowed into the temple; nor were they even considered to be citizens. Third Isaiah ends with the certainty of God's justice with his people and the assurance of his salvation. A summary of the prophet's message can be found in Isaiah 66:2–3: There are two ways to live life: in humble obedience or with arrogant disregard. 🔲

FOR REVIEW

1. List the eight visions that Zechariah recounted. Summarize the overall message he delivered.

2. Through the prophecy of Malachi, what did God promise the people if they were faithful in their tithe?

3. What was wrong with the priestly sacrifices offered in Malachi's time?

4. What did Third Isaiah say about people of other nations and eunuchs?

5. What message did Haggai deliver to the older generation about the glory of the rebuilt temple?

FOR DISCUSSION

How are Isaiah 61 and the Sermon on the Mount (in Matthew 5) similar? In what ways are we as a society living in accordance with or in ignorance of these commands? What are some ways for us to more fully conform?

ACTIVITY

Based on your discussion, choose eight symbols that would convey God's message for today's society. Refer to Zechariah's night visions, then choose symbols relevant to our culture. Make a poster to display your symbols and be ready to explain it.

Rose Philippine Duchesne

Saint of the Sacred Heart

Rose Philippine Duchesne was born into a wealthy family in Grenoble, France, in 1769. Early in life she developed a concern for people who were poor, and by age eleven she was giving them her weekly allowance. She loved to read books about missionaries and dreamed of helping Native Americans someday. By the time she was twelve, Duchesne knew she wanted to pursue the religious life. Much against her father's wishes, she entered the Visitation Order at the age of seventeen.

During the French Revolution, all religious orders in France were disbanded, yet the young Philippine continued her service to others. She cared for people who were sick or poor, sheltered fugitive priests, visited prisoners, and taught children. After frustrated attempts to reestablish the Visitation Order at Grenoble, she and a small group of nuns in 1804 joined the Society of the Sacred Heart, a community recently founded by Madeleine Sophie Barat.

In 1816, Bishop William DuBourg visited the Paris convent seeking nuns to come to America to open schools on his frontier mission. (He lived in St. Louis, but the Louisiana Territory comprised his diocese.) Philippine enthusiastically volunteered, and, at the age of forty-eight, she and four other nuns embarked on a ten-week voyage across the Atlantic, followed by a forty-day trip up the Mississippi to St. Louis. Upon their arrival there in 1818, however, the bishop informed the weary nuns that he had chosen the town of St. Charles—some twenty miles further west—for their first mission. Disappointed in her desire to work with Native Americans, Mother Duchesne obeyed the bishop and worked admirably in the midst of abject poverty.

The log cabin that had been rented for the nuns became the convent for five nuns, boarding school for three young ladies from St. Louis, and a free school for local pioneer children who sometimes numbered as many as twenty-one. After one year of unstable enrollment, the decision was made to abandon St. Charles and open a school on the St. Louis side of the Missouri River in Florissant. It was not until 1828 that the

Rose Philippine Duchesne remained obedient to God and led a life of service to others.

nuns were urged by the Jesuits to return to St. Charles to reopen the school near their newly established parish church.

Although she was plagued by a sense of inadequacy, Mother Duchesne went on, in the next twenty years, to establish schools in Missouri and Louisiana that would survive to the present time. Her schools became models for educational excellence in the cities where they existed, and Philippine's missionary zeal was the beginning of the spread of the Society of the Sacred Heart to countries around the world.

Her childhood desire to work with Native Americans never faltered, and in 1841, at the age of seventy-two, Philippine was finally permitted to accompany other Sacred Heart nuns and Jesuit priests to a Potowatami mission in Sugar Creek, Kansas. Although she considered herself a failure because of her inability to master the Potowatami language, she deeply impressed the natives by her habit of constant prayer. They reverently named her *Quah-kah-ka-num-ad,* "Woman who prays always."

Mother Duchesne spent only one year on the Kansas prairie. In frail health, she returned to her beloved St. Charles where she lived ten more years in prayerful, humble service before dying on November 18, 1852, at the age of eighty-three. On July 3, 1988, she was canonized a saint by the Catholic Church.

Claiming the Future

Together we can make decisions to better our lives and the lives of others.

JourNaL

Think of a relationship you have—with a parent, sibling, relative, friend, neighbor, or classmate—that is strained. What can you do to improve the relationship? Make a list of actions and words you can use to restore the relationship.

anawim a Jewish term referring to people who are in need of assistance

STARTING OVER

When the exiled Jews were allowed to return to Jerusalem, the city was in ruins and needed to be restored. This period was a time of new beginnings. The restoration of this ancient city can provide a metaphor for our lives. We have opportunities in our own daily lives to restore and rebuild ourselves and our community.

For instance, the start of a new grading period at school—a new semester—is a time of restoration, another chance. We have the opportunity to start fresh and get things right. Whatever mistakes we may have made before that, whatever difficulties we may have had, can all be overturned when we start anew. Given another chance, we can make even better grades than before.

We may think that another chance is given to us only once in a while, or only if we're lucky. This is not true; we're given another chance daily. Have you had a difficult relationship with someone? Have you had a relationship that "went sour"? Have you had to deal with an adversary? All of these situations can be made better. Just as Ezra called for the people of Israel to renew their commitment to God, so, too, can you rebuild and restart your life. ■

The Book of Malachi describes dismal conditions: people who view worship of God as a burden, men who have divorced their Jewish wives to marry rich non-Jewish women. Similarly, in the Book of Haggai, poverty is widespread, and rich people care only about themselves. There is a clear need for reform.

Our world today has its share of problems, such as poverty, hunger, war, disease, and prejudice. As in the time of the prophets, there is a need for reform. The Church's role is clear: to show love for all of God's people and to help them live in a just and peaceful society. The life of Saint Rose Philippine Duchesne provides us with a poignant example of such compassion and dedication to improve the lives of others.

The Jewish word *anawim* means "little ones" or "forgotten ones." It is used to refer to people in need, such as widows, orphans, and those who are poor. The Church today continues to relieve suffering and provide aid to people in difficult circumstances, such as those who are poor, homeless, lonely, or the victims of injustice. In many ways you have the opportunity to do your part to serve others in God.

HOW CAN I HELP?

It may be overwhelming to think, I've got to solve the world's problems. And no one can do this alone. The problems are large and require time and the cooperation of others to solve. You can only do your part to the best of your ability. When Nehemiah began to rebuild the city of Jerusalem, he did not do it alone. He had a crew of volunteers and workers who, together, completed the work. Each person made his or her own personal effort, and as a whole the group was successful. You can do the same.

Think about where you live. What situations could you and other Christians make better in your community? The opening story provides the example of working at a homeless shelter, serving lunch to people who are poor and hungry. Are there any hospitals or homeless shelters nearby where you might be able to volunteer your time or services? Perhaps you live near a care center where the elderly could use your good company. You may be able to brighten an older person's day by just being there to listen and offer encouragement. In your own school, there may be an individual or small group of students who might need your help as a tutor. Can you join or establish a "service club" for your school? ■

JouRNaL

What can you personally do to help restore society?

GOD'S PROMISES OF PEACE AND SALVATION

While the world has its share of problems and we must do our part to help solve them, it is also important to look forward to the future. We must stay focused on our faith and look ahead to God's promises of peace and salvation. Just as God answers the Jews' plea for forgiveness and help, as Third Isaiah tells us, God will always be with you as you claim the future.

For Review

1. List some of the major problems today's world faces.

2. Who are the anawim of today?

For Discussion

In your opinion, what is the most significant problem in the modern world? Why do you think so? What makes this problem worse than other problems?

Activity

Conduct research in newspapers, magazines, and on the Internet. Research at least five problems in the world and ways in which people are trying to solve them. Clip out all the articles and paste them on a poster board. Place the problems on the left and the solutions or efforts on the right.

Summary

The prophets worked to preserve the tradition of their people. The stories of Ezra, Nehemiah, Haggai, Zechariah, and Malachi helped to restore and renew Israel as a religious community, not as a nation. The people had become scattered and had strayed from their traditions and commitment to God. Rebuilding the temple was a significant event in attempting to restore their spirituality and fidelity to God.

In a sense, the return from exile and the movement to the diaspora continue today. For Jews around the world, preserving their tradition comes through faithfulness to the covenant. Christians also strive together to maintain their faith and covenant with God. Each of us is given challenges and further chances in life to fulfill our roles and responsibilities to our families and communities—our world—and to God.

The LORD is my rock, my fortress, and my deliverer,
  my God, my rock in whom I take refuge,
    my shield, and the horn of my salvation, my stronghold.
I call upon the LORD, who is worthy to be praised,
  so I shall be saved from my enemies.

Psalm 18:2–3

With trumpets and the sound of the horn
    make a joyful noise before the King, the LORD.
Let the sea roar, and all that fills it;
    the world and those who live in it.
Let the floods clap their hands;
    let the hills sing together for joy
at the presence of the LORD, for he is coming
    to judge the earth.
He will judge the world with righteousness,
    and the peoples with equity.

Psalm 98:6–9

Events at the Time of the Struggle for Jewish Independence

221 B.C.

Ch'in Shih Huang-ti is first
emperor to unify China

C. 180–140 B.C.

Mayan game Pok-ta-pok played on
I-shaped court with rubber ball

262 B.C.

Mauryan Emperor Asoka reorganizes
India and builds monuments to Buddha

C. 220 B.C.

Nazca People (of Peru) excel at
textiles, weaving, and pottery

C. 168 B.C.

Maccabees begin their revolt
against the Greeks

CHAPTER 10

A Future Built on Promise

CHAPTER GOALS

Increase knowledge of the meaning of the Old Testament and deepen understanding of its value by studying the following:

- literary characteristics of speeches, legends, fairy tales, folktales, and irony
- the Hellenistic Age and the Hasmonean dynasty
- God's providence in the lives of the faithful
- role of missionaries in evangelization

CHAPTER OUTLINE

Literary Interpretation: Moralistic Narratives

Historical Interpretation: Struggle for Independence

Theological Interpretation: Faith and Providence

Witness: Francis Xavier

Personal Challenge: Missionary Work

Summary

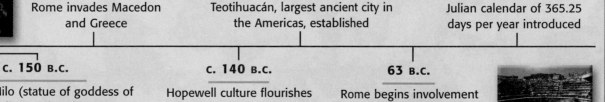

146 B.C.
Rome invades Macedon and Greece

c. 100–60 B.C
Teotihuacán, largest ancient city in the Americas, established

45 B.C.
Julian calendar of 365.25 days per year introduced

c. 150 B.C.
Venus de Milo (statue of goddess of love, Aphrodite) sculpted in Greece

c. 140 B.C.
Hopewell culture flourishes in Ohio

63 B.C.
Rome begins involvement in Palestine

You are at your friend's house after school one day to work together on a project. The batteries are dead in the tape recorder you need for the project, so your friend suggests that you walk together to the drug store to buy new ones.

At the drug store you walk down one of the aisles, and there you see some birth control products. It starts to make you think: You know that the Catholic Church is against artificial birth control, yet here in the United States, birth control products are legal. And then there's the issue of abortion; the Church takes a strong stand against it, while the nation's laws permit it. How, you ask, can I live in a nation whose laws conflict with the teachings of the Catholic Church? You grapple with the problem, wondering how the laws of Church and country can apply to you simultaneously. You wonder which one is the right one.

Once you and your friend have the batteries, you walk to the cash register to purchase them. There you see cigarettes and tobacco for sale. You realize that there are many things in this country and this world that can tempt you—alcohol, cigarettes, and over-the-counter drugs that can be used for unintended purposes.

You come to realize that the fact that something is legal or accepted by a group of people doesn't mean it's right for you or even morally right for anyone. The society that you live in is made up of many different kinds of people who all make different choices.

By the time you and your friend are back at the house working on the project, you have a deeper understanding of the relationship between national laws and Church laws.

Keep this story in mind as we study the Books of Maccabees, Daniel, Tobit, and Judith. God's people often use God's laws to measure the laws of a nation or a ruler.

Literary Interpretation

Faith Sharing

Three times this week, consider the various factors that go into your decision making.

- Whose advice should you follow?
- How can you be certain that you are living according to what Jesus taught?
- What can you do to stay on the right path?

The books toward the end of the Old Testament offer commentary on the conditions during the last centuries before Christ. The writers of these books focus on God's plan for his people and sometimes emphasize hope for the coming messiah. They envision a future built on promise. The opening story provides a reminder that in times of conflict, or when faced with a moral dilemma, it is crucial for us to remain focused on God and his promise. The Jews of ancient times had that same struggle. ■

Apocalyptic Symbolism

In Chapter 9 we looked at the apocalyptic visions in the Books of Zechariah and Joel. However, the Old Testament book best known for its apocalyptic symbolism is the Book of Daniel. The book is made up of six stories (chapters 1–6) and four dream-visions (chapters 7–12), followed by a collection of short stories (chapters 13–14). Revelations of the end times are received by Daniel and are explained to him by an angel. As we learned in Chapter 9, this is a common characteristic of the apocalyptic genre. ■

Activity

Oppressed groups have often identified with biblical figures who were delivered from adversity by an act of God. Listen to a recording of "Didn't My Lord Deliver Daniel?" (or read the lyrics together as a class if a recording is not available). How does this African American spiritual convey the message that God will provide deliverance for all who are downtrodden?

According to the story, Daniel was thrown into a lions' den twice and was saved by his faith in God both times.

LEGEND CYCLE

legend an unverifiable story that is passed down from generation to generation and accepted as true or partly true

JouRNaL

Describe a time in your life when you had to cling to your faith in the face of adversity. How was God there for you in your struggle?

Read Tobit 1:1–3:6.

The **legends** in the Book of Daniel are primarily centered on a character named Daniel and his companions. These narratives form a legend cycle, a pattern in which a religious figure is confronted with temptation but remains faithful to God and is delivered from danger. This cycle was most likely developed in an oral form before being written down. The stories tell of Daniel's legendary skill at interpreting dreams (chapter 2); Shadrach, Meshach, and Abednego in the fiery furnace (chapter 3); the writing on the wall (chapter 5); and Daniel in the lions' den (chapter 6, verses 16–24 and chapter 14, verses 28–42). In the story of Susanna, the legend cycle is seen in the life of a devout woman who is saved by Daniel (chapter 13). ■

MORALISTIC FAIRY TALE

The Book of Tobit is often classified as a fairy tale, due to the progression of events within the story and its happy ending. The book provides interesting information about life in ancient times. The story's characters are fully developed through monologues and dialogues, which give the reader insight into their thoughts and emotions throughout the narrative. In addition, the story often is classified as moralistic because it is filled with prayers and hymns, wisdom sayings, and concepts from angelology (study of angels). ■

JouRNaL

Have you ever felt as if you were being punished for doing something good? Were you eventually rewarded in some way for your action?

Read Tobit 3:7–8:21.

FOLKTALES

The Book of Tobit revolves around secular folktales. The first is the story of the Demon-Lover (also known as the Monster in the Bedchamber) and the Dangerous Bride. With this story, an evil creature is in love with a beautiful woman and kills her husband on their wedding night. A version of this folktale is also found in the Indian epic called *Ramayana*. This epic tells the tale of a brave young man named Rama and his beautiful bride, Sita. Soon after their wedding, Sita is carried off by the demon-king Ravana, and the heroic Rama must rescue his beloved. The occurrence of this folktale across different cultures shows us that it was part of a secular oral tradition prior to being incorporated into various written works.

A second folktale within the Book of Tobit is the tale of the Grateful Dead: A man is first impoverished, then rewarded, for burying an abused corpse. Using widely recognized, secular folktales helped the writers of Tobit capture the interest of their audience, thereby enabling them to deliver an important moral lesson.

There are other ways to look at the book. Tobit is presented as a comic character, thus chiding those who are rigid in their piety. The book uses symbolic names as well: Raphael means "God heals"; Tobiah means "God is good."

The Indian epic Ramayana, *like the Book of Tobit, is built around the folktale of the Demon-Lover and the Dangerous Bride.*

Ironic Folktale

irony contradiction between an expectation and the actual occurrence

Read Judith 8.

There is a great deal of situational **irony** in the Book of Judith, which is often classified as a folktale. The story of Judith is the tale of an unlikely heroine who overcomes her fears and defeats a powerful enemy of her people. The first point of irony in the story is that a woman, rather than a man, saves Judah. This was ironic within the patriarchal and sexist society of Judah. Judith is a particularly unlikely heroine in that she is a childless widow and, therefore, has low standing. It is also ironic that Judith defeats Holofernes not with military prowess, as would be expected, but with her beauty and charm. She wields her beauty as a weapon and destroys the enemy. ■

JouRnaL

Have you ever been in a situation that struck you as ironic? Describe the situation and explain its irony.

Read 1 Maccabees 13:3–6.

NARRATIVE STYLE OF MACCABEES

The two books of Maccabees are filled with elaborate speeches, persuasive arguments, and other types of commentary on events in Israel's history. Like the Deuteronomic History, Maccabees focuses on the theological significance of historical events. The books tell the story of a family and the role they played in bringing about Jewish independence.

An example of the elaborate speeches used in Maccabees can be found in the stirring speech Simon delivers in 1 Maccabees 13:3–6, inspiring the people to elect him as their ruler. He passionately reminds the people of his proven dedication to the laws and the sanctuary and that all his brothers have perished for the sake of Israel. ■

The author of 2 Maccabees places emphasis on holiness, on the fact that God defends his temple, and on other religious matters. Because of this emphasis, 2 Maccabees is sometimes described as "temple propaganda." It also tends to be less precise and less reliable for historical facts than 1 Maccabees; numbers tend to be inflated and events are exaggerated to have more of an emotional appeal. The second book also focuses more on individual stories of heroism rather than the larger historical events.

OpeNING THE WoRD

Read 1 Maccabees 4:52–59. Then read 2 Maccabees 1:2–2:18. This festival is known today as the Jewish feast of Hanukkah. Why do you think it was important for the people to observe this feast?

For Review

1. What is the legend cycle within the stories of Daniel?

2. Name two folktales that are incorporated within the Book of Tobit.

3. Why is the story of Judith ironic?

For Discussion

Think of a situation in which world leaders might either exaggerate or downplay certain statistics. What would the intention be for altering the numbers?

Activity

Examine the similarities between a secular legend, folktale, or fairy tale of your choice and a story told in Daniel, Tobit, or Judith. Organize these similarities in a chart.

The Struggle for Jewish Independence

As noted in preceding chapters, world events outside of Palestine often had a direct impact on the historical events of Jewish history. Jewish independence was a direct result of power struggles in the ancient Near East that came closer and closer to home for the Jews. Finally, the events literally came so close to the center of the Jews' religion, the temple, that the only choice for some Jews was rebellion against the ruling power of the day. One story of rebellion is told in 1 and 2 Maccabees.

The stage was set for the rebellion in the fourth century B.C. by Alexander the Great who, as a lover of all things Greek, hellenized the ancient Near East. The Jews, individually and as a community, had to make difficult decisions when the rules of the governing powers were not in agreement with God's law, much like the situation in the opening story.

Alexander the Great

Philip of Macedon had unified the warring Greek city-states. This was quite an accomplishment, since he was an outsider from Macedon, especially since Macedon was a less-civilized country north of Greece. Philip's son, Alexander, inherited his father's military skill and his mother's belief that because he was a descendant of the Greek war hero, Achilles, he was destined for a divine mission. The Greek philosopher Aristotle was Alexander's tutor, and this instilled in him a greater appreciation of Greek, or Hellenic, thought and its way of life.

Greek concert halls, such as this one in Turkey, were built near the market.

With the assassination of Philip of Macedon, Alexander inherited the throne in 336 B.C., at the age of twenty. Alexander, who had served in the field under his father, began his conquests with vengeance on his mind. He had 35,000 Macedonian and Greek soldiers and wanted to punish the Persians for their invasion of Greece almost a century and a half before he was born. Alexander defeated the Persian army in three major battles and quickly took hold of Syria, Palestine, Egypt, and Asia Minor—the lands dominated by the Persian empire. With his troops he pushed east beyond the Indus River. As the East and West became unified, trade centered in the East and flowed easily. This was due in part to Alexander having issued a standard coinage. Alexander created about seventy cities, settling them with his military and administrative personnel and their families, many of whom were Greek. In so doing, Alexander began the hellenization of the ancient world.

After Alexander died unexpectedly in 323 B.C. at the age of thirty-two, his heirs and generals fought for control of the empire. Eventually three of his generals divided it into three kingdoms.

THE SELEUCID AND PTOLEMAIC EMPIRES

Ptolemy, a Greek general, eventually won control of Egypt and with it the former Israelite kingdoms. Ptolemy allowed the Jews to pursue their religion without much interference. By this time, Egypt had become well populated with Jews, who began to use the Greek language politically and socially as well as commercially. The fact that during this time the Scriptures were translated into Greek (the translation referred to as the Septuagint), shows the predominance of the language. Some Jews, however, did not agree with this hellenization of the Scriptures and with the inclusion of books not in the existing Jewish canon, some of which were originally written in Greek.

Around 200 B.C. a Seleucid ruler, Antiochus III, turned his attention toward Egypt and Palestine and won control of the region away from Ptolemy. Under Antiochus, who dealt fairly with the Jews, the temple was given a government subsidy, and its personnel were exempt from taxes. Most importantly, Antiochus III issued an edict that proclaimed that the Jews were allowed to live in accordance with their law. The books that come from this part of the Hellenistic period (Esther, Tobit, Daniel 1–6) often deal with problems that could occur under the rule of outsiders, with happy endings for Jews who stay faithful to their traditions. This changes with the later persecution.

Unfortunately for the Jews, Antiochus III dared to take control of a part of Greece that was under Roman domination. At this time, Rome was emerging as a new superpower. The Romans chased Antiochus III back to Asia and forced him to yield all of Asia Minor to them, provide hostages, including one of his sons (Antiochus IV), and pay Rome a large sum of money. The sum was so large that Antiochus III raided temples to pay the Romans. In 168 B.C. Antiochus III was succeeded by Antiochus IV, who came to play a major role in the religious crisis for the Jews that led to their rebellion.

1 and 2 Maccabees provide the basis for the Jewish feast of Hanukkah.

ANTIOCHUS IV SETS THE STAGE FOR REBELLION

Upon returning from his time as a hostage in Rome, Antiochus IV found that his kingdom was on shaky ground. The Ptolemaic king in Egypt was prepared to fight to regain control of Palestine and the coastal trade region of Phoenicia. The Romans were looming on the horizon in Greece, and Antiochus IV knew firsthand what the Romans were capable of doing. He decided it was time to unify his people as a preparation for facing these threats. The way to unify them was to enforce a more Hellenic way of life. Antiochus IV "sent an Athenian senator to compel the Jews to forsake the laws of their ancestors and no longer to live by the laws of God" (2 Maccabees 6:1).

The Hellenic way of life Antiochus wanted the Jews to adopt differed greatly from their way of life. While the Jews were monotheistic, the Greeks were polytheistic. The Greek gods had good and bad human attributes, statues and idols could represent them, cities built temples in the gods' and goddesses' names, and sacrifices were made in their honor. Central to the Greek way of life was the gymnasium, and a gymnasium was established in Jerusalem.

In ancient Greece, the gymnasium was a public institution where training for public competition occurred, as did the teaching of philosophy, literature, and music. The gymnasium was dedicated to the Greek gods Hercules and Hermes. For Jewish men to participate in athletics in the gymnasium was to openly admit to a belief in Hercules and Hermes. They were calling into question the very thing that made them Jewish—their monotheistic belief. While some Jews did participate in the athletics in the gymnasium, many refused to do so. ■

Antiochus IV went even further in his disrespect of the Jews. To further his cause of hellenization, he put into place a royal commissioner to help the high priest (of the Greek religion). The commissioner treated Jerusalem as an adversary and built a citadel in the vicinity of the Jewish temple. A colony of hellenized polytheists occupied the citadel, and, as a result, the temple became a Greek shrine. Zeus, the major Greek god, was to be worshiped alongside the God of the Jews. While many Jews were deeply offended, many others went along with the edict. In 1 Maccabees 1:43 we are told: "All the Gentiles accepted the command of the king. Many even from Israel gladly adopted his religion; they sacrificed to idols and profaned the sabbath." As a result of Jewish resistance to this change, Antiochus IV annulled his father's earlier concessions to the Jews.

Journal

Have you ever been pressured to participate in something with which you did not agree? How did you handle the situation? If you refused, how did the people pressuring you respond?

THE FIGHT FOR INDEPENDENCE

OPENING THE
WORD

Read 1 Maccabees
3 and 4. How
would you describe
Judas as a leader?
Cite specific verses
to support your answer.

A Jewish family of priestly descent—a man named Mattathias and his sons—led a rebellion in response to Antiochus IV's decrees. They encouraged other Jews who believed in God and his law to join them. They waged guerrilla warfare against Antiochus IV's followers and the Jews who had joined them. After Mattathias's death, his third son, Judas Maccabee, turned the rebellion into a full scale struggle for Jewish independence. With Judas's repeated successes against the Seleucid generals, more Jews joined the cause for independence.

Judas eventually marched into Jerusalem, reclaimed and cleansed the temple, and restored the priests who had remained faithful. After the temple was cleansed, it was rededicated. The feast of Hanukkah is a celebration of this historic event. ▧

THE HASMONEAN DYNASTY

The descendants of the Maccabee family came to be known as the Hasmonean dynasty. Its members began their rule in 142 B.C. The triumph by Judas allowed the Jews to be politically independent after centuries of subjection to Persian and then Greek rule. His was the first in a long line of successes in which the people of the dynasty continually fought for and won the right to practice their ancestral religion. The result was an independent and influential Jewish Palestine that was recognized in treaties with Sparta and Rome. The success came to an end when the Romans started to intervene in Palestinian politics about 63 B.C. Two branches of the Hasmonean dynasty quarreled, and the Romans put Herod, who was half Jewish, into office as governor of Palestine.

For Review

1. How did Alexander the Great spread the Hellenic way of life into the lands he conquered?

2. What does the Septuagint signify about Egypt at the time it was written?

3. Why did Antiochus IV try to unify his people? How did he do this?

For Discussion

Greek became the common language of the ancient world. Discuss the advantages and disadvantages of people using a common language other than their native tongue.

Activity

Look up the word *macabre* in the dictionary. Linguists have noted that this word shares the same root as *Maccabees*. How do you think the definition of *macabre* reflects the content of 1 and 2 Maccabees? Cite Scripture to support your assertions.

With the persecution of Antiochus IV, there was a change in the response of the Jews to outside rule. The optimistic approach of the earlier books no longer seemed believable. The persecution brought two responses: armed revolt (Maccabees) and the prediction of a dramatic divine intervention without the need to take up arms (the apocalyptic visions in Daniel 7–14). Each response may be appropriate in different circumstances.

DANIEL

OPENING THE WORD

Read Daniel 13:28, 51–62 and 14:10–22. How are these two stories similar to detective novels?

Read Daniel 3:1–30.

JOURNAL

Write about an instance when you took a stand for something despite the possible consequences. Did you have friends supporting you in this? How did that help?

The legends in Daniel are presented to relay a spiritual message. Each is a depiction of the lifestyles of Jewish exiles in Babylon. Daniel's message was one of hope, with clear delineation of the boundaries necessary to live as a Jew in a non-Jewish world. Each story stresses the need to stay faithful to the Jewish traditions and law despite the demands of the Babylonian culture.

In chapter one, Daniel and his companions are servants to the Babylonian king and are trained in the Babylonian language and literature. They willingly participate and actively excel at these studies. They do not refuse nor ask for special treatment or exemptions, but also remain true to their faith without compromising. Shadrach, Meshach, and Abednego stand together in their dedication to God and unequivocally refuse to bow down to Nebuchadnezzar's golden idol. The three heroes of the story clearly state in Daniel 3:17–18 that they are prepared to die for their faith. ■ ■

This mosaic from a monastery church in Greece portrays the three young men in the fiery furnace protected by an angel of God.

According to the story, God protected Daniel in the lions' den. Painting of "Daniel in the Lion's Den" is by Austrian artist Adrian Kupman (1910).

Daniel's superior ability in interpreting the king's dreams was a God-given gift. Daniel refused to take the many perks offered for his gift of interpretation, but he agreed to interpret the writing the king saw on the wall (Daniel 5:5, 17). He did not compromise his integrity by being paid; this purity allowed him to tell the truth without qualms.

The story of Daniel's sojourn with the lions helps readers understand the political climate. Because Daniel had many adversaries striving for his position, King Darius was tricked into putting Daniel in with the lions. Daniel defied the king's law by praying faithfully and openly three times a day (Daniel 6:10–11). To have hidden his praying would have shown fear.

Clearly, Daniel's is a message of obedience and courageous loyalty to God's law. King Darius's parting words to Daniel as he is lowered into the den are evidence of Daniel's strong impact on him: "May your God, whom you faithfully serve, deliver you!" (Daniel 6:16); Daniel's integrity had not gone unnoticed. The king's relief at finding Daniel still alive the following day shows the fondness King Darius held for Daniel, and the event also led to the king's decree, recorded in Daniel 6:26–27. Daniel's daily life and actions were testimony to the power of God. Regardless of the governing political system, God is in control and all will resolve itself in his time. Believing this, we trust in his providence. ■

In the numerous visions that Daniel interprets for the king are symbols of God's justice and righteousness. Daniel and his friends give strong evidence to the power behind prayerful faithfulness to God's law.

A unique feature of Daniel is that it is the only book of the Hebrew Bible that clearly affirms resurrection for the individual (Daniel 12:2–3). (The belief is also found in 2 Maccabees 7, but this book is not included in the Hebrew Bible, that is, the Old Testament portion of the Bible accepted by Jews and Protestants.) Other books speak of restoration for the nation, but the Book of Daniel asserts that individuals will be resurrected.

Read Daniel 5.

ActiviTy

Research the Columbine High School shootings that took place in 1999. Look particularly for accounts of how Christians at the scene responded. Check Christian book and magazine sources, as well as the Internet. How does the faith of these teens compare to that of Daniel?

Read Tobit 3:1–6
and 3:10–15. How
are the responses
of Tobit and Sarah
to their personal
suffering similar?

JOURNAL

Have you ever felt
overwhelmed
by a life situation?
Write about the
incident, your feelings, and
how you coped.

Read Tobit 4:12–21, 8:5–8.

JOURNAL

Have you ever
surrendered a
problem to God?
If so, how did
you feel? From whom do you
seek support when dealing
with your problems? How
does that help?

*The Venetian artist Giorgio
Giorgione (c. 1477–1510)
captures the strength and
beauty of the heroine Judith.*

TOBIT

Tobit is a fairy tale of two people who are faithful yet unjustly suffer through difficult life situations. Tobit and Sarah pray, fast, and give to people who are poor. Yet Tobit becomes blind while performing an act of mercy, and Sarah is widowed seven times. ■ ■

The prayers of Tobit and Sarah were a final surrender to God. It is at this juncture that the solution to their struggles begins to manifest itself. The solution comes from God through another person, Tobias. Once they prayed, they saw who to ask for help. ■

According to the story, answers come to Tobit and Sarah through the intervention of an angel. On the other hand, Sarah's plight, her husbands' deaths, are the result of a demon. These images represent a clear conflict between good and evil. Raphael acts as the mediator at God's throne to bring about deliverance from persecution for Sarah and Tobit. They, like Daniel, remain true to their faith and continue in obedience despite mistreatment.

Tobit's counsel to his son was the counsel of a Jew living in a hostile culture. His admonishment to marry only within the faith echoed the admonitions of many prophets before him. The history of Israel is ripe with evidence of the folly of watering down the Jewish faith. Tobit's message is a strong call to the community to maintain their faith.

Tobit and Sarah prayed for protection, in praise and in thanksgiving, and their deliverance increased their dedication to God and their obedience to his covenant. This Scripture passage is an available option for use in wedding ceremonies.

JUDITH

Judith's heroism in saving Judah from the wrath of Nebuchadnezzar is another example of an individual using her wit and particular gifts to bring about God's victory. The name *Judith* means "Jewish woman," so the folktale of Judith commemorates all women of faith who are pivotal in carrying out the Lord's plan. Because she is a childless widow, Judith remains on the bottom rung of the ladder of Jewish social hierarchy. Yet she is God's chosen instrument for the rescue of his people. Her ironic weapons of wit, feminine wile, courage, and strength are clearly God's choice for this particular job at hand.

Read Judith 16.

JourNaL

Write a gratitude list of all the accomplishments or victories you and your family have experienced. Include stories of success and God's providence that your ancestors, as well as your immediate family, have encountered. Title your list "Great Things God Has Done," and use it as a prayer of praise to God.

JourNaL

Based on your research on the Columbine shootings, how do you think the Christian students' understanding of resurrection impacted their actions during the ordeal?

Judith's wisdom was readily acknowledged by Uzziah. Judith knew what her gifts were and prayed that God would bless her mission. In the male-dominated society portrayed in the Book of Judith, a woman's primary and strongest weapon was her beauty. In that sense, Judith put on her full armor, sparing neither perfume, jewelry, nor finery, and had her maid carry an extravagant meal along. With these tools, and with the drunken state of Nebuchadnezzar's chief general, Judith successfully defeated him and preserved her chastity as well. God was clearly at work, proving that he will free his people if they obey him and rely on his covenant.

While the priests and elders were content to pray and surrender to Holofernes, Judith prayed and was led to action. Like Tobit and Sarah, Judith did more than admit powerlessness. And, like Daniel, she actively resisted the assault on her faith. ■

1 AND 2 MACCABEES

Maccabee means "hammer," and this was the nickname of Judas Maccabeus, the leader of the revolt against Antiochus. Both 1 and 2 Maccabees describe the military response to Seleucid persecution of the Jews. Like Judith, three generations of the Maccabee family worked to free the Jews in God's name. Judas is presented as the ideal Jewish warrior, praying before and after battle and honoring Jewish rituals.

Antiochus's institution of an altar to Zeus within the Jewish temple was unacceptable and blasphemous to the Maccabees. As a result, they used guerrilla warfare against Antiochus, employing the gifts of wisdom and quick thinking, as had Judith. The sanctity of the temple was fiercely defended, and Antiochus was ousted. The stories in 2 Maccabees affirm the role of martyrs in the restoration of Israel and include the incentive of resurrection for those who die for their faith (2 Maccabees 7:9, 14, 23; 14:46). With the same spiritual fortitude as Daniel, the Maccabees died in protecting the Torah. ■

For REVIEW

1. What did Nebuchadnezzar see when he looked in the furnace?

2. Why did Daniel continue to openly pray when he knew that it was against the king's law?

3. What did Judith accuse Uzziah and the leaders of doing to God?

4. What act of Antiochus inflamed Judas Maccabee into action?

For DISCUSSION

Using the examples of the daily faith of Daniel, Tobit, Judith, and the Maccabees, what are the key steps to living a life of integrity? How can we spread the news about God's salvation? How can our leaders?

Francis Xavier

Patron of Foreign Missions

Knowing the right path to take can sometimes be difficult. Saint Francis Xavier's path led him across the world to do great missionary work. He was a prophet of multiculturalism and believed strongly in the importance of serving God through missions to far-off countries.

Francis was born at the castle of Xavier in Navarre, Spain, in 1506. In the early 1530s, while studying at the University of Paris, he met a Spanish ascetic named Ignatius of Loyola. Francis became one of the original six young men who joined with Ignatius to form the Society of Jesus, the Jesuits, in 1534. Francis was ordained a priest in 1537.

In 1541, Francis was named the apostolic nuncio to Asia, giving him the freedom and responsibility to do missionary work there. At the request of Portugal's king, Francis immediately set off for Goa, a section of India controlled by Portugal. He arrived after a perilous thirteen-month voyage. Francis thus became the first Jesuit missionary.

Christianity had already been established in Goa, but the Church was poorly run and in bad shape. With Goa as his base, Francis traveled down the coast of India and to islands in southern Asia, immersing himself in the local language in order to communicate the good news of Jesus to the people. He converted many individuals through his preaching, mostly people from the poor lower castes.

As he continued his missionary work, Francis heard many reports of the highly advanced kingdom of Japan. He was determined to make the place his next mission and arrived there on August 15, 1549. At the time, Japan was going through a period of political instability, so it was easy for people from other countries to enter. As he settled in, Francis was impressed with the sophistication of the Japanese culture.

Saint Francis Xavier, the first Jesuit missionary, set an example of appreciating other cultures and showing proper respect toward those individuals he hoped to convert to Christianity.

Francis's work with the Japanese helped him develop a new approach to missionary work. He realized the need to understand the local culture, comprehend its inherent strengths and virtues, and find ways to make connections to the gospel message. By being a cultural observer and tapping into, rather than subjugating, the practices of other peoples, Francis can be considered a prophet of cross-culturalism.

After Japan, Francis set his sights on an even more challenging frontier, China, which at the time was closed to people from other nations. Francis felt compelled to go, eager to minister in this virtually unknown land. In 1552, after numerous attempts to travel there, Francis finally found a ship willing to transport him to China. With his dream about to be realized, he became seriously ill, was taken off the ship, and was placed on an island off the coast of China. There his health deteriorated, and he died at the age of forty-six. His dream of ministering to the people in China was unfulfilled. Francis Xavier was canonized a saint in 1622, and in 1927 he was named patron of missions to other countries.

Missionary Work

evangelization giving witness to one's faith by proclaiming the good news of Jesus Christ to the world through words and actions

A missionary is a person who devotes his or her life to **evangelization** and service. Missionaries work in home missions or missions in other lands. In addition to evangelization, missionaries work to improve education, medical care, employment, and agricultural methods, and to provide help during natural disasters such as earthquakes, floods, famines, and storms.

Christian missionary activity began nearly 2,000 years ago. Enthusiastic missionary work by Saint Peter, Saint Paul, and others led to the rapid spread of Christianity. The faith had spread throughout the Roman Empire and to North Africa by 300 A.D. By the Middle Ages most of the people of Europe were Christian. The next far-flung missionary work occurred in the 1500s, when Catholic missionaries began to travel with European soldiers and explorers to Africa, Asia, and the Americas. It was at this time that Saint Francis Xavier began his important trip to Asia.

Catholicism in the United States would not have developed so quickly and so well without the work of men and women missionaries. Many Catholic missionaries in the world today come from the United States and travel to Asia, Africa, Latin America, and many Pacific Islands. Missionaries today use modern technology and scientific knowledge to help the people they serve, and they cooperate with the local churches. Missionaries share their faith, but do not impose it. ■

Although there are missionaries all over the world doing the work that needs to be done, there are never enough. But our own society also has many problems and people in need. You can do God's work in another land or right in your hometown. ■

Activity

Use the Internet to find out how many Christian missionaries were martyred in the last year.

Journal

Would you like to be a missionary to another country? Why or why not?

From the beginning of Christianity, missionaries have taken the gospel to far-flung parts of the world. With what missionary work are you familiar?

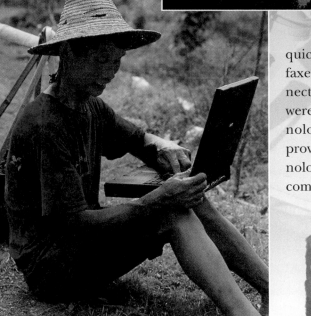

Christians today use many types of technology to help communicate the gospel.

COMMUNICATING YOUR FAITH

As you learned in Chapter 9, the community of Jews scattered outside Israel came to be known as the Diaspora. The Jews of the Diaspora had very limited methods of communication or mutual support. It was difficult for them to stay united and remain in contact with each other.

Today modern technology allows us to communicate quickly and easily. With telephones, teleconferencing, faxes, and E-mail, people across the world can stay connected. Imagine if you and a community of 1,000 Christians were scattered across the world today. With modern technology available, you could easily communicate and provide support for one another. Communications technology can be a powerful resource within the Christian community worldwide. ■

JOURNAL

How can you utilize modern communications technology to help others? In what ways could you use it to help spread God's word?

For REVIEW

1. In what ways do missionaries provide for the needs of the people they are evangelizing?

2. To what parts of the world do missionaries travel?

3. What methods of communication do we have today that were unavailable to the Jews of the Diaspora?

For DISCUSSION

Some native people have objected to missionaries in their countries because missionaries have, at times, believed European or North American culture to be superior to the native culture and tried to change local customs. Should missionaries always accept native cultures as they are, or are there instances when some change is good? Support your opinion.

ACTIVITY

Request information from your local parish about missionaries who travel to other countries. What problems do they attempt to help solve? What obstacles do missionaries encounter? What are the statistics on individuals converted to Catholic Christianity through missionary work?

The Jews of the ancient Near East faced many challenges, but they remained true to their faith in the promise of God. While under Persian and Greek control, the Jews endured great hardships. By living according to their faith and acting against the laws of the governing body that contradicted their religious laws, the Jews placed themselves in a position of potential martyrdom—they risked dying for their beliefs.

As the opening story suggests, Christians today must continue to critique national laws in the light of Church teaching. Following God's law is not always the popular thing to do. While it is unlikely that anyone today will throw us into a lions' den or fiery furnace as punishment for adhering to our faith, we may at times find ourselves persecuted in other ways. We can find support for our personal struggles by reading in the Scriptures about the challenges faced by God's people over the centuries.

I will give thanks to you, O LORD, among the peoples,
and I will sing praises to you among the nations.
For your steadfast love is higher than the heavens,
and your faithfulness reaches to the clouds.

Psalm 108:3–4

Let my cry come before you, O LORD;
   give me understanding according to your word.
Let my supplication come before you;
   deliver me according to your promise.

Psalm 119:169–170

Timeline of Wisdom Literature

c. 1290–1250 B.C.
The Exodus

1000–600 B.C.
Egyptian *Instruction of Amen-em-opet* written

2000–1000 B.C.
Egyptian and Mesopotamian wisdom literature flourishes, including Babylonian poem resembling Book of Job

c. 1000–961 B.C.
Reign of King David

961–922 B.C.
Reign of King Solomon

CHAPTER 11

The Wisdom of Israel

CHAPTER GOALS

Increase knowledge of the meaning of the Old Testament and deepen understanding of its value by studying the following:

- psalms, proverbs, and love poems as literary forms
- structure and significance of the Book of Job
- historical context of wisdom literature
- the development of the Liturgy of the Hours

CHAPTER OUTLINE

Literary Interpretation: Wisdom Literature

Historical Interpretation: Wisdom in the Ancient Near East

Theological Interpretation: Liturgy of the Hours

Witness: Thomas Merton

Personal Challenge: Worshiping in Community

Summary

600–400 B.C.
Book of Job composed

500–400 B.C.
Proverbs compiled into its final form

c. 180 B.C.
Book of Sirach (Ecclesiasticus) composed

587–539 B.C.
Exile of Jews in Babylon

c. 450–400 B.C.
Song of Songs edited into its final form

300–200 B.C.
Book of Ecclesiastes (Qoheleth) written

One day during math class, a friend of yours receives a message to gather her things and report to the school office. She looks perplexed but does as she is told. She doesn't come back to class, and you don't see her later in the day in your science class either. She doesn't even show up for track practice after school. You begin to get worried. When you get home from practice, you call her to find out if everything is okay. The phone rings multiple times before she picks up the phone and says very quietly, "Hello?"

You ask her what happened, and she tearfully explains that her father has died in a train collision. He was on his way home from a business trip. She keeps repeating, "How could this have happened? Why him? Why did it have to be my dad?" You find yourself at a loss, not knowing how to comfort her. All you can say is how sorry you are for her loss. After collecting herself, she thanks you for calling, but says that she really doesn't want to talk about it right now.

After you hang up the phone, you can't stop thinking about what you have just heard. Your friend is one of the nicest, most caring people you have ever met. Of all the people in the world, why did this have to happen to her? How could God take away her father and make her suffer like that? In addition, you know that her father was very involved in community service. He was always putting the needs of others above his own. Why would God allow him to die so young when he could have gone on to do so many good things? Isn't God supposed to protect those who follow him? Isn't he supposed to deliver them from hardship?

Why do bad things happen to good people? Keep this story in mind as you study the wisdom literature of the Old Testament.

Faith Sharing

Faith Sharing

Over the next week, think about the following questions: What positive thing could come out of a person's suffering? How can God use a negative circumstance to bring about something positive? Have you ever seen or heard of something good come out of what was initially a painful circumstance?

Journal

Record three wisdom statements by which you live. At least one should be your own rather than wisdom from someone else. If you can't think of three, scan the Book of Proverbs for appropriate sayings.

"David and all the house of Israel were dancing before the LORD with all their might, with songs and lyres and harps and tambourines and castanets and cymbals."

2 Samuel 6:5

The opening story poses a question: Why do bad things happen to good people? This question appears in many forms throughout wisdom literature as people try to understand events in their lives. The writers of wisdom literature question the necessity of suffering, and they sometimes cannot find an answer. But they also place their faith in the providence and wisdom of God and praise him for his deliverance and guidance. ■

Wisdom Literature

The wisdom literature of the Old Testament provides a commentary on the faith of Israel. Wisdom literature generally asserts that wisdom leads to prosperity and folly leads to destruction. This type of literature uses examples from daily life and teaches readers how to cope with everyday struggles. While wisdom instruction appears throughout the Old Testament, it is more highly concentrated in these texts.

Much of the wisdom literature is attributed to King Solomon, for his name was almost synonymous with wisdom. He prayed to God for wisdom above all other favors, and wisdom is what made Solomon a great leader. Many of the psalms, however, are attributed to King David. Attributing writings to these great leaders in Israel's history was a way of honoring them. Most of the literature was most likely produced by scribes and intellectuals in Israelite society, often in the style and usually in the spirit of the person to whom the writing is attributed. ■

PERSONIFICATION OF WISDOM

Personification is the literary technique by which something nonhuman, such as an object or abstract quality, is described by using human characteristics. For example, justice, good luck, bad luck, death, and time have all been personified in literature. Wisdom is often personified as a female with positive characteristics, thereby emphasizing the desirability and elusive nature of wisdom. The use of the words *her* and *she* in reference to wisdom or knowledge signify the personification. The personification of wisdom appears in the Book of Baruch, the Book of Wisdom, and in Proverbs 1–9.

OPENING THE WORD

Read Baruch 3:9–4:4, Wisdom 7, and Proverbs 8. Create a list of similar concepts and terms used in these personifications of wisdom.

In this icon Sophia (Wisdom) is attended by the virtues of faith, hope, and love. All four are personified as woman.

PROVERBS

The Book of Proverbs is a collection of moral and religious sayings, poems, and warnings, many of which are attributed to King Solomon. **Proverbs** establish strict dichotomies of good and evil, wise and foolish—there are no "gray" areas. Proverbs are usually two lines of parallel thought that offer wisdom, often in a style similar to that of a riddle. These sayings of folk wisdom are of such universal appeal that many have become accepted as figures of speech. You may even recognize some of them. The proverb form is also used in the Books of Sirach and Wisdom and occasionally in the Book of Ecclesiastes.

The Book of Proverbs includes proverbs of comparison, such as Proverbs 11:18, and proverbs of command, such as Proverbs 14:7. Other proverbs are of fact, such as Proverbs 20:12, or of condemnation, such as Proverbs 24:20. Proverbs provide similes, as in Proverbs 26:14, or offer encouragement, as in Proverbs 29:25. Many proverbs are numerical sayings, such as Proverbs 30:15.

OPENING THE WORD

Read the acrostic poem in Proverbs 31:10–31 on the characteristics of a good wife. Compare this portrait to the one found in Sirach 26:1–4.

ACTIVITY

Select ten proverbs—five that you think are useful for life today and five that you feel are no longer clearly applicable. Write one sentence for each proverb you have chosen, defending your choice. Chart your selections and explanations.

ACTIVITY

In a small group read aloud Gerard Manley Hopkins's poem "Pied Beauty" or "God's Grandeur." Discuss how the poem is similar to a psalm.

ACTIVITY

Listen to a recording of a hymn or other choral music based on a psalm. Read along in the Scriptures as you listen.

prologue the introduction preceding a literary work that gives information to help the audience understand the story that follows

epilogue the conclusion to a literary work

PSALMS

The psalm is a literary form that occurs throughout the Old Testament; see, for example, Hannah's prayer in 1 Samuel 2:1–10. The Book of Psalms is a collection of 150 songs and poems that were used in Israelite worship and continue to be used in religious services today. The word *psalm* is derived from the ancient Greek word *psalmoi*, which designates the instrumental music that originally accompanied the lyrics. The psalms are divided into five books, as was the Law of Moses in the Pentateuch. The typical structure of a psalm includes an invocation or praise of God, a description of a particular situation, and an affirmation of God's power. The longest psalm, Psalm 119, is a 176-verse meditation on God's law and commandments. ■ ■ ■

Type of Psalm	Description	Examples
Hymns	songs of praise	Psalms 46, 48, 76, 84, 87, 122
Songs of Thanksgiving	celebrating deliverance, recognizing God as the rescuer	Psalms 18, 30, 40, 66, 116, 118
Laments	prayers for help	Psalms 6, 7, 22, 38, 41–43, 51, 69
Royal Psalms	celebrating a coronation or other royal occasion	Psalms 2, 18, 45, 72, 101
Wisdom Psalms	wisdom sayings	Psalms 1, 33, 37, 49, 73
Question & Answer	question and answer format	Psalms 15, 24, 50, 82

There are many types of psalms and many different ways to classify them.

PATTERN AND STRUCTURE WITHIN THE BOOK OF JOB

The story line within the Book of Job follows a pattern of tests of faith and subsequent suffering. The thematic progression is similar to the legend cycle discussed in Chapter 10. The book is structured in such a way that prose narratives in the **prologue** and the **epilogue** frame an internal poetic debate. This literary structure highlights the pattern of thematic content within the story line.

Read Job 1 and 2.

Opening the Word

In a small group, read aloud Job 28 and discuss the meaning of this hymn.

Read Song of Songs.

sensory images images that appeal to any of the five senses

In the prose prologue (Job 1–2), God gives Satan permission to test the righteous Job. This is followed by Job's discussions with his friends about the reason for suffering in this world (Job 3–31). These discussions are in the form of poetic dialogue. Following these dialogues is a monologue by another person, Elihu (Job 32–37). Then there are two speeches made by God and two subsequent submissions by Job (Job 38–42:6). Finally, in the prose epilogue, we read about Job's restoration (Job 42:7–17). ■

LOVE POEM

The Song of Songs, also called the Song of Solomon or the Canticle of Canticles, a collection of love poems, is often grouped with the wisdom literature, even though it has a different character and purpose. One reason for this is its presumed connection with Solomon. Each song is an independent work of deliberate artistry, perhaps composed by a professional singer. Although the songs were written by multiple unknown authors, similarities in vocabulary, imagery, form, and content unify the text as a whole.

The songs alternate points of view as the lovers take turns describing one another and their erotic relationship. The lovers describe each other using natural and **sensory images.** What develops through the dialogue of these lovers is a description of an ideal form of love—free of restraint, direct, honest, and mutual. The love portrayed is a communion of souls, and the man and woman are portrayed as equals. As an allegory, the Song of Songs can be understood as the love story between God and Israel or, from a Christian viewpoint, between Jesus and the Church.

For Review

1. What is the typical structure of a psalm?

2. List four types of psalms.

3. How do the prologue and epilogue of the Book of Job differ from the internal dialogues?

For Discussion

What is the biblical definition of wisdom? Of the political leaders today, who seems to demonstrate wisdom? Which leaders do not?

Activity

On the Internet, research the proverbs or wisdom sayings of another culture. Create your own "book" of wisdom by compiling and illustrating a selection of these sayings.

Journal

Do you think it is appropriate for the Old Testament to contain a collection of love poetry? Why do you think the Song of Songs is part of the Bible? Have you read any other love poetry that seemed spiritual? Why was it spiritual?

WISDOM AND THE OLD TESTAMENT

The Books of Proverbs, Job, and Sirach differ from other books in the Old Testament in a very distinct way. While other books focus on the twists and turns of Israel's history and on Israel's unique relationship with God, these books deal with universal human experiences of any time or place and are not tied specifically to events in Israelite history.

These books were compiled in postexilic times when Israel was most concerned with being a community that worshiped the God of Israel, yet this is never mentioned. Instead, these books offer advice on living a meaningful life and dealing with the perplexing problems of being human. Similar advice, or wisdom, was a part of life in the ancient Near East. The wisdom tradition probably started orally and eventually came to be recorded and used in royal courts and schools. This process is referred to as the wisdom movement, and evidence of this movement is found in the wisdom literature of the Old Testament.

WISDOM IN THE ANCIENT NEAR EAST

Ancient texts provide insight into the wisdom movement and its place in ancient Near East society. One such text is the *Counsels of Wisdom,* a Mesopotamian text of a reflective nature that resembles the Book of Proverbs. Around 2450 B.C. in Egypt, a collection of sayings from a *vizier,* or adviser to a pharaoh, was compiled. This collection provided instruction regarding the path to material and political success and recommended hard work and strict discipline. Other Egyptian texts—labeled *seboyet* (meaning "instruction")—counseled the court of the pharaoh. Reflective literature also existed in Egypt, as in the text *Dispute with His Soul of One Who Is Tired of Life.*

THE WISDOM MOVEMENT IN ANCIENT ISRAEL

In preexilic times, wisdom was important to the king. According to 2 Samuel 16:23, David listened to the advice of a counselor and took his advice very seriously: "Now in those days the counsel that Ahithophel gave was as if one consulted the oracle of God; so all the counsel of Ahithophel was esteemed, both by David and by Absalom." During Absalom's rebellion, David receives advice from a wise woman of Tekoa. The fact that she is sought after by Joab indicates that she had a professional standing as a wise person and that such a class of people existed (see 2 Samuel 14:2).

The wisdom movement in Israel was prominent enough for the prophet Jeremiah to acknowledge it. Jeremiah 18:18 states that " . . . instruction shall not perish from the priest, nor counsel from the wise, nor the word from the prophet." The sages who represented the movement had enough of a presence in Israelite society to be compared to priests and prophets. The sages even had enough sway to influence events.

Although wisdom was seen as an attribute of the God of Israel, the female personification of wisdom bears a striking resemblance to the Egyptian goddess Maat (pictured below) and the Canaanite goddess Asherah.

THE PATRIARCH OF THE WISE

Much of the wisdom literature in the Old Testament is attributed to Solomon. Solomon's wisdom was renowned, and scribes in his court may have written down some of his sayings, although this is not known for sure. Solomon was recognized as a ruler who welcomed regional influences and had many diplomatic ties, which also may have influenced the collections in Proverbs.

Proverbs

The Book of Proverbs as we know it was probably compiled in the fifth century B.C. to help the people live in harmony with God. Some of the proverbs are attributed to Solomon as a tribute to him as a wise leader. Other sayings are attributed to a professional class of sages and are labeled "The Words of the Wise" (Proverbs 22:17–24:34). There is also a record of proverbs compiled by royal advisers: "These are other proverbs of Solomon that the officials of King Hezekiah of Judah copied" (see Proverbs 25–29). In keeping with Solomon's diplomatic stature, some proverbs are attributed to foreign kings: "The words of Agur son of Jakeh" (see Proverbs 30). Proverbs 22:17–24:34 closely resemble the Egyptian *Instruction of Amen-em-opet*, which was written for a pharaoh around 1000 B.C. The writers of Proverbs recognized the universal human experience and truth found within these writings, adapted it, and incorporated the wisdom within the Book of Proverbs. ■

Some biblical scholars believe that the female personification of wisdom in the Books of Proverbs, Wisdom, and Baruch was a way to counteract the ancient Near Eastern practices of goddess worship. Wisdom bears a striking resemblance to the Egyptian goddess Maat (meaning "truth") and to the Canaanite fertility goddess Asherah. While the biblical writers condemn worship of the goddess, archaeological evidence suggests that some Israelites were devoted to Asherah, perhaps worshiping her as a female counterpart to the God of Israel. The wisdom books in the Old Testament preserve the qualities of the goddess, but apply them to the wisdom of the one true God.

JOB

While little is known about the origins of the Book of Job, the author may have been influenced by other ancient Near Eastern wisdom literature. A Mesopotamian text has a central character who is wealthy and well, but then is suddenly subjected to illness and trouble. The character complains that the will of a god is beyond understanding. At the end of the story, as in the Book of Job, the god returns him to his previous healthy condition.

A Babylonian text comes even closer to matching the Book of Job, not only in content but in form. In the *Dialogue about Human Misery*, the main character, who questions the justice of the gods, is joined by a friend. The dialogue between the main character and his friend resembles Job's dialogue with his friends.

The inspired writers of the Book of Job were able to take the form of these writings and refashion them into a testament to God's impact on human life. Questioning one of the tenets of conventional wisdom—that God rewards the righteous—is one of the things that sets the Book of Job apart from most of the wisdom literature.

King Solomon's name is synonymous with wisdom.

OPENING THE WORD

Read Proverbs 31:1–9, wise sayings attributed to the mother of King Lemuel (a non-Israelite). Compare the advice given to the advice you receive from your mother or other important women in your life.

SIRACH

The Book of Sirach is a unique work among wisdom literature in that the entire book was probably written by the person to whom it is ascribed (circa 180 B.C.). Sirach was a scribe who traveled widely and acquired "much cleverness" (Sirach 34:11). He states that he has written his book—which is a collection of diverse sayings, psalms of praise and lament, and moral maxims—". . . for all who seek instruction" (Sirach 33:18). He probably had a school or an academy for young men from wealthy families. These students would probably, like Sirach himself, become scribes.

ECCLESIASTES

The author of Ecclesiastes is referred to as "The Teacher," and the book was written in the third or fourth century B.C. Because of its wisdom focus, the book was often incorrectly attributed to Solomon. The wisdom in the book is contrary to "popular wisdom." Hard work and righteousness do not always lead to reward (we would say, in this life); see 1:2–11; 9:1–3, 11–12. And coming to know God does not happen in the way people have come to expect; see 3:10–15; 5:1. But "Wisdom makes one's face shine . . ." (8:1).

For Review

1. How does the wisdom literature in the Old Testament differ from other Old Testament books?

2. What are some of the literary influences on Israel's wisdom literature?

3. What kind of standing did wise counselors or sages have in ancient Israel?

4. According to some scholars, what may have influenced the writers of the Old Testament to use a female figure (rather than a male figure) to personify wisdom?

For Discussion

Except for scribes, priests, those of royalty, and people who were very wealthy, most of the people in ancient Israel were illiterate. Discuss how your life would be different if you were illiterate. What kind of power comes with literacy?

Activity

Make a list of "wisdom" sayings that you frequently hear. Maybe you have had a teacher who always said the same thing before sending you home to study for a major test. Perhaps there is a family member who dispenses wise advice on a regular basis. Look for parallels to these sayings in the Book of Proverbs.

Journal

Why do you think wisdom literature is included in the Old Testament? How did you respond to the selections you read from it?

In the first ten chapters of this text you read about Israel's unique experience with God. The relationship between God and the Israelites is dynamic and active. The relationship traverses through cycles: The covenant is made, the covenant is broken, Israel is punished, a savior overcomes suppressors, the Israelites return to right relationship with God. Throughout this cycle, the Israelites (and later the Jews) found ways to preserve their religious community. Laws and rituals were formulated into religious practices, and the temple provided a place for worship. Prayer came to embody the individual and communal experience of God.

PSALMS

You are probably familiar with psalms because they are incorporated into the prayer life of the Church. The Book of Psalms, or Psalter, is a group of religious songs that address a wide range of topics. You may have noted this variety in the opening and closing psalms of each chapter in this text. Chapter 3 of this text opens with a psalm about the wonderful works of God. Chapter 5 begins with a psalm about God and victory.

Some of the psalms were created for the ritual life of the temple. The psalms also were part of great festivals held for celebrating the renewal of the covenant (Psalm 24). Singers, trumpeters, dances, and shouts for those festival days contributed to the psalms we have today (Psalms 68, 89, 149). These festivals also included gifts and feasts that are the subject matter of some psalms.

The subject matter varies, as does the speaker—from the most intimate and personal expression to the voice of a large group or community. Other psalms are hymns of thanksgiving and of praise, or pleas for help. In the Book of Psalms you may find an individual crying to God or a community lamenting some distress or great crisis or crying for help.

In individual laments, the psalms often speak against enemies and ask God to intervene. An individual voice in the psalms may also ask for a personal rescue from wickedness or sickness. Like some of the stories in the Old Testament, many psalms contain a cycle or a structure that includes a complaint or an appeal to God, a plea for God to intervene, and God's answer, response, or acknowledgment. Another psalm form is one of praise and then thanksgiving to God as king.

The psalms express how the Israelites experienced God in **liturgy.** The word *liturgy* is based on a Greek word for "public" and originally meant a "service in the name of or on behalf of the people" or a "public work." The liturgy is designed to bring people together into a common experience of worship. ■

OPENING THE WORD

Read Psalm 50. What does this psalm illustrate? Why might this psalm have been part of a festival in ancient times?

liturgy a group of words and ceremonial acts for public worship

Although the Liturgy of the Hours is prayed by many Catholics, it provides the structure of the day for contemplative communities such as Trappists and Trappistines.

THE LITURGY OF THE HOURS

A *canonical hour* is a term from Jewish customs that eventually passed into the vocabulary of Christians. For Christians, canonical hours are the Church's cycle of daily prayer consisting of prayers, readings, hymns, and psalms. This Liturgy of the Hours is divided over several times during the day and night.

Prayer is understood as an individual and a communal act. Many of the psalms contribute to our understanding and appreciation of basic elements of prayer. The canonical hours are based on the praying of the psalms and the consecration of every hour to God. The Book of Psalms is often referred to as "the prayer book of the Church." Some or all of the canonical hours are prayed in monastic communities and by members of the clergy, religious, and many laypeople.

The Liturgy of the Hours developed from the practice of praying and singing communally as a vigil prior to a holy day. In the early days of the Church, a prayer service was held in three parts on the night before a feast day. Vespers, matins, and lauds in the canonical hours are related to these three parts. Monks prayed vespers as an evening prayer, matins in the middle of the night (around three o'clock in the morning), and lauds or morning prayer in the early dawn. Then they would go back to bed. Later, the monks created a second morning prayer called prime. Compline was a second night prayer—the last canonical hour or prayer before bed.

In the beginning, prayer of some kind was offered every three hours, day and night. Human limitations (tied to the need for more than two hours of sleep per night) led to changes that make the canonical hours usable by more people today. ■

JOURNAL

Imagine what it would be like to live in a monastery of monks or nuns. How would you feel at dawn in this environment? What sights or sounds might you experience? How might such an environment facilitate prayer for you?

The Liturgy of the Hours

Matins
Middle-of-the-night or early morning prayer: nine to eighteen meditative psalms, readings from Scripture and Church fathers

Lauds/Morning prayer:
hymn, psalms, short reading, canticle, prayers of intercession

The Little Hours
Prayer through the day: terce (mid-morning), sext (noon), and none (mid-afternoon)

Vespers
Evening prayer: hymn, psalms, short reading, canticle, prayers of intercession

Compline
Night prayer: examination of conscience, offering of the actions of the day to God

The Office of Readings
Any time of day: pray; read Scripture, homilies, or biographies of saints; meditate

Matins

The Liturgy of the Hours is designed to help people on their spiritual journey. The canonical hours are a guide for each time segment of each day; they are linked to a particular need of that time of the day. Matins, for example, was originally prayed in the early morning hours, around three o'clock in the morning. (You may have first learned to pray before you went to bed. This practice is consistent with the idea of matins from early times.) Matins is still prayed during the night in many monasteries, but it is prayed at other times by many people.

Invitatory Psalm

The invitatory psalm serves as an introduction to the canonical hours. It may be recited prior to lauds (morning prayer) or before reciting the office of readings. If vespers is all that is recited, then the invitatory psalm precedes vespers.

Lauds: Morning Prayer

Lauds is a celebratory canonical hour. Symbols of this hour include dawn, the awakening of nature, and the resurrection; they are connected symbolically to our rise from slumber and an awakening of the human spirit. The psalms included here are songs of praise.

The Little Hours

The "little hours" are known as prayer throughout the day. These brief pauses in the day help us to raise our hearts to God. The hymns of the little hours are related to the themes corresponding to a point of the day. Terce is at nine o'clock in the morning. Sext is at noon; the day is at its climax and it is understood that this is the most challenging time of the day. The individual is called to beware of sin. None (pronounced to rhyme with *loan*) is from three o'clock to six o'clock in the evening. The day is slowly ending. This canonical hour corresponds also to a recognition of the end of life. Perseverance is the theme of this canonical hour.

Vespers and Compline: Evening Prayer and Night Prayer

The evening prayer of the Church is vespers. This canonical hour takes us from the end of the day to the calm of the evening. Compline is the second evening prayer; it asks for peace with God. Symbols present here are the sun and light and the divine life. In darkness we search for God, symbolized by light, and pray for a happy death. The prayer sums up the day's events and themes and contains four parts: God is invited to dwell with us (visitation), God is the guardian of our soul, the angels are also invited to dwell with us, and we call for God's blessing throughout the night. ▪

The Office of Readings

As part of recent changes to the canonical hours, the Liturgy of the Hours includes canonical hours that may be prayed at any time of the day. This Office of Readings includes a first reading from Scripture and a second reading from a writer of the early centuries of the Church or from the lives of the saints. Men and women religious who do not live in a monastery and laypeople may pray fewer canonical hours and may do so alone.

The Liturgy of the Hours is a rich weaving of prayer and praise on behalf of the entire Church. When the psalms are used for the Liturgy of the Hours, they are understood as universal in their themes and sentiments. We apply them to our own lives and use them to face challenges and crises. The meaning of the psalms for the Israelites is paralleled in our lives today; we too experience moments of victory, grace, and love, for instance. These moments are intrinsic to the human experience—and as such they are timeless. ▪

OPENING THE WORD

Read Psalm 6. Identify a canonical hour that might include this psalm.

JOURNAL

Find a psalm that relates to a current situation in your life. Describe how your emotions are similar to those expressed in the psalm.

For Review

1. What is liturgy?

2. What is the Liturgy of the Hours (canonical hours)?

3. How are the psalms that are used in the Liturgy of the Hours related to the history or the practices of the Israelites?

4. What is matins and how is this included in the Liturgy of the Hours?

For Discussion

In the last 500 years, what changes have occurred in the ways that people live that warranted changing how the Liturgy of the Hours is prayed?

Activity

Research illustrated versions of books of hours or the Book of Psalms (Psalter) from medieval Europe, England, and Ireland. Write an essay describing the importance of these works and the time devoted to creating them. How does the beauty of these books express reverence for wisdom literature?

Thomas Merton

A Man of Wisdom

Thomas Merton was born in Prades, France, on January 31, 1915. For a time, Merton studied at Cambridge University in England; he later attended college in the United States. In 1939 he received a master's degree from Columbia University. During this time he slowly converted from being an agnostic to a devout Catholic, being baptized in 1938.

After spending some time teaching English and working in a Harlem settlement house, Merton decided he wanted to become a monk. In 1941 he chose the Trappist order because of its emphasis on solitude and silence, and was ordained a priest in 1949. Within Gethsemani Abbey, which is outside Louisville, Kentucky, Merton served as master of students and novices. His twenty-seven years there led to profound changes in his views of himself and the world, as is revealed in his many writings.

Merton's many published works included poems, essays, meditations, articles, and works of social criticism and made him the leading Catholic author of his time, as well as a prominent figure in American literature. His autobiography, *The Seven Storey Mountain*, was published in 1948. It became an instant bestseller and propelled him onto the world stage. The book has sold over one million copies and has been translated into twenty-eight languages. Although he was first and foremost a monk, Merton continued to write and publish more than sixty books. He frequently wrote about the Liturgy of the Hours in his many journals.

Merton's social criticisms raised public awareness. He became a strong supporter of the nonviolent civil rights movement, calling it "certainly the great example of Christian faith in action in the social history of the United States." He believed racial tolerance and world peace to be the two most urgent issues of his time. However, many people—Christians and people of other faiths—felt that monks should not involve themselves in politics and, as a result, Merton was severely criticized, as well as admired.

Thomas Merton was a man of wisdom who became known for his writings on prayer and contemplation. He also wrote social commentary and attempted to bridge the gap between Eastern and Western religions.

During his later years, Merton became interested in Eastern religions, particularly Zen Buddhism. He saw many parallels between Buddhism and Christianity, especially in the areas of prayer and meditation, and he began writing about them and promoting an East-West dialogue. When Merton met with the Dalai Lama in 1968 in the Far East, the Dalai Lama praised Merton for having a more profound understanding of Buddhism than any other Christian he had known.

While attending an ecumenical conference of Buddhist and Christian monks in Bangkok, Thailand, Merton suffered a tragic accident on December 10, 1968, and was electrocuted by a faulty wire on a fan.

Thomas Merton's life continues to inspire others in maintaining right relationship with God. Since his death, Merton has become recognized as the greatest monastic figure of the twentieth century.

Finding Meaning

The wisdom books of the Old Testament show us how to pray, love the Law, and live a good life. For the Israelites, these books might read like a sort of self-help book. You have probably come across self-help titles in bookstores; there are books to improve health, take college entrance exams, and overcome shyness. However, the purpose of the wisdom books is to show people how to find integrity in living a good life. In a broader sense, the entire collection of Scriptures is a guide for living.

What is a good life? How do you recognize wisdom? Part of the challenge in reading the Old Testament (including the wisdom books) is to apply it to your experience today. How can you keep the word alive in yourself? How are your actions a response to what you have read and learned?

Wisdom can come in the form of instruction about moral conduct. Each day you are confronted with choices big and small, and each choice is an exercise of the strength of your character. Some of the choices may not present much of a challenge: If your friend approaches you in a time of trouble, you would extend yourself and help. The opening story in this chapter is an example of a situation in which you would need to extend yourself to a friend, trying to comfort the person during a difficult time.

Wisdom can come into our lives through the advice and comfort of a friend. Wisdom takes friendship to a deeper level where it will endure through the stress and difficulties of everyday life.

Old Testament wisdom literature is a strong component of Catholic worship prayers and hymns.

You might not come to a decision so easily for other choices: If you find a $100 bill on the sidewalk outside of a home, would you knock on the door of the home and return it? If someone starts an argument with you over something small, would you walk away? Wisdom comes from experience, which the sages expressed in sayings, observations, and psalms. The opening story illustrates how life's events can seem unfair and confusing. How might a proverb or psalm help you find wisdom and guidance? How might worshiping with others aid healing in your life? ■

Remember that prayer can bring peace to a troubled mind and heart. Prayer with a community brings even greater strength. A community of faith seeks religious expression. Thomas Merton wrote many books on the subject of prayer and contemplation in order to guide people in expressing their faith in prayer and worship. You have read about the Israelites and how they shared a need to express their understanding of God. Some of these expressions dealt with love of God, God's love for them, and their commitment to live in justice and peace—in right relationship with God. Many of these ideas have been passed from one generation to the next, all the way to your generation.

The Church's religious expression can be seen in the liturgy and the sacraments. Understanding these expressions helps you experience Church and understand the Scriptures, which were written thousands of years ago. You are living in the mystery of God as your ancestors lived in God in their day. The messages still hold true, and they are carried forth in the worshiping community. You are the believers of today. In community, you share, encourage each other, and celebrate your experience of God. The community challenges you to live in right relationship with God and others. ■

OPENING THE WORD

Read Psalm 23, the well-known psalm that compares God to a shepherd. Why do you think this psalm is so loved? What images might be used to express the same sentiments today?

JOURNAL

Write a personal psalm based on one of the structures of psalms.

For REVIEW

1. List one situation from your life that relates to the subject of a psalm.

2. What are two benefits of worshiping within a community?

For DISCUSSION

What services do local churches provide for the community? Discuss the spiritual and physical gifts that come from community churches.

ACTIVITY

Research e. e. cummings's poem "i thank you God for most this amazing day." How is this poem similar to a psalm?

The wisdom literature of the Old Testament draws on universal human experience and truth to provide practical instruction for its readers, directing them toward right relationship with God. Through a variety of forms, wisdom literature explores an ideal form of love, the meaning of suffering, and the importance of faith in the providence of God. Wisdom, often personified as a female, is held up as an attribute of God and as a quality to be desired above all others; the contrasting consequences of foolishness are also presented.

There is substantial evidence suggesting that there were many influences on the Old Testament Scriptures that came from the surrounding cultures. The wisdom literature of Israel was part of a larger wisdom movement throughout the ancient Near East. Scribes and intellectuals in Israelite society recorded wise sayings of wise men and women within their society and drew upon the wisdom of surrounding nations, incorporating it into the wisdom literature of the Old Testament, in order to help the people live in harmony with God.

Much of the wisdom literature can be found in the prayers of Christians and Jews today. Words and ceremonial acts that developed in early Judaism and Christianity have been incorporated into the sacraments, hymns, and the Liturgy of the Hours. We are invited to participate in all of these forms of prayer and worship.

The mouths of the righteous utter wisdom,
*   and their tongues speak justice.*
The law of their God is in their hearts;
*   their steps do not slip.*

Psalm 37:30–31

Blessed art Thou, O Lord our God, King of the Universe, who hast kept us alive, sustained us, and permitted us to reach this time of joy.

Traditional Jewish Blessing

The Old Testament— The Word of the Lord

Jewish People Today

From the time of the Diaspora approximately 2,000 years ago until 1948, Jews had no country of their own and, therefore, formed communities worldwide. Although they compose a small percentage of the world's population, Jews live in Europe, Asia, India, Africa, Australia, and the Americas. The Jewish religion is a living faith; it is a continuing religion and people. The essential element of the Jewish faith is the belief that Jews are God's chosen people. God spells out this relationship in Exodus 19:5: "Now therefore, if you obey my voice and keep my covenant, you shall be my treasured possession out of all the peoples." God is faithful and has not revoked his covenant with his chosen people. Likewise, his people understand themselves to be obligated to keep his law, an obligation reinforced throughout Jewish liturgy. While someone from outside the faith may see this obligation as a burden, a Jew sees it as an expression of his or her love for God.

The covenant of God was made with the descendants of Abraham. For this reason, the Jews see themselves as a nation, sharing a particular ethnic heritage, as well as a faith. Due to the importance of remaining devoted to their faith, Jews are traditionally encouraged to marry people who are Jewish. Although marrying outside the faith is discouraged, doing so would not cause a Jew to fall out of the covenant relationship with God. A Jew has to deliberately convert to another religion in order to step outside the bounds of the covenant, and even then the way is always left open for his or her return.

Prayer and the study of Scripture and the Talmud are essential activities for Orthodox Jews. This man is wearing a tallith and phylactery during morning prayer. Look up these two terms.

Talmud a collection of Jewish oral law and commentary; a guide for conduct in particular circumstances

rabbi an ordained Jewish teacher and spiritual leader

JourNaL

Do you know any Jews? What steps can you take to improve your relationship with them?

ORTHODOX AND NON-ORTHODOX JUDAISM

Within the Jewish faith, there are many different branches—Orthodox, Hasidic, Conservative, Reconstructionist, Reform, and Humanistic. The separation of Jews into these groups is based on differences in interpretation of the Scriptures and their daily application. Even within these branches, there are many differences in belief and practice between individuals. Orthodoxy is a strict, traditional observance of the law in which emphasis is placed upon diligent study of the **Talmud.** Hasidism is a branch of Orthodoxy in which personal piety and spiritual devotion are stressed, and worship is more mystical and joyful.

Conservative Judaism maintains that while some biblical traditions are permanent, others were meaningful during a certain period of time. They believe in responding to the changing times; for example, as of 1983, women can be ordained as **rabbis** within the Conservative movement. Reconstructionism, which grew out of Conservative Judaism, retains many traditional practices but does not impose a belief in the divine revelation of the Scriptures.

The Reform movement called for dispensing with what they considered to be outdated rituals in order to focus on a more purely ethical way of life. Reform Jews believe in the equality of men and women regarding capability to be religious leaders, and many Reform temples have female rabbis. Humanistic Judaism developed out of the Reform movement and, like Reconstructionism, believes that Judaism is a human creation rather than a religion inspired by a divine being. Humanistic Judaism embraces a variety of beliefs and practices. ■

ROLE OF SCRIPTURE

Judaism is a continuing religion from biblical times. There is an ongoing process of rabbinical interpretation of God's word and its application. The Law continues to be interpreted in its modern context to meet the challenges of a changing society. Among the non-Orthodox, it is accepted that the Jewish Law must be adapted for it to be applied to modern life.

The primary Scripture of the Jewish faith is the Torah (Pentateuch). Generally speaking, it is recognized as the written law of God and is treated with utmost reverence. The other books of the Old Testament are considered to be less directly inspired than those in the Pentateuch. The historical and prophetic books are grouped in the Nevi'im ("Prophets"), while the other books are grouped in the Ketuvim ("Writings").

Mishna Jewish oral law

The **Mishna,** which was compiled in the second century A.D., is a record of the oral tradition of the ancient Jews. It provides ritual and ethical decisions made by generations of rabbis and is part of the Talmud. The Talmud is a record of deliberations between sages and rabbis pondering the implications of the Torah and the provisions of the Mishna. The text known as the *Jerusalem Talmud* was compiled in the fourth century, and the later text known as the *Babylonian Talmud* was compiled in the sixth century.

SYNAGOGUE

Jewish synagogues are community centers as well as places of study and worship. Many contain classrooms and libraries, and synagogues often serve as administrative offices for Jewish charities. The synagogue is structured to direct the focus of the congregation to a large cupboard that symbolizes the Ark of the Covenant. The Ark contains the parchment scrolls on which the Torah is written, and it is considered a great honor to open or close its doors or to read from the scrolls. As a sign of respect, the congregation stands whenever the Ark is opened.

In Orthodox synagogues, men and women in the congregation sit apart so that the men will not be distracted by the women. In non-Orthodox synagogues, separate seating is not required; this enables families to sit together.

These Torah are covered in velvet and housed in the Ark when not in use.

SABBATH

Mirroring God's day of rest after the creation, the Sabbath (Shabbat) is to be a day of rest. No work is to be done, including such things as writing, sewing, cooking, cleaning, and shopping. Jews observe the Sabbath every Saturday, beginning at sunset on Friday. There are also special Sabbaths connected with Jewish festivals. On the Sabbath, Jews are to rest, relax, spend time with friends and family, study the Torah, and worship God. The Friday night meal, complete with special songs and ritual blessings, is an opportunity for the family to spend time together while following God's commandment. Orthodox Jews do not use any electricity or motorized transport on the Sabbath, while secular and Reform Jews focus more on spending time with their families rather than following a strict observance.

At the synagogue on the Sabbath, the liturgy contains prescribed readings from the Torah, a reading from prophetic literature, and specialized prayers. There is a morning service and an afternoon service. Three meals are eaten on the Sabbath, with a discussion of the Torah often being the topic of conversation at the table. The day concludes with a ritual ceremony in the home. Observing the Sabbath enhances family solidarity, tranquillity, and prayerfulness.

FAMILY AND COMMUNITY VALUES

The Jewish community has traditionally been a model of family values. The community nourishes strong bonds between generations and generally seems to have fewer broken families than non-Jewish communities. Children are considered a blessing, and traditionally large families are common. A traditional Jewish mother is devoted to meeting the material needs of her family and encouraging her husband and children in their studies. Husbands are commanded to love and respect their wives, and children are commanded to honor their parents.

At the Sabbath meal the mother lights the candles and prays the benediction. She prays for the health and honor of her children, that they may grow up as good Jews open to the Torah.

Jewish Holy Days

Holy Day	Description	Relevant Scripture
Passover (Pesah)	harvest festival and celebration of liberation from Egypt	Exodus
Weeks (Shavu'ot)	also called Pentecost, celebrating the gift of the Torah	Exodus, Ruth
Tabernacles (Sukkot)	harvest festival and reminder of wanderings in the wilderness	Leviticus
Lights (Hanukkah)	celebrating victory of Maccabees	1 and 2 Maccabees
Esther (Purim)	commemorating the deliverance of Persian Jews by Jewish queen	Esther
Rosh Ha-Shanah	New Year, start of Ten Days of Penitence	Genesis, Numbers, 1 Samuel, Jeremiah, Micah
Fast of Yom Kippur	Day of Atonement, concludes Rosh Ha-Shanah	Leviticus, Numbers, Psalms, Ecclesiastes, Isaiah, Jonah
Tishah b'Av	anniversary of the destruction of the first and second temples	Isaiah, Lamentations ∎

ActiviTy

Research one of the Jewish holy days shown in the chart above to find out more information about the significance of the occasion and how it is observed.

As members of the larger community, Jews are encouraged to support those in need and to give generously to charitable organizations. They are called upon to observe the spirit of God's law as well as the letter of the law. A Jew is to be truthful and fair, kind and compassionate, working toward peace at all times. Having been called upon to be "a light to the nations" (Isaiah 42:6), Jews maintain an ethical obligation to promote social justice. ∎

FOOD LAWS

kosher fit for consumption; conforming to the Jewish laws of Kashrut; meat and dairy products must be stored, prepared, and served separately

An interesting custom within the Jewish community is the observance of the food laws of Kashrut and the **kosher** designation. As in every aspect of Jewish theology, different branches of the religion make varying allowances regarding observance of the food laws. Some Jews follow a strict interpretation and observance of the laws, while others have different interpretations and practices. For instance, a non-Orthodox Jew might maintain a kosher kitchen at home, but relax those restrictions when in a secular social situation.

ActiviTy

Research Jewish and Catholic charities in your community. Based on your research, what are some common values and goals among Jews and Catholics?

Many Jews continue to follow the strict dietary laws dictated by God in the Old Testament. For an animal to be fit for consumption, it must have a cloven hoof and chew cud (Deuteronomy 14:6). Thus, Jews do not eat meat from pigs or rabbits. The meat must also be prepared in a particular manner: the slaughter of the animal is to be as painless as possible, and minimal blood is to remain in the meat. Deuteronomy 14:9 specifies that only fish with scales and fins shall be consumed, thereby forbidding the consumption of shellfish (shrimp, crab, lobster, oysters, clams). Dairy products must be stored, prepared, and served separately from meat.

Accompanied by her parents, this Jewish girl reads from the Torah at her Bat Mitzvah.

CEREMONIES

The family unit plays an important role in the Jewish tradition. Tradition is handed down from generation to generation, so the home environment is a crucial training ground. For this reason, the birth of a child is a highly celebrated event within the Jewish community. It is customary for parents to visit the synagogue soon after the birth of a child to offer a prayer of gratitude to God. Newborn boys are circumcised in a ritual ceremony, during which a professional circumciser called a *mohel* performs the surgery. Newborn girls receive a blessing in the synagogue. Every Jewish child is given a Hebrew name, often during the circumcision service or blessing ceremony.

When a Jewish boy reaches the age of thirteen, his adulthood is celebrated in a rite of passage. A **Bar Mitzvah** ceremony is held in the synagogue, during which the boy reads from the Torah scroll. The term *bar mitzvah* means "son of the covenant," and the ceremony symbolizes the boy's duty to keep God's commandments. In non-Orthodox Jewish communities, girls are given a similar ceremony at the age of twelve or thirteen. It is called a **Bat Mitzvah,** meaning "daughter of the covenant." Among the Orthodox, girls are not allowed to read from the Torah in the synagogue, but they do receive recognition of having reached adulthood. This celebration is generally held in the home rather than in the synagogue.

As young people reach a marriageable age, they are encouraged by the Jewish community to marry within their faith. The family members are highly involved in the courtship, often encouraging their child to marry a certain person. In a traditional Jewish wedding, the couple stands together under a marriage canopy, and a marriage contract is signed. A common marriage benediction is "Blessed art Thou, O Lord, who hast hallowed Thy people Israel by the rite of the wedding canopy and the sacred covenant of marriage." Wedding ceremonies vary among the different Jewish communities but are always joyous events involving the family and friends of the couple.

Bar Mitzvah Jewish coming-of-age ceremony for thirteen-year-old boy

Bat Mitzvah non-Orthodox Jewish coming-of-age ceremony for twelve- or thirteen-year-old girl

STATE OF ISRAEL

The Jewish sense of identity as a nation is strongly tied to the land of Israel—the promised land. As we learned in earlier chapters, God's chosen people struggled to take possession of the promised land. They were forced into slavery and exile but held onto the belief that they would settle once again in the land promised to Abraham by God.

After World War I, anti-Semitism ran rampant. Adolf Hitler (1889–1945), chancellor of Germany, publicly voiced his hatred of the Jews. Between 1933 and 1945 Hitler's Nazi forces attempted to annihilate the Jews through a system of concentration and extermination camps. By the end of World War II, six million Jews had lost their lives—approximately one third of the Jewish population. Survivors of the **Holocaust** tried to return to their homes, only to find that they were unwelcome. Many European Jews found themselves homeless and sought to return to Israel. On May 14, 1948, the independent State of Israel was formally established.

The Holocaust and the establishment of the modern State of Israel significantly influenced the Jewish community worldwide. Laying claim to the promised land provided hope and renewal for a people who had felt abandoned by their God during the war. Today the Jewish community worldwide is united in the belief that the State of Israel must be maintained as a homeland.

Upon the United Nations' recommendation for a Jewish state after World War II, there was turmoil in the Middle East. Arab peoples also saw Israel as their homeland and resented the Jewish claim to the land. Between 1948 and 1993 battles and terrorist attacks resulted in thousands of deaths on both sides. Finally in 1993 Israeli prime minister Yitzhak Rabin formed a peace agreement with Yassir Arafat, the leader of the Palestinian Liberation Organization (PLO). However, after the assassination of Rabin, the peace process deteriorated. The turmoil in the Middle East continues to be a heated issue in the twenty-first century. ■

Holocaust the destruction of Jewish people by Nazi forces between 1933 and 1945

Activity

Research and discuss: What do you see as the challenges that an Orthodox Jew faces living in modern America? What challenges does a secular Jew face in Israel?

The Hall of Remembrance in the United States Holocaust Memorial Museum in Washington, DC, provides a place to reflect on the victims of the Holocaust and on the dangers of the hatred and bigotry still present in our society.

WISDOM OF POPE JOHN PAUL II

Pope John Paul II has been outspoken about the need for a Jewish-Catholic dialogue. He stressed the importance of treating Jews with respect and pointed out many similarities between Jewish and Christian liturgies. On March 6, 1982, the pope said in an inspiring speech, "May God allow Christians and Jews really to come together, to arrive at an exchange in depth, founded on their respective identities, but never blurring it on either side, truly searching the will of God the Revealer."

On a later date, he reminded his audience that Christians and Jews share a spiritual inheritance and the spiritual bond between them is a sacred one (October 28, 1985). In a historic visit to Israel in March 2000, Pope John Paul II met with Jewish and Arab leaders in an effort to help reconcile the Jewish, Arab, and Christian communities.

For Review

1. Name the four non-Orthodox branches of Judaism.

2. What biblical texts are shared by Jews and Christians?

3. Which Jewish holy day celebrates the gift of the Torah?

For Discussion

Why do you think it is important for Christians to learn about the Jewish faith?

Activity

Use the Internet to research the "Declaration on the Relationship of the Church to Non-Christian Religions" *(Nostra Aetate),* the decree from the Second Vatican Council in which the spiritual bond between Christians and Jews is recognized (see # 4). Choose two statements from this section on Judaism, and write a paragraph on what the statements mean to you.

It is our duty to magnify the Lord of the Universe and to acknowledge the greatness of God . . . He is our God, there is no other . . . Acknowledge it today and take it well into thy heart that God, the Lord, is above in Heaven and down on the earth, He and no other.

Jewish Alenu Prayer

Glossary

acrostic—(ə ˈkrȯs tik) an ordered poem in which the first letters of individual lines or verses, when combined in order, form their own pattern, phrase, or word

allegory—a story with symbolic characters that presents religious truths or generalizations about human nature

anawim—a Jewish term referring to people who are in need of assistance

anthropomorphism—(an thrə pə ˈmȯr fi zəm) the attributing of human characteristics to non-human realities

antihero—a character who is placed in the role of a traditional hero but is not idealized in any way

apocalypse—(əˈpä kə lips) a revelation of future events

archetype—(ˈär ki tīp) recurrent character type, image, or theme in literature

Ark of the Covenant—an ancient symbol of God's protection and presence; a portable throne in ancient times that included a seat that was believed to be occupied by God

Babylonian Exile—period of history when the Babylonians forced most of the inhabitants of Judah to migrate to Babylon; the Exile

ban—ancient custom of completely destroying everything in a defeated city

Bar Mitzvah—(bär ˈmits və) Jewish coming-of-age ceremony for thirteen-year-old boy

Bat Mitzvah—(bät ˈmits və) non-Orthodox Jewish coming-of-age ceremony for twelve- or thirteen-year-old girl

chronicle—a listing of historical events; an historical account or narrative with a purpose; a creative reinterpretation of historical events

covenant—a sacred agreement between God and his people; a solemn agreement between two people or groups of people

Diaspora—(dī ˈas pə rə) the community of Jews in Babylonia after the Exile; **diaspora**—communities of Jews who have scattered all over the world, including places such as India, Africa, and Spain.

Divided Kingdom—the result of the division of Israel into two separate nations: Israel and Judah

divine justice—the moral standard by which God judges human conduct; the realization of that standard by God; an expression of God's righteousness, pity, love, and grace

dynasty—a succession of rulers in the same family line, frequently father to son

epic—a long, exaggerated, and idealized narrative about a hero or heroine who goes through various trials

epilogue—the conclusion to a literary work

evangelization—giving witness to one's faith by proclaiming the good news of Jesus Christ to the world through words and actions

exile—an individual banished from his or her home; banishment from one's land

Exodus—departure of the Israelites from Egyptian slavery under the leadership of Moses, who was led by God

fairy tale—a myth with an earthly setting, human characters, and a happy ending

Fertile Crescent—region of rich farming and grazing land extending in an arc from Mesopotamia to Canaan

folklore—composite of traditional customs, art forms, tales, and sayings preserved among a people

genealogy—an account of ancestry

hapiru—a class of people living in the countryside of Canaan, some of whom were former slaves; they may have been ancestors of the Hebrews

Hebrews—peoples enslaved in Egypt who eventually became the community known as Israel

Holocaust—the destruction of Jewish people by Nazi forces between 1933 and 1945

idolatry—false worship; honoring and revering a creature in place of God

inspiration—divine influence; God flows into and influences the human intellect, will, imagination, memory

irony—contradiction between an expectation and the actual occurrence

Israelites—a people who unified around 1050–1000 B.C. and included Canaanites, the hapiru, the shasu, Sea Peoples, and the original Hebrews

Jews—term originally used to describe the people who resettled in the area of Judah following the Babylonian Exile; most commonly used to refer to followers of Judaism

judge—one of twelve charismatic military leaders of the Israelites during the period between the conquest of Canaan and the establishment of the monarchy

Kingdom of Judea—the kingdom south of Israel that existed from the time following Solomon's death in 925 B.C. until the destruction of the temple in 586 B.C.

kosher—(kō `shər) fit for consumption; conforming to the Jewish laws of Kashrut

legend—an unverifiable story that is passed down from generation to generation and accepted as true or partly true

liturgy—a group of words and ceremonial acts for public worship

messiah—king or deliverer expected by the Jews; the "anointed one"

messianism—belief in a messiah as the savior of the people

Mishna—(`mish nə) Jewish oral law

monarchy—rule by a single head of state, often a hereditary office

monotheism—(`mä nə thē i zəm) the worship of one god

myth—a symbolic story that gives insight into ultimate questions about beliefs, natural phenomenons, or practices of a particular people

narrative—prose or poetry story

natural moral law—the moral order that is part of God's design for creating the law that expresses the original moral sense, enabling people to discern good and evil through the use of reason

novella—a suspenseful tale that revolves around a specific situation

oracle—a message from one who speaks for God; also the person through whom God speaks

oral tradition—unwritten, memorized accounts of historical events and stories

original sin—the human condition of the need for salvation based on the first humans' choice to disobey God

parable—story with a moral or religious lesson

Passover—refers to when the Israelites were "passed over" by the angel of death as dictated by the tenth plague; a holiday celebrated by Jews as a day of deliverance

pastoral—drawn from a rural setting or rustic way of life

patriarch—male leader of a family or tribe; **patriarchs**—the ancestors of the Israelites, particularly Abraham, Isaac, and Jacob

Pentateuch—(`pen tə tük) the first five books of the Old Testament; the Torah

personal sin—the free choice to disobey God; to do something that is the opposite of the good

personification—something nonhuman is described with human characteristics

persuasion—an appeal intended to convince a specific audience to share a particular belief or perform a certain action

polytheism—(`pä lē thē i zəm) the worship of many gods

prologue—the introduction preceding a literary work that gives information to help the audience understand the story that follows

prophecy—the words of God, delivered through a spokesperson known as a prophet; generally calls for the Israelites to live justly and avoid idolatry

prophet—a person who has a close relationship with God and communicates a divine message

proverb—a brief statement that conveys a general truth or rule of conduct

providence—divine guidance and care

rabbi—(`ra bī) an ordained Jewish teacher and spiritual leader

remnant—exiles and former exiles who remained faithful to God

revelation—God's deliberate and gradual disclosure to humans of himself—his nature, his plan, his providence, and what he wants from people

salvation history—historical events through which God saves; how God enters into history to bring the salvation he has promised; God's saving actions in human history

satirical humor—humor that exposes human folly through a form of ridicule in order to achieve a moral purpose

satrapy—(`sā trə pē) an administrative province ruled by a governor called a *satrap*

sensory images—images that appeal to any of the five senses

social justice—practice by which social rules and government procedures follow a standard of righteousness and fair treatment

social sin—a collective, societal act or sign that society has distanced itself from God

Talmud—(`täl mùd) a collection of Jewish oral law and commentary; a guide for conduct in particular circumstances

Ten Commandments—the laws given by God to Moses that prescribe moral obligations for the Israelites as part of God's covenant with them

theocracy—(thē `ä krə sē) a nation ruled by God

Torah—(`tōr ə) Hebrew, "law"; Jewish name for the first five books of the Old Testament; the Pentateuch

vow—a solemn promise

worship—to honor or revere a divine being, usually within a religious ritual

Index

* defined in text margin

patriarchs, 12*, 46*, 52–56

peace in the Middle East, 223

Pentateuch, 6*, 29*–32, 65–69, 87, 219

Persian Empire, 167–170, 187

personal sin, 31*

personification, 202*

persuasion, 127*

Philistines, 92, 110, 112

plagues, the, 75

poetry in the Old Testament, 108–109

polytheism, 12*, 74, 92, 188

Pope John XXIII, 139–139

Pope John Paul II, 18, 224

prayer of the Church, 209–211

Priestly tradition, 31

primeval history, 33

promised land, the 85–102, 171

prophecy, 126*, 145–147

prophet, 69*

prophets, the,

    major,

        Ezekiel, 147, 149, 153

        Isaiah, 145, 147–148, 151

        Jeremiah, 149, 152

    minor

        Amos, 125–126, 133–134

        Elijah, 130–131, 136–137

        Elisha, 137

        Habakkuk, 154

        Hosea, 125–126, 131, 134–135

        Micah, 146, 148, 154

        Nahum, 146, 148, 153

        Second Isaiah, 149, 153

        Zephaniah, 155

    of post–exilic Israel

        Ezra, 170

        Haggar, 171

        Jonah, 165, 171

        Malachi, 174

        Nehemiah, 169–170

        Third Isaiah, 175

proverb, 202*

Proverbs, Book of, 113, 202, 206

providence, 191*

psalms, 108, 147, 203, 208–211, 214

Psalms, Book of, 203, 208–211

Ptolemaic Empire, 14, 187–188

Ptolemy, 187

purpose of the Old Testament, 7, 11, 15

R

rabbi, 218*

Rabin, Yitzhak, 223

Rachel, 12, 46

Rebekah, 12, 46, 54

Reform Judaism, 218

religious art, 119

religious laws, 66

remnant, of Israel, 151, 170

responsibility, 39, 58–59, 81–82, 101–102, 139–140,
    157–158, 177–178, 195–196, 213–214

revelation, 15*, 17

Ruth, Book of, 8, 87, 90, 94, 101–102

S

Sabbath, 220

salvation history, 37*, 45

Samson, 89

Samuel, 110, 112, 114

Samuel, Book of, 102

Sarah, 12, 46, 50, 52–54

satirical humor in the Old Testament, 164*

Saul, 13, 110–112

Sea Peoples, 12, 71–72, 91–92

Second Isaiah, 153

Seleucid Empire, 14, 187–189

sensory images in the Old Testament, 204*

Septuagint, the, 187

setting priorities, 118–120

Shasu, the, 12, 71, 91

short stories in the Old Testament, 8

sin, 35, 37, 98, 114, 173f. (see prophets)

Sinai, Mount, 77–78, 88, 118, 137

Sirach, Book of, 207

social justice, 147*, 157–158

social sin, 37*

Solomon, 13, 109, 113, 115, 163, 201, 204, 206

Song of Solomon (Book), 113, 204

sources of the Old Testament, 6

state of Israel, 223

storytelling in the Old Testament, 25–28

structure of the Old Testament, 5–6

symbolism in the Old Testament, 68–69
synagogue, 219

T

Talmud, the, 218*, 219
temple, the, 115, 167–169, 171–172, 193
Ten Commandments, the, 12, 15*–17, 77–78, 118
Teresa, Mother, 18
theocracy, 114*
theological virtues, 39
Tobit, Book of, 184, 192
tolerance, 101–102
Torah, 6*, 15, 29–32, 193, 219–220, 222
Tower of Babel, the, 37
Twelve tribes of Israel, 46, 49
two kingdoms of Israel, 13, 124–141

V

vow, 109*

W

war and Israel, 96–98
Wisdom, Book of, 113
wisdom in ancient Near East, 205
wisdom literature of the Old Testament, 201–211
    Ecclesiastes, 207
    Job, 203, 206
    Proverbs, 202, 206
    Psalms, 203, 208–211
    Sirach, 205, 207

Song of Songs (Solomon), 204
wisdom movement in ancient Israel, 205
witnesses to faith, stories of,
    Azélie Marie Guérin, 57
    Francis of Assisi, 38
    Francis Xavier, 194
    Joan of Arc, 100
    Louis Martin, 57
    Martin Luther King Jr, 156
    Mother Teresa, 18
    Pope John XXIII, 138
    Rose Duchesne, 176
    Stephen Bantu Biko, 80
    Thomas Merton, 212
    Thomas More, 117
women leaders of Israel, 94
worship, 77, 115*
written sources of the Old Testament, 6

X

Xavier, Francis, 194

Y

Yahwist tradition, 30
YHWH, 30

Z

Zechariah, Book of, 164, 172–173
Zephaniah, Book of, 155
Zoroastrianism, 169